ON THE SOCIAL LIFE OF POSTSOCIALISM

NEW ANTHROPOLOGIES OF EUROPE

Daphne Berdahl, Matti Bunzl, and Michael Herzfeld
FOUNDING EDITORS

On the Social Life of Postsocialism

MEMORY, CONSUMPTION, GERMANY

Daphne Berdahl

—⚊⚊—

EDITED AND WITH AN INTRODUCTION BY
MATTI BUNZL

FOREWORD BY
MICHAEL HERZFELD

INDIANA UNIVERSITY PRESS
BLOOMINGTON AND INDIANAPOLIS

This book is a publication of

Indiana University Press
601 North Morton Street
Bloomington, IN 47404-3797 USA

http://iupress.indiana.edu

Telephone orders 800-842-6796
Fax orders 812-855-7931
Orders by e-mail iuporder@indiana.edu

∞ The paper used in this publication meets the minimum requirements of the
American National Standard for Information Sciences—Permanence of Paper for
Printed Library Materials, ANSI Z39.48-1992.

Manufactured in the United States of America

Library of Congress Cataloging-in-Publication Data

Berdahl, Daphne, 1964–2007.
On the social life of postsocialism : memory, consumption, Germany / Daphne Berdahl ; edited and with an introd. by Matti Bunzl ; foreword by Michael Herzfeld.
p. cm.
Includes bibliographical references and index.
ISBN 978-0-253-35434-1 (cloth : alk. paper) — ISBN 978-0-253-22170-4 (pbk. :
alk. paper) 1. Political anthropology—Germany. 2. Politics and culture—Germany.
3. Post-communism—Germany. 4. Consumption (Economics)—Germany.
5. Germany—History—Unification, 1990 6. Germany—History—1990–
7. Germany—Politics and government—1990– 8. Germany—Social life and
customs. I. Bunzl, Matti, date II. Title.
GN585.G4B45 2010
306.0943'09049—dc22

2009026624

1 2 3 4 5 15 14 13 12 11 10

CONTENTS

—ᴍ—

FOREWORD

—⁄ル—

MICHAEL HERZFELD

Daphne Berdahl's tragically curtailed life framed an anthropological career of extraordinary resonance. An astute observer of transition in Germany during the dramatic years surrounding the dismantling of the Berlin Wall, she was also one of the architects of another transition: the coming in from the cold—if we might borrow a metaphor from John Le Carré, a very different writer on German themes—of Europeanist anthropology. While she was by no means the first to take ethnographic method to the industrialized and powerful countries of Europe's western and northern reaches, she did so in a way that we now know to have been deeply consequential for the anthropology of globalism, postsocialism, and the reformulation of national identities in the pluralistic world that emerged with the end of the Cold War and the rapid spread of the new technologies of information.

The reunification of Germany provided her with an ideal platform for thinking through these issues. With a wry sense of irony that could open up new perspectives as effectively as her theoretical mastery, she was actively engaged in debunking the West's triumphalism and self-congratulation as the formerly socialist states scrambled to redefine themselves in the capitalist firmament. She also helped to shift the emphasis away from mechanistic accounts of the political changes in Germany and toward the process—still incomplete—of ending the absurd scholarly division of Europe into specializations representing the symbolic east and west of the Cold War. Especially in her later work, she showed how the peculiar vicissitudes of European citizens caught in the grip of neoliberalism could illuminate the global impact of this economic ideology and its attendant, often wrenching dislocations. A benchmark for what the series New Anthropologies of Europe was intended to achieve, her work exemplifies the generation of new theoretical insights out of the ethnographic specificities of Europeanist research.

Her approach was classically anthropological, highlighting in the most mundane details of everyday life refractions of massive geopolitical shifts to illustrate the impact of those shifts on the lives of the people she came to know during her field research. These people were her personal friends as much as they were her informants, a choice of relationship that with characteristic aplomb she confronted directly, in full awareness that to some colleagues she might appear to be transgressing sacred boundaries between scholarship and affect. She described her friends' daily struggles and achievements, as well as her own subjective reactions—sometimes as full of exasperation as of affection, as so often happens with true friends. In so doing, she brought to vividly painful life the frustration and self-doubt that assail every sensitive ethnographer faced with the apparent recalcitrance and inevitable cultural blockages that arise from radically different life experiences.

Here her writerly skills are the centrally important vehicle of her extraordinary ethnographic sensibility. By making the tiniest details sing, she achieved an immediacy and poignancy of description that few have matched. Her modest, level-headed, but beautifully articulated scholarly voice thus came to challenge some of the conventional assumptions—theoretical, political, methodological, and ethical—that had become the received wisdom of the discipline.

Take, for example, the passage in which she describes a friend's agonizing over whether to leave her collar pointing upward or downward. Daphne used this seemingly trivial matter to illuminate the excruciating existential decisions that confronted citizens of the former German Democratic Republic as they struggled to define their position within the new, largely hostile, and culturally and socially impatient new Germany. One friend, after a prolonged period of worried vacillation about which way to wear the collar, eventually appeared with one side of the collar up and the other down. Daphne's uncertainty and hesitation about how to interpret her friend's appearance at that moment mirror the perplexities of interpretation—and thus also of impression management—that were the daily torment of these East Germans. She did not try to impose an authoritative interpretation on such a moment of doubt. Instead, her empathy in describing the shabby, familiar, well-worn clothing of her friend brings alive the very fabric of everyday life during that time of transition—the resentments, the desires, the sheer bafflement, and above all the indecision that flowed from suddenly having to confront entirely unfamiliar codes of interaction.

Daphne did not try to eliminate uncertainty from her ethnographic descriptions. On the contrary, she celebrated it, sympathizing with those for whom it represented the existential pain of trepidation but also drawing from their vicissitudes a rich array of insights into the relationship between cultural hegemony and the practical dilemmas of lifestyle. She was as determined to challenge easy interpretations of the transition as she was to reveal just how ridiculous the complacency of Western observers could be, and, wherever possible, she let her friends' voices and actions provide the substance of her critiques and serve as sounding-chambers for her own, deeply reflexive uncertainties.

In this radically ethnographic modality, Daphne Berdahl made an especially vital contribution to understanding the significance and the ramifications of the curious nostalgia that East Germans displayed, soon after unification, for the symbols and daily utensils of life in the GDR. Fully cognizant of the irony whereby West Germans were sometimes the architects of this newly east-directed commodification of nostalgia, she nonetheless also pushed analysis in other and still more revealing directions. She especially explored what this nostalgic modality meant for its consumers. Her choice of focus sometimes meant probing the most intimate dimensions of her informants' lives, which she always did with respectful sensitivity to their continuing predicaments. In this regard, her work also represents an ethical standard of rare intensity and responsibility.

Through her attention to the physical and discursive details of everyday existence, she probed the dynamics of shifting identity formation as the former GDR citizens struggled with their assigned role as despised *Ossis* and slowly, and at widely differing paces, reached for the encompassing role of sophisticated German consumers and even of critics of the consumer society. In her pages, ordinary Germans do not just come alive, warts and all; they *explain*—but they do so by example, embodying, in her descriptions, the fundamentally empirical charge of anthropological work, and thus opening up new questions and resolutely refusing the comforts of simplistic answers.

There is in Daphne Berdahl's work a powerful sense of conviction—indeed, an honesty that compels attention to the very details that, as she noted, were often despised by other observers. Her own humanity emerges clearly in the caring that she expresses for (and tries to bring to) her seriously ill friend and in the dismay she experiences as she confronts the complexity of her own emotions and conflicted entanglements with the friend's support network. It also appears in her fierce refusal to engage in deliberate judgmentalism even as she chides herself for her own sometimes stern judgments of others—notably of the priest who welcomed her and her family to the village of Kella but then became something of a potential adversary over the appropriate course of action for her ailing friend. In recounting such experiences, or in showing us why a villain from the perspective of Frankfurt becomes a hero from that of Leipzig, she reveals her own total commitment to an ethical honesty that transcends easy solutions and speaks to the relentless responsibility that goes with the privilege of being an anthropologist—of, as she decisively shows, having friends.

We too, who have worked with Daphne as colleagues, were—and are—her friends. Hers is the kind of anthropology that, in the face of massive geopolitical torment, brooks no alternative. Her humane generosity lives on in these pages and shows us what we must do—in conducting research, in writing, in teaching, in engaging in debate—to realize in our own work the intense honesty and commitment that infuse her anthropology; that made her a gifted and popular teacher; and that here offer us an exciting and yet—for such is the power of recognition in the best of anthropological writing—profoundly and disconcertingly familiar vision of the human condition. Those of us who knew her cannot easily accept that we will never again hear her actual voice—lightly bantering, amused, passionately serious, analytic, by turns and sometimes all at once—in classrooms and at the dining table, at conferences and in casual meetings on the street. But we can recall and celebrate that voice, especially when we re-read her wise words; and we can be sure that this volume will convey something of its quality to those who never had the privilege of knowing her in person. Anthropology is already a better place for her writings; and in publishing this volume we hope to ensure that they will remain, in the words of Thucydides, a possession for all time.

ACKNOWLEDGMENTS

—w—

"Voices at the Wall: Discourses of Self, History, and National Identity at the Vietnam Veterans Memorial." *History & Memory* 6(2) (1994): 88–124.

"Consumer Rites: The Politics of Consumption in Re-Unified Germany." In Jutta Lauth Bacas and William Kavanagh, eds., *Border Encounters: Proximity and Asymmetry at Europe's Frontiers* (New York: Berghahn, 2009).

"'(N)Ostalgie' for the Present: Memory, Longing, and East German Things." *Ethnos* 64(2) (1999): 192–211.

"'Go, Trabi, Go!': Reflections on a Car and Its Symbolization over Time." *Anthropology and Humanism* 25(2) (2001): 131–141.

"Mixed Devotions: Religion, Friendship, and Fieldwork in Post-Socialist East Germany." In Hermine DeSoto and Nora Dudwick, eds., *Fieldwork Dilemmas: Anthropologists in Post-Socialist States* (University of Wisconsin Press, 2000), 172–194.

"The Spirit of Capitalism and the Boundaries of Citizenship in Post-Wall Germany." *Comparative Studies in Society and History* 47(2) (2005): 235–251.

"Local Hero, National Crook: 'Doc' Schneider and the Spectacle of Finance Capital." Previously unpublished.

"Expressions of Experience and Experiences of Expression: Museum Re-Presentations of GDR History." *Anthropology and Humanism* 30(2) (2005): 156–170.

"Goodbye Lenin, Aufwiedersehen GDR: On the Social Life of Socialism." In Maria Todorova and Zsuzsa Gille, eds., *Post-Communist Nostalgia* (New York: Berghahn, 2009).

INTRODUCTION

—m—

MATTI BUNZL

DAPHNE BERDAHL WAS A PIONEERING anthropologist and an exceptional person. A leading scholar of central and eastern Europe, she was a key theorist of the transition from state socialism to capitalism and one of the finest ethnographers the discipline ever produced. She also made important contributions to the anthropology of borderlands, memory, and consumption. This book, collecting Daphne's articles and essays, is a testament to her extraordinary accomplishments as well as to the vibrancy and enduring relevance of her work.

Daphne was born in 1964, the daughter of a German historian. She grew up in Eugene, Oregon, and attended Oberlin College, where she studied history and German. Following her 1986 graduation, she spent a year each at the University of Tübingen and the University of Illinois, preparing for graduate study in anthropology. In the fall of 1988, she enrolled in the Ph.D. program at the University of Chicago, where she studied with Bernard Cohn, Sharon Stephens, and James Fernandez, who became her dissertation advisor.

At the University of Chicago, Daphne was part of a vibrant group of graduate students who worked on Europe, which, at the time, was still considered marginal to anthropology at large. With her sights set on Germany and a particular interest in borders, she decided to undertake ethnographic research in the Eichsfeld region, an area that was bisected by the inner-German border. Daphne arrived in the village of Kella in 1990, witnessing firsthand the immediate aftermath of the *Wende* (the transition) and Germany's re-unification. After 2 years of pioneering fieldwork on the postsocialist condition, she returned to Chicago, where she completed her doctorate in 1995. She spent the following 2 years at Harvard University, first as a postdoctoral fellow and then as a lecturer in the Department of Anthropology. In the fall of 1997, she accepted a position at the University of Minnesota, where she received tenure in 2000. At the time of her passing, she was associate professor of anthropology and global studies.

Within the discipline, Daphne is most strongly identified with the anthropology of postsocialism. As one of its pioneers and leaders, she mounted an important challenge to "transitology," dominated as it was until the late 1990s by political scientists and economists. Against their "linear" and "teleological" narration of the transition in terms of "capitalist 'triumphalism'," Daphne championed a view that emphasized "the contradictions, paradoxes, and ambiguities of postsocialism" (Berdahl 2000: 1).

Daphne accomplished this objective to universal acclaim in her pathbreaking book *Where the World Ended: Re-Unification and Identity in the German Borderland* (1999a). Based on her dissertation (Berdahl 1995) and an additional stint of fieldwork in 1996, it is an exemplary study of the transition. Set in Kella, it is first and foremost an account of the radical and sudden transformations in the village. But in the fashion of anthropology's best ethnographers, Daphne readily discerned in such local realities the processes of German re-unification at large. The village's proximity to the former border was crucial in this respect. Daphne treated the boundary as both symbolic and real, allowing her to view her interlocutors' frequent border crossings in both their immediate and historical significance. The result was an on-the-ground account of the emergence of a new East German subjectivity, the *Ossi,* whose genealogy in the former GDR was imprinted on her body and behavior and dramatized in her encounters with the west and its *Wessis.*

In beautifully constructed chapters, Daphne traced this development in such areas as social structure, religion, and historical memory. Analyzing social transformations in the east, for example, she typically found an analytic inroad in a telling joke: "What is the most difficult [adjustment] for the Ossis since the Wall fell? Having to survive without connections" (Berdahl 1999a: 115). Explicating the joke through her rich ethnographic material, Daphne documented how social differentiation in the GDR was marked by an individual's level of *Beziehungen,* her networks and access to nodes of power. In the new era, *Vitamin B* (for "Beziehungen") no longer spelled success, one of the many lessons Ossis had to absorb in the wake of the Wende.

Where the World Ended is ethnography at its best. Daphne captured the sights, sounds, and smells of Kella. But what really came to life were its inhabitants. As an ethnographer, Daphne used her tape recorder only sparingly, drawing her data almost entirely from participant observation and the copious notes she took at the end of each day. The resulting representations had novelistic qualities, with fully realized settings and characters seamlessly blending into the larger arguments about the transition and German re-unification. These qualities have also helped make *Where the World Ended* a hit in classrooms, where it is equally at home in graduate seminars and introductory undergraduate courses. In her review of the book, Katherine Verdery captured this unique quality: "It is not often that reading a book for review has led me to rewrite a syllabus I was about to hand out, but that is what happened when I read *Where the World Ended*" (Verdery 2000: 545).

Where the World Ended is a classic that will be read for generations to come. But it would be unfortunate to flatten Daphne's career into one book, even one as brilliant as her ethnography of Kella. There was so much more to Daphne's scholarship, and this is what the present book seeks to capture. In particular, it sets out to accomplish two goals: First, it aims to restore the entirety of Daphne's corpus to view by collecting her essays in one volume. Some of these texts are classics in their own right—like her piece on the Trabi—while others are little known or previously unpublished. Second, it shows that *Where the World Ended* should not be understood in isolation, but as part of a larger intellectual trajectory. The publication of the later pieces is especially important in this regard. They allow us to observe Daphne's ongoing thinking about the postsocialist transition, which she continued to research for well over a decade following her initial fieldwork in Kella.

The book is structured along the lines of Daphne's research trajectory, with the three parts recalling the fieldsites of her career. This organizational principle is also meant to underline Daphne's unwavering commitment to ethnography. It is important to start in Washington, D.C., where Daphne undertook her first in-depth research. The year was 1989, and the result was a master's thesis on the Vietnam Veterans Memorial. Daphne completed the piece in 1990, and a revised version appeared in the journal *History & Memory* in 1994. It was Daphne's first scholarly publication and has remained virtually unknown among her Europeanist colleagues. But it is well worth the read, both in its own right and as a remarkable document in Daphne's intellectual trajectory. While set in a different national context, it foreshadowed her interests in such key domains as history, memory, and national identity, theorizing their intersection in ways that directly anticipated her work in Germany. It also introduced Daphne's lasting theoretical approach, grounded in the concepts of experience, performance, narrative, and dialogue. This orientation reflected the enduring influence of Ed Bruner, Daphne's first teacher in anthropology, who had mentored her during the year she had spent at the University of Illinois (cf. Bruner 1984, 1986a, 1986b).

The rest of the book is devoted to Germany, its two parts allowing us to follow Daphne's dynamic thinking across foundational fieldwork experiences. "Kella" is made up of essays that primarily draw on Daphne's fieldwork in the village in 1990–1992 and 1996. As a whole, the essays complement and augment *Where the World Ended,* with the individual pieces also striking out in new directions. "Consumer Rites" is an elegant distillation of key parts of *Where the World Ended,* emphasizing the book's material on consumption and beginning its ambitious retheorization in the context of the "globalization of consumption-oriented market economies, particularly in postsocialist societies" (this volume: 34). "'(N)Ostalgie' for the Present" and "Go, Trabi, Go!" also bring the Kella ethnography into conversation with later concerns. The former is Daphne's definitive statement on *Ostalgie,* the nostalgia for East Germany. Published in *Ethnos* the same year that saw the appearance of *Where the World Ended,* it is a widely read piece that continues to influence scholarship on the subject (e.g., Boyer 2008). "Go, Trabi, Go!" is another favorite. Written on the occasion of an AAA session in honor of James Fernandez and published in a 2001 special issue of *Anthropology and Humanism,* it is a masterpiece of lighthearted prose and razor-sharp analysis. An homage to Fernandez's approach to symbolic anthropology, an important inspiration throughout Daphne's career, it also continues to have a most productive afterlife (cf. Fernandez 1986; Zivkovic 2008). Finally, "Mixed Devotions" is a deeply moving piece whose tragic overtones only amplify its pertinence. A self-reflexive essay originally published in a volume on fieldwork in postsocialist eastern Europe, it illuminates the religious dynamics of postsocialism and comments meaningfully on the cultural construction of illness and health. Most importantly, though, it brings us very close to Daphne herself.

"Leipzig" collects pieces that were written on the basis of research Daphne carried out in the East German city, starting with an exploratory trip in 1998. A longer stay followed in 2001, and a final stint took place in 2003. The essays evince Daphne's continued and deepened interest in two crucial domains: the intersection of consumption and citizenship, on the one hand, and the significance of memory and nostalgia, on the other. "The Spirit of Capitalism and the Boundaries of Citizenship in Post-Wall Germany" squarely falls in the former. An important 2005 article in *Comparative Studies in Society and History,* it is followed by the previously unpublished "Local Hero, National Crook," a beautiful essay that anchors Leipzig's postsocialist transformation in the vagaries of neoliberalism. The final two pieces return to the question of Ostalgie. "Expressions of Experience and Experiences of Expression," written for an AAA session in honor of Ed Bruner and published in another special issue of *Anthropology and Humanism,* addresses the musealization of the GDR. The representation of East Germany also takes center-stage in "Goodbye Lenin, Aufwiedersehen GDR," a brilliant reading of the 2003 film *Good Bye, Lenin!* as social text and cultural phenomenon.

In Daphne's design, the four essays in "Leipzig" formed parts of two separate book projects. The first was a monograph with the working title "Citizenship and Mass Consumption in Post-Wall Germany"; the second a collection of essays to be called "On the Social Life of Socialism: Memory, Nostalgia, Things." These were exceedingly ambitious projects; and while Daphne's untimely death prevented their completion, her optimism and endurance in the face of terrible illness allowed for the completion of the pieces we do have.

They also allow us to discern the trajectory of Daphne's theorization of postsocialism, particularly in regard to her key themes of consumption and memory. *Where the World Ended* had already emphasized consumption as a crucial domain of the transition. In this, Daphne seemed to follow the dominant representation of the Wende as, first and foremost, one big shopping spree. But this kind of triumphalism was far from her agenda. Instead, she paid close attention to the actual experiences of East Germans as they encountered the commodity-driven world of capitalism. Frequently accompanying villagers on their shopping trips across the former border, she brilliantly described their "lack of a certain cultural fluency." The passage is echoed in "Consumer Rites," where it is followed by a typically subtle piece of ethnography:

In the first years after the Wende, the stereotypical insecure Ossi walked with her head down and asked the store clerk not "where" a specific item was, but "do you have it?" Whereas West Germans could refer to certain products by their brand names—such as "Tempo" for a tissue or "Uhu" for glue—East Germans would describe their function. When people described differences between East and West Germans, they frequently pointed only to consumption practices. "Ossis compare prices," I was often told. "Wessis always know what they want to buy." It was usually during shopping trips in an adjacent western town that people would recriminate themselves for behaving like an Ossi. "Now she probably knows I'm an Ossi," one woman whispered to me about the bakery clerk. "I didn't know what that bread was called." (this volume: 38)

The key insight, in other words, was that it was in the inherently unequal realm of consumption that the citizens of the former East Germany became Ossis.

By the time Daphne commenced her research in Leipzig, she came to see the domain of consumption in even more embracive terms. After the Wende, it had engendered the inadequate subjects shopping at western supermarkets. But with the full-fledged arrival of capitalism in the east, consumption became the key to the transition itself. The starting point of this investigation was the realization that the new order ultimately turned on the production of citizens as consumers. The transition, in other words, was less about the achievement of political freedoms (the right to vote in free elections) than the attainment of consumptive privileges (the right to make choices during shopping). This, in turn, led Daphne to an investigation of citizenship. Influenced by theorists of neoliberalism like Jean and John Comaroff who had diagnosed a general shift from production to consumption in the constitution of the normative national subject (Comaroff and Comaroff 2000), she came to see Germany's postsocialist transition as a particularly dramatic instantiation of this process. It had certainly been the most rapid.

Leipzig was a particularly apt place for such an investigation of the shift from production to consumption. In the years since the Wende, it had lost 90 percent of its manufacturing jobs. At the same time, it emerged as a commercial center for the new states. Building on Leipzig's long history of trade fairs, the process had been spurred by the creation of vast malls on the city's outskirts. It had also entailed the renovation of the downtown area and its transformation into an upscale shopping district.

Daphne set out to investigate the "making of citizen-consumers" in this rapidly deindustrializing world (this volume: 87). *Wendegewinner* and *Wendeverlierer* (the winners and losers of the transition) were the key figures in her analysis. In "The Spirit of Capitalism and the Boundaries of Citizenship in Post-Wall Germany," the focus was on the latter. With characteristic sensitivity and great ethnographic subtlety, Daphne related their stories of defeat and captured the "image seminars" that promised them "individual fulfillment, self-discovery, and even healing through consumption" (this volume: 98). The new form of citizenship, Daphne showed, was both normalizing and exclusionary.

"Local Hero, National Crook," by contrast, addressed an apparent Wendegewinner, "Doc" Schneider. A West German real estate tycoon, he had been the principal force behind downtown Leipzig's post-Wende revitalization. In 1994, however, his empire collapsed when it became clear that he had run a pyramid scheme based on fraud and corruption. The West German banks that had financed his scheme were left with billions of Marks in losses. In the west, this made Schneider a villain; but in the east, especially in Leipzig, he came to be celebrated as a kind of Robin Hood, a "trickster who [had] outsmarted the capitalists" and done so for the good of the city (this volume: 110). Daphne brilliantly theorized Schneider's rise and fall as emblematic of the contradictions of neoliberalism in re-unified Germany. To her, it perfectly captured the "Faustian bargain" in the East German embrace of capitalism (this volume: 110).

Memory was the second enduring theme in Daphne's work on postsocialism. There, too, the present volume allows us to appreciate the trajectory of her thinking, particularly in regard to Ostalgie. Daphne had been one of the first academics to seriously contemplate the nostalgia for state socialism. Scholars in other disciplines tended to regard the phenomenon as a trivial side effect of the large-scale transformations. Daphne, by contrast, recognized it as integral to the transition itself, a position that became the topic of a memorable exchange between her and historian Charles Maier at a 1998 conference in Vienna.[1] Daphne had presented her first analysis of Ostalgie, which was received with surprising skepticism, even hostility, by Maier and several of the other participants. To them, Ostalgie was no more than a growing pain, an attitude, Daphne felt, that belittled the real frustrations associated with the massive upheavals. As she later explicated, Maier's account of the Wende, widely considered definitive, had been "relatively uninterested in the voices and experiences of ordinary Eastern Germans" (Berdahl 2000: 3; Maier 1997). Daphne sought to restore these very aspects of everyday life to scholarly view; it was in that context that Ostalgie became a dominant theme of her work.

In the broadest sense, Daphne regarded Ostalgie as a form of resistance, showing that East Germans did not simply internalize the hegemonies of the west but actively negotiated them, even if they did so on the dominant terms. She also insisted that Ostalgie had its own cultural logic and dignity, helping people give meaning to the massive transformations that had upended their lives.

In the essays collected here, we can see that Daphne charted three phases of Ostalgie. A first occurred in the direct aftermath of the Wende; and preceding its widespread recognition as a relevant cultural phenomenon, it could be labeled a kind of vernacular Ostalgie. The women of Kella returning to wearing their smocks, as related in "Consumer Rites," is a good example. In the immediate wake of the Wende, women had abandoned their smocks in the recognition that they were not "modern" (i.e., western) and thus marked them as Ossis. After some time, however, they resumed wearing the old garments, an "assertion," Daphne argued, of their "identity as East Germans" (this volume: 43).

The second phase of Ostalgie is brilliantly captured in "'(N)Ostalgie' for the Present," which analyzed the mid-1990s "birth and boom of a nostalgia industry" in the former GDR. In the article, Daphne charted the proliferating sites of Ostalgie, from *Ost-Discos* to supermarkets specializing in East German products (this volume: 48). Conceptually, the piece was a retort to the widespread criticism of these phenomena as GDR romanticism mobilized by clever entrepreneurs. Daphne's main evidence against such dismissals was an investigation of "Ostalgic practices" on the ground (this volume: 59). Among them was her moving account of playing the Ostalgie game *Ferner Osten* with friends, documenting the great affirmation they derived from its validation of East German knowledge. Daphne ultimately concluded that the Ostalgie boom was the "expression of a kind of counter-memory" in the asymmetrical context of the new Germany—an "attempt to recuperate, validate, and anchor a collective memory of a shared past" (this volume: 55). In that sense, Ostalgie was not about "identification with the former GDR"; instead, it was about generating meaning for the present via forms of "oppositional solidarity and collective memory" (this volume: 56).

The 2000s, Daphne argued, witnessed the arrival of a third mode of Ostalgie. In contrast to earlier forms that had "captured feelings of profound loss, longing, and displacement in a period of intense social discord," this new form was more self-referential and "dominated by a certain cynicism, irony, and parody" (this volume: 131). "Expressions of Experience and Experiences of Expression" is a key essay in this regard, comparing, as it does, three museum-based memory practices in early twenty-first-century Leipzig: the federally sponsored Forum of Contemporary History (with its "western" representation of the GDR past), the "Witnesses to History" project (with its earnest collection of East German environs and goods), and a fashion show of East German clothing (with its "playful appropriation and ironic parody of Ostalgie" itself [this volume: 122]). It was the last example that stood for the new kind of Ostalgie, representing a moment when "East German things became 'camp' rather than objects of nostalgic longing or counter-memory" (this volume: 122).

Daphne was intrigued by this development in the history of Ostalgie, which she saw most fully expressed in the cultural phenomenon that was *Good Bye, Lenin!* Her account, presented at several conferences and recently published in an important volume on post-communist nostalgia, was a tour de force. It combined a subtle reading of the film and its symbolism with an analysis of the movie as a social phenomenon. The latter included a marketing bonanza, the clearest evidence for the new phase of Ostalgie. With theaters decked out in GDR paraphernalia and employees and audience members encouraged to don young pioneer scarfs and Free German Youth shirts, that phase may have been marked by its "hypercommercial and self-parodying form," a set of practices that "celebrate[d] and naturalize[d] capitalism as the inevitable outcome of socialism's demise" (this volume: 131). But even then, Daphne argued, Ostalgie remained an important framework for the ongoing negotiation of the transition—a mode in which "capitalist forms and practices" could be "contested *and* affirmed" (this volume: 132). It was the recognition of that dialectic that ultimately stood at the heart of Daphne's work on Ostalgie and postsocialism more generally.

Daphne's two books-in-progress were widely anticipated, their importance recognized by prestigious fellowships (including a Guggenheim for "Citizenship and Mass Consumption in Post-Wall Germany") and invitations to speak at numerous distinguished conferences. Her death deprives us of their completion. But we are lucky to have some of the parts. It is in the nature of a volume like this to have some repetition between individual texts. But the encounter of such redundancies seems a minor price to pay for the reward of reading Daphne's beautifully crafted essays and the ability to appreciate them in the context of her scholarship at large.

It is appropriate that this book should appear in a series Daphne founded and co-edited, a testament to her intellectual generosity and limitless capacity. So is the fact that the book is framed by her work on memory. From the Vietnam Veterans Memorial to *Good Bye, Lenin!* she showed that the act of remembering is at the heart of the human condition and that our present is only made meaningful by our past. As we mourn the passing of Daphne Berdahl, we know that she will always be a part of our present.

ON THE SOCIAL LIFE OF POSTSOCIALISM

PART ONE

—⚏—

WASHINGTON, D.C.

1

VOICES AT THE WALL
Discourses of Self, History, and National Identity
at the Vietnam Veterans Memorial

VISITORS TO THE VIETNAM VETERANS Memorial in Washington, D.C., respond to its stark, haunting beauty in a multitude of ways. Some come here to weep, pray, mourn, and to remember; others come to witness the emotion of the place. Many knew someone whose name is now engraved on the Wall; most do not. Some stay for hours, standing alone in silent contemplation and reflection, tracing a name with their fingers, taking a rubbing of a name, or leaving behind an offering to the dead; for others the memorial is a brief stop on a tour of the nation's capital. A public place where private communions with and mourning for the dead occur, this most visited monument in Washington, D.C., has come to be called "a national healing shrine"; many visitors come here not as tourists, but as pilgrims.

Much of the memorial's power stems from its simple design. Situated between the Washington Monument and the Lincoln Memorial, two black granite walls are wedged into the earth of America's most sacred and symbolically loaded landscape. The walls meet in an obtuse angle whose sides point to the towering white marble tributes to the country's most revered presidents. Instead of climbing steps as at the Lincoln Memorial or taking an elevator as to the top of the Washington Monument, the visitor here walks down a gently sloping ramp alongside the 494-foot wall. A line of five names on a ten-inch panel begins at each end where the Wall emerges from the earth. The lines of names multiply quickly as the height of the memorial's panels increases and it rises to its ten-foot apex, where one is confronted with the reflecting blackness of the polished granite and thousands of names.

More than 58,000 names of American men and women killed or missing in Vietnam are inscribed on the memorial in chronological order by date of casualty. The ordering of names chronicles the escalating destruction of the Vietnam War, creating not a static monument, but rather a journey into the past that begins by moving from a name in the directory[1] to a name on a panel that contains all the others who were casualties on that same day. The memorial's architect conceived of the Wall as a boundary between the living and the dead as well as a journey; the individual visitor decides when the journey is over.

Unlike most monuments that can be regarded passively by the observer, the Vietnam Veterans Memorial demands that the visitor "actively participate in the space defined by the work" (Blum 1987: 128) in order to experience it. The handprints that smudge the Wall's polished black granite surface are evidence of visitors' active participation, testament to the need to interact with and touch this memorial. A striking contrast to the traditional national war memorial, the Tomb of the Unknown Soldier, where uniformed military guards stand watch and keep visitors at a distance, this monument invites the observer to make contact with the names of the known casualties (Wagner-Pacifici and Schwartz 1991; cf. Mosse 1990).

My principal aim in this paper is to explore the relationship between public space, private histories, and the production of cultural practices, historical memory, and national identity. Drawing on Bakhtin's theories of dialogic processes and discourse as language in its social form (Bakhtin 1968, 1981; cf. Bruner and Gorfain 1984), I examine a discourse generated at the memorial in which self, history, and national identity are constructed, reconstructed, and frequently contested. All are in a state of production and flux at the memorial, defined and redefined by the "multiplicity of social voices" that speak here (Bakhtin 1981). The Wall has become a place for metasocial commentary, where people as well as a nation tell themselves stories about themselves.

The organization of this paper parallels what I see to be a progressive development in the memorial's discourse. After briefly discussing how a notion of silence and healing became part of the memorial's discourse from the start, I examine how the construction of the memorial produced struggles over the control of historical knowledge and representation. My analysis then turns to the voices and stories that speak at the Wall that conflate personal memory with collective history and national identity. Arguing that the multitude of utterances, narratives, and offerings here are in a dialogic as well as power relationship to one another, I suggest how every act of remembering may also be an act of forgetting. Finally, I consider how the reproduction of this discourse in mass culture and media representations has routinized and structured practice, creating and sanctioning culturally coded responses to the Wall.

BREAKING A SILENCE: BACKGROUND

Vietnam was America's longest and, except for the Civil War, its most controversial war. Over three million served between 1959 and 1975; their average age was 19. Those who returned, 75,000 of whom were permanently disabled, faced their own personal battles amidst a turbulent nation opposed to the war. Traditional homecoming rituals for returning warriors like ticker-tape parades were never held; soldiers returning from Vietnam slipped in the country's back door—often 24 hours after leaving the combat zone—and were ignored. There was no public commemoration or recognition of veterans who served in Vietnam. Although Congress had authorized a Tomb of the Unknown Vietnam Soldier in 1973, and a white marble cover had been installed over an empty crypt at Arlington National Cemetery in 1974, these plans were abandoned in 1975 after the fall of Saigon. The marble cover was removed and replaced with a red granite slab that concealed the presence of an empty tomb.[2]

The idea to build a memorial to honor the men and women who served in Vietnam was conceived by a Vietnam veteran, Jan Scruggs, who, as the legend goes, became obsessed with building a monument containing the names of those killed and missing in Vietnam after seeing the movie *The Deer Hunter* in 1979 (Wagner-Pacifici and Schwartz 1991). Together with two other Vietnam veterans, Robert Doubek and John Wheeler, Scruggs organized a non-profit Vietnam Veterans Memorial Fund (VVMF), which launched a massive nationwide lobbying and fund-raising campaign. By July 1980, the VVMF had succeeded in getting a bill through Congress and signed into law, authorizing them to build a memorial on a two-acre site near the Lincoln Memorial. The fund had insisted on this location in the shadow of Lincoln to symbolize national reconciliation.

This theme of reconciliation and redemption became a major trope in the early discourse of the memorial. The aim of the memorial project was to "heal the nation's wounds" from the Vietnam War by commemorating the soldiers who fought rather than the war itself (by "separating the war from the warriors"). In making a case for the memorial, fund-raising efforts called upon stories of the mistreatment of vets after the war, like this one recounted in Scruggs's book:

> Back home, no one wanted to hear what you'd been through. If people saw you in uniform they might spit, call you a murderer, or—most painfully—ask you why you were stupid enough to go. And if you'd been seriously wounded . . . someone might come up and say "served you right." Even ten years after you came back, the easiest way to clear a room was to mention Vietnam. (Scruggs and Swerdlow 1985: 11)

In the discussions of the memorial, this silence was not perceived as an imposed suppression of knowledge of the past, nor as a reluctance to speak on the part of veterans; rather it was viewed as a product of the American public's desire to forget the controversial war.

There is little question that such a silence existed following the war, and that it did suppress the voices and stories of veterans and quelled the expression of pain related to the war and loved ones lost, as letters to the fund accompanying donations illustrated ("My son was killed and I can't bring it up at a party" [Scruggs and Swerdlow 1985: 25]). But once part of the memorial rhetoric, the notion of healing a nation through breaking a silence became part of a dominant narrative[3] of the public history and memory of Vietnam.

Having secured its site on the Mall, the VVMF called a national design competition, open to anyone over 18, professional or amateur. The enormous response was unprecedented: over 1,400 entries were submitted, "some obviously prepared in high-tech studios, others sweated out on kitchen tables."[4] The jury of professional architects, sculptors, landscape architects, and an art critic were selected and asked by the fund to adhere to specific criteria in their selection of a design: the memorial could not make any political statement about the war; it had to contain the names of those who had died in conflict and who were still missing; it had to be reflective and contemplative in character; and it should harmonize with its surroundings. First prize went to Maya Lin, then a 21-year-old Chinese American undergraduate at Yale. Lin later wrote of her design:

> I had designed the memorial for a seminar on funerary architecture . . . We had already been questioning what a war memorial is, its purpose, its responsibility . . . I felt a memorial should be honest about the reality of war and be for the people who gave their lives . . . I didn't want a static object that people would just look at, but something they could relate to as on a journey, or a passage, that would bring each to his own conclusions . . . I had an impulse to cut open the earth . . . an initial violence that in time would heal . . . It was as if the black-brown earth were polished and made into an interface between the sunny world and the quiet dark world beyond that we can't enter. The names would become the memorial. There was no need to embellish. (*National Geographic* 1985)

As the history of the construction of the Vietnam Veterans Memorial demonstrates, commemorations are socially produced and negotiated events involving struggles over the control of knowledge. Once announced, the design of the memorial became the object of intense controversy and opposition. Calling it a "black gash of shame," "an insult to those it intends to memorialize," "bizarre," and "a black trench that scars the Mall," opponents argued the memorial made an obvious anti-war statement and failed to honor surviving veterans. A scathing criticism in the conservative journal the *National Review* voiced the opponents' objections on the grounds that it symbolized a silence the memorial was supposed to overcome:

> Our objection to this Orwellian glop does not issue from any philistine objection to new concepts in art. It is based upon the clear political message of this design. The design says that the Vietnam War should be memorialized in black, not in the white marble of Washington. The mode of listing names makes them individual deaths, not deaths in a cause: they might as well have been traffic accidents. The invisibility of the monument at ground level symbolizes the unmentionability of the war. (*National Review* 1981)

In what came to be called "the battle of the Vietnam Memorial," "the controversy," and "the war on the Wall," debates centered around the purposes and responsibilities of public art. The need for a monument to be both aesthetically pleasing as well as symbolically appropriate, methods for its selection, the relationship between professional elite standards and popular taste, and the appropriateness of abstract symbolism or realist representation were at issue in the heated controversy that threatened to end the project. James Watt, Reagan's conservative secretary of the interior, refused to grant a construction permit to build the memorial until these issues were resolved.

After much deliberation and debate, a compromise was finally reached in January of 1982 to add a realistic statue and an American flag to the memorial site at a later date. "The idea was grotesque that you could design a memorial through this backroom debate—let's put up a statue—that it could be brokered like that," Robert Doubek, co-founder and project director of the VVMF, later remarked in an interview (August 9, 1989). But it worked; Watt granted the permit, construction began in March 1982, and Lin's memorial was completed 8 months later.

However, the battle over the memorial was not only a debate over the nature of public art; it was a struggle over the control and appropriation of history through representation and commemoration. It was not only an aesthetic controversy between advocates of modernism and proponents of realism; it was a political debate that mirrored much of the controversy surrounding the war itself. But it was not necessarily an argument between hawks and doves, between those who had supported the war and those who demonstrated against it; it was also a dispute between a group of primarily professional military men who strongly believed the memorial should make a political statement about the righteousness of the war's cause, and the veterans who believed it should remain apolitical by focusing on the individual casualties.

However, a non-statement about the war—either through lack of commemoration or in an ambiguous, apolitical memorial design—does make a statement. The open-endedness of the design itself conveys the message that a unified, monolithic statement about the war cannot be made. As Robert Doubek pointed out:

> To a certain extent we [the Vietnam Veterans Memorial Fund] expressed doubt about the war by not making any statement about it. There was obviously some doubt in our minds. (Interview on August 9, 1989)

Jan Scruggs also conceded that the memorial's ambiguity makes a particular statement about war:

> I always thought that the opponents were basically right, that the memorial is kind of an anti-war statement. It is not an anti–Vietnam War statement, but a kind of universal statement on war. I think it really focuses on the tragedy of the loss of individual lives. I do not think, nor have I ever thought, that the memorial makes a political statement about that particular war. (Interview on August 11, 1989)

A devoted long-term National Park Service volunteer at the Wall, John Bender, most clearly articulated the type of statement made by the memorial's open design:

> The memorial says: this is the price we pay. It doesn't say whether it was right, it doesn't say whether it was wrong, it doesn't say whether it was worth it or not. It simply says "this is the cost of war."

The controversy surrounding the memorial also concerned the issue of who controls memorialization in society. This was not a project initiated and fought over by the state but rather by the people the memorial was to commemorate.

Funded entirely by over $7,000,000 in private contributions, the memorial project's success was largely due to the way its discourse of silence and commemoration resonated with individual experience. Many letters to the fund and stories told at fundraisers expressed a longing for space, both discursive as well as a physical site, in which veterans and their families could tell their stories, as the following excerpt illustrates:

> If I can touch the name of my friends who died, maybe I will finally have time to react. Maybe I will end up swearing, maybe crying, maybe smiling, remembering a funny incident. Whatever it is, I will have time and the focal point to do it now. (Scruggs and Swerdlow 1985: 126)

AN EXPLOSION OF PERSONAL NARRATIVES

While the struggle to build the memorial established the tropes of silence, healing, and redemption as part of the memorial's discourse, the Wall's dedication in November 1982 affirmed and reproduced the notion that a national silence had been broken. The week-long National Salute to Vietnam Veterans triggered an explosion of personal narratives, creating a permanent discursive space as well as a physical site from which the voices could continue to emerge.[5] The Vietnam Veterans Memorial immediately became a collective point in the manner of Bakhtin's medieval carnival and marketplace (characterized by the expression of voices and the use of language otherwise suppressed), as well as a culturally framed space and "memory site" where people could tell their stories (Nora 1989). Veterans quickly named it "the last firebase,"[6] a metaphor that reveals their perceptions of the Wall as a safe place, a gathering point, a final stop before leaving the war behind them.

Organized by and for Vietnam veterans, the long-overdue national tribute and homecoming was a convincing "definitional ceremony,"[7] giving veterans visibility and allowing them to define their experiences in their own terms, with their own voices. Aiming to "exorcise in a national ritual" the logic that blamed those who fought in the war for the war itself (Scruggs and Swerdlow 1985: 126), the week-long salute included wreath-laying ceremonies, workshops related to veterans' concerns about such issues as the effects of Agent Orange and post-traumatic stress disorder, and a 3-day, round-the-clock candlelight vigil in the National Cathedral where the names of all servicemen and women killed or missing in Vietnam were read aloud. The week's activities culminated in an old-fashioned parade down Constitution Avenue—carried live on Cable News Network—of color guards, grand marshals, floats, cadets from military academies, and 15,000 Vietnam Veterans in wheelchairs, on crutches, and in old combat fatigues or new suits; the dedication ceremony at the memorial attended by an emotional crowd of 150,000 took place later that same day.

Veterans from all over the country flocked to their belated homecoming and first national recognition. For the first time since their return, veterans were thanked and appreciated: civilians attending the dedication ceremony and parade were anxious to shake their hands, people carried signs saying "Thank you Vietnam Veterans" and cheered as they paraded past. Cab drivers refused fares, strangers bought them drinks, a group of college students stood and applauded a table of veterans one night in a restaurant. Along with the veterans' longing for catharsis was the country's need for redemption; even the generation too young to have experienced the Vietnam era had assumed a sense of collective guilt over the treatment of veterans following the war.

Most remarkable about the dedication and national salute was the opportunity it provided veterans to tell their stories—and they seized it, claiming a space for their voices, narratives, and experience in the public discourse. Buttons worn on old army jackets, bumper stickers on wheelchairs, and placards carried in the parade expressed veterans' attitudes toward the war as well as current concerns: "We killed, we bled, we died for worse than nothing," "Agent Orange Victims of New Jersey," "Next Time, Let Us Win It," "Why Were the Privileged Exempt?" or "I Need a Job." Their stories erupted spontaneously at reunions of battalions, fortuitous meetings of old buddies, over drinks, and at the memorial. Veterans approached each other asking, "When were you there?" "Who were you with?" The words most frequently overheard during the week were uttered during a handshake or embrace: "Welcome home, brother." The ordering of names evoked painful memories and personal stories of the war: "There are the names of guys who took bullets for me," "There's my whole platoon together," "That's the day my helicopter went down" (Scruggs and Swerdlow 1985: 148). The outpouring of emotion in an atmosphere of *spontaneous communitas* was overwhelming. Following the week's ceremonies the *Washington Post* reported that "rarely in this city have so many men been seen to break down in tears in public, to embrace another as they remembered a shared past."[8]

The recognition of individual lives was a central part of the press coverage of the dedication: newspapers, popular periodicals, and the broadcast media focused on individual experiences of veterans and their families. The *Washington Post* ran articles throughout the week on veterans' reactions to the Wall, different experiences of the war, as well as pilgrimages to the memorial in memory of a loved one. Essays by veterans themselves tended to recount their own experience of the war in relation to someone whose name was on the Wall. Like the memorial, the articles, profiles, essays, and letters contained names—names and stories of men and women on the Wall, names and stories of those who survived.

The dedication thus established the centrality of individual histories in the memorial's discourse. The offerings that littered the base of the Wall following the ceremony focused on the loss of individual lives. In addition to the traditional memorial icons of wreaths, crosses, and flowers, people had left cowboy boots, photographs, notes, and a teddy bear. The way stories are told here is as important as what they have to say: a brief message scrawled on a torn piece of paper, apparently on the spur of the moment; a poem, carefully written, typed, and framed; a letter to someone on the Wall, placed in a plastic bag to protect it from the rain. Stories may be told verbally to family, friends, or National Park Service volunteers. Some offerings tell stories that are known only by the donor and the person whose name is now inscribed on the memorial: a senior prom picture, a wedding bouquet, a bottle of Jack Daniels, a dollar bill with the note written across the front, "A debt so long unpaid and the beer I promised"; a blood-stained Ace bandage; or red lace panties alongside an empty bottle of tequila. People have occasionally chosen to communicate a story in a letter mailed by Federal Express or flowers sent by FTD (Florists' Transworld Delivery) to someone on the Wall.

With each spoken, written, or even non-verbal utterance, a story becomes embedded in the memorial; or, as Edmund Leach has pointed out, "story and place are mutually supportive" (Leach 1984: 358). Edward M. Bruner's description of the relationship between stories and sites helps explain a similar interaction at the Vietnam Veterans Memorial (cf. Basso 1984; Bruner and Gorfain 1984):

> Names may construct the landscape but stories make the site resonate with history and experience. Stories introduce a temporal dimension, making sites the markers of the experiences of groups and historical persons, not just markers of space. In spite of the inevitable changes that occur with each retelling of the story, the now culturally constituted landscape, in its solid materiality and sequentiality, authenticates the story. The permanence of the site becomes an anchor for an elusive story. (Bruner 1984: 4)

The stories told by visitors at the Vietnam Veterans Memorial are ephemeral, ever-changing, and often contradictory to one another. Multiple voices coexist here in a dialogic relationship to each other; the memorial collects and authenticates the stories they have to tell.

STORIES, HEALING, AND THE
CONSTRUCTION OF SELF

Since the memorial's dedication, the discursive practices that immediately became a part of the site have continued, multiplied, and evolved. Because the nature of the discourse generated at the Wall focuses on individual experiences of the war, I will first consider the content of such personal narratives in order to explore the relationship between individually constituted histories, public space, and a national memory of the Vietnam experience.

The Wall's alleged potential for individual and national "healing" has become a prominent part of the stories told here. A poem in honor of the memorial and its dedication describes the nature of this "healing" effect:

> Our Wall stands in Washington
> Proclaiming its best
> Built to honor our fallen
> And put young souls to rest

It's time to reunite fellow veteran
For this is finally our day
With the strength of our convictions
America will see it our way

To all closet veterans
Who carry scars from the past
Step out of your darkness
And be heard at last

If we all stand together
And demand to be heard
Our many unresolved illnesses
Can finally be cured. (Unknown in POW/MIA n.d.)

The memorial has been called "a healing shrine" and "the Wall that heals." The National Park Service brochure on the memorial describes it as "beginning the healing process," and the Friends of the Vietnam Veterans Memorial, "a non-profit, non-political membership organization dedicated to furthering the positive effects of the Vietnam Veterans Memorial" formed in 1986 to "undertake projects that will enhance and extend the healing nature of the memorial for all Americans" (Friends of the Vietnam Veterans Memorial n.d.).

Implicit in the notion of healing is an assumption of illness, rarely explicitly defined but understood to be the political divisiveness of the war and the silence that followed it—a national "dis-ease" (Williams 1987). Like the sickness, the memorial's healing is secular, associated with "coming to terms with the Vietnam War," remembrance, redemption, and catharsis. There is a presumed connection between individual and national healing here, a sense that the collective healing of individual griefs can heal a national consciousness as well.

The memorial's reputed healing power has contributed to the Wall's status as a sacred shrine, to which people come as pilgrims. A terminally ill veteran hopped in his car on an impulse and drove straight from Texas to see the memorial. "I told my wife I just had to get here to set this part of my life behind me," he told me. "It really is worth the 1,300 miles." Another veteran saved for years, put on his now snug-fitting old combat fatigues, and left a bush hat with "Saigon Sweetheart" stitched across the front. As at other pilgrimage shrines, people at the Vietnam Veterans Memorial leave votive offerings and communicate with the dead, making the memorial a kind of "spirit medium" (Cheree and Hocking 1988). People describe feeling closest to their loved one or buddies here at the Wall. "It's the one place in the world where I feel as if I am given the opportunity to communicate with my father and tell him how much I love him and respect him and wish we could have shared a life together," one visitor explained (Palmer 1988: 95). The wife of a soldier killed in Vietnam said, "I felt like I wanted to tiptoe because I was with all these men's spirits. Although I knew Bob's body was buried . . . at home, I felt like he was there [at the Wall]" (Palmer 1988: 156).

Visitors' behavior at the memorial reflects this feeling of closeness. One National Park Service volunteer witnessed a man dressed in jungle fatigues approach the Wall and hit it lightly, jokingly, as if one might hit a friend. I observed a similar interaction as a veteran dressed in a dark business suit leaned against the memorial and slowly caressed a name with shaking hands, crying silently. He then suddenly pulled back, clicked his heals together and saluted the Wall. Most people attribute this sense of connection to the names: "It's because of the names—the spirit of them—you can sense they are there because of the names," a Park Ranger who is also a Vietnam veteran explained, "You really can feel it!"

The mythology, legends, and folklore of the Wall have endowed it with spiritual and supernatural qualities much like those of pilgrimage sites. Like apparitional shrines, some people have claimed to see ghosts here; others say they can see the dead soldiers behind the names in the black granite: "If you look closely you can see their faces," a combat veteran explained, pointing between the names. When it rains, people say "the Wall cries." Visitors, volunteers, and most people who have spent much time at the Wall describe a similar experience of finding a name without looking it up in the directory or searching for it. This happened to me while working as a volunteer before I had heard this story and I asked another volunteer who agreed: "I don't believe in this kind of thing, but I've often gone to look for a name, stop before a panel, and there it is." "The names call out to you," people say. While the discourse and mythology of the Wall has attributed human, spiritual, and magical capacities to the memorial, the source of its healing power is not perceived as supernatural.

The perception of healing, I would argue, stems from the telling of a story in a culturally as well as physically framed space. But it is not the storytelling alone that heals; it is the public nature of the performance—self-knowledge acquired through display (Myerhoff 1986: 281)—that is therapeutic. When enacted in performance, stories become transformative (Bruner 1986a: 7).

For veterans, whose interaction with the Wall is different from that of friends and relatives because it is influenced by survivor's guilt and the experience of war, telling a story at the Wall enables them to define, constitute, and impose meaning on painful or haunting experiences during and after the war. A fifty-page handwritten narrative left at the memorial details a soldier's enlistment, arrival in Vietnam, court martial and time spent in an Army stockade, and combat:

> All night I thought about putting my friends in body bags, picking up pieces of their bodies, a boot with a leg, no body, arms, feet, heads, the night went on forever. I've never been the same since.

By describing key events of his tour in Vietnam, this veteran explains to himself and to others the problems he faces today:

> I've been a P.O.W. in my own mind for twelve long years, flashbacks every day, sometimes a few in one day...
> ...Nobody wanted to hear Vietnam... we all had enough of the war, but for me the war isn't over yet... When will it be over, when can I turn the light out at the end of the tunnel? I hope the light at the end of the tunnel isn't the sun. (Palmer 1988: 139–141)

Most veterans' stories are told in letters to "brothers"; these speak not only to people on the Wall, but to others at the Wall—the visitors who are the audience for the performance—as well. Many are confessions:

> To the Soldiers of the 101st Airborne:
> In 1968 we spent some time together. We tried not to get close for reasons only you and I can understand, however we did laugh, drank beer, played cards, and even cried together . . . The memories are the worst. From seeing Billy in tears and laying into his bayonet to the soccer game with a VC head . . . The worst memory for me is the day I sent the 76 men out of your 85 to their deaths. I have to explain and I pray to God you will understand. (VVMC, x1,901)[9]

Several messages contain apologies, often hastily scribbled on a torn piece of notebook paper:

> I'm so sorry Frankie—I know we left you—I hope you didn't suffer too much— give them hell. (VVMC, x612)

Other letters vividly articulate veterans' agonizing guilt and ask for forgiveness:

> We did what we could but it was not enough because I found you here. You are not just a name on this Wall. You are alive. You are blood on my hands. You are screams in my ears. You are eyes in my soul. I told you you'd be all right, but I lied, and please forgive me. (VVMC, x1,875)

The messages and letters of veterans express, define, and sometimes claim to purge them of this guilt. One note attached to a gold wedding band explained it had belonged to a Viet Cong fighter who was killed by a Marine unit in 1963. The author of this note had carried this ring—an emblem of his guilt—for 18 years and was liberating himself of the guilt by leaving it, along with the ring, at the Wall. "It's time for me to lay it down. This boy is not my enemy any longer" (Fish 1987: 39).

Bitterness and resentment toward those who avoided the war and "shunned their duty" may also be asserted in these messages:

> You "peace boys" pant from your easy chairs
> But you don't know what it's like over here.
> You have a ball without even trying
> While over here the boys are dying.
> You burn your draft cards and march at dawn.
> Plant your flags on the White House Lawn.
>
> Use your flags, your drugs, and have your fun.
> Then refuse to use your gun.
> There's nothing else for you to do.
> And just think, I'm supposed to die for you.
>
> I'll hate you till the day I die.
> You made me hear my buddy cry.
> I heard them say, "This one's dead." (VVMC, x1,189)

The following letter reads almost as if it were a response to these accusations, and thus reflects how voices at the Wall exist in a kind of dialogic relationship to one another. Addressed to all names on the Wall from someone who stayed behind, it reveals a different sort of survivor's guilt:

> I feel guilty when I think about you. I felt the war was justified and went to college with a school deferment. I don't know how any of you felt about the war; I do know you fought and died. Not even the lottery required me to exert my courage . . . I don't wish that I fought and died. Rather I wish for an opportunity to put myself on the line, to put my courage up for my convictions. Hopefully it will make up for my lack of guts the last time around. (VVMC, x1,904)

Non-verbal offerings at the Wall can also tell or represent a story. Veterans typically leave items recalling combat: medals, dog tags, combat boots, C-Rations, unit patches, and helmets covered in graffiti ranging from "kill gooks" to peace signs. A maroon beret decorated with fifteen ribbons, headgear of the 37th Aerospace Rescue and Recovery Unit that saved many lives, identifies the soldier who probably wore it as a senior crewman, a master parachutist, and someone who participated in three campaigns in the Vietnam War. An M-14 rifle with the words "USMC, Chu Lai, 1965–1966" and fifteen notches carved in the fore-stock embodies a story known only by the soldier who went to the trouble to get the gun out of Vietnam. By leaving behind the part of them that represents the soldier, many veterans say they are able to rid themselves of the war itself and "come home." One veteran explained:

> If you leave something there, if you leave a little bit of your emotion, if you leave a little part of you, no matter what it is, that little part of you is going to stay there also. Because you've given up fighting that second fight, you've come home. (Fish 1987: 39)

A visit to the memorial may also be part of a process by which a veteran asserts his identity as a Vietnam veteran. Men come to the Wall wearing hats that say "Vietnam Veteran and Damn Proud of it," or T-shirts with the words "America is #1 thanks to its vets" or "Vietnam combat vet" printed on the front. Veterans refer to the memorial as "our Wall" and check it regularly for cracks or vandalism. Within this defined space, veterans are invested with authority to talk about the war or answer questions about the Wall; several men, referred to as "professional vets," are regulars there.

Another way veterans claim the Wall heals is by finding a name, bidding farewell, and letting go. Frequently soldiers never knew whether a comrade wounded in combat had survived; many veterans go to the memorial to find out. In Vietnam, soldiers were not able to go through the funeral ritual that bid a final farewell to fellow servicemen—they never had a chance to say good-bye.

> It is only now on my second trip to this monument that I can admit that you, my friends, are gone forever—that I can see your names, call you my friends, and speak of your deaths.
>
> I've cried for you so many times. I've been dead for so long trying to keep you alive.
>
> I've carried the anguish of your deaths for so long, but I think I can stop looking for you now. I think I can start living without letting you die. (VVMC, x967)

Another letter expresses a similar message:

> Perhaps, now I can bury you; at least in my soul . . . We crept point together and we pulled "drag" together. We lay crouched in cold mud and were drenched by monsoons . . . When you were hit, I was your medic all the way, and when I was blown 50 feet by the mortar, you were there first. When I was shaking with malaria, you wiped my brow.
>
> . . . You got a bronze star, a silver star, survived 18 months of one demon hell after another, only to walk into a booby trapped bunker and all of a sudden you had no face or chest.
>
> I never cried. My chest becomes unbearably painful and my throat tightens so I can't even croak, but I haven't cried. I wanted to, I just couldn't.
>
> I think I can, today. Damn, I'm crying now.
>
> Bye Smitty. Get some rest (VVMC, x1,998)

Veterans' stories not only articulate, interpret, and thereby construct their experience of Vietnam as well as their visit to the Wall itself, they also define a relationship with someone on the Wall. They not only tell their own stories, but may also tell stories for buddies who no longer can.

Offerings left by friends and family similarly express painful personal loss, but offer a different perspective on that loss by forcing a recognition of the individual life—and death—a name represents. They leave photographs of young men in uniforms and little boys, giving meaning to a name by attaching a face to it. A note left at the Wall reminded visitors: "each of these names has a face." Parents leave stuffed animals, calling attention to the fact that each name is also somebody's child. Children leave roses and cards on Father's Day for someone they love, but never knew: "You are the perfect father because I have no memory of you."

Leaving an offering at the memorial also enables people to define themselves in relation to a particular memory. A large poster board with photographs, a newspaper clipping of a death announcement, and a typed narrative entitled "A 1968 Story" neatly arranged and laminated for display told of the day its author learned of her fiancé's death. The process of selecting photographs, deciding to include the news clipping, and the writing of the narrative itself framed, interpreted, and reconstructed this individual's experience. It was a story she told herself and others about herself.

The public telling of private stories at the Wall is thus crucial to a process of self-definition. The following letter from a mother to her son was left wrapped in plastic on a neatly constructed stand for public presentation; it is addressed to her son, but intended for others:

> Dear Bill,
> Today is February 13, 1984. I came to this black wall again to see and touch your name, and as I do I wonder if anyone ever stops to realize that next to your name, on this black wall, is your mother's heart. A heart broken 15 years ago today, when you lost your life in Vietnam.

> . . . They tell me the letters I write you and leave here at this memorial are waking others up to the fact that there is still much pain left, after all these years, from the Vietnam war.
>
> But this I know. I would rather have had you for 21 years, and all the pain that goes with losing you, than never to have had you at all.
>
> Mom
>
> (Edelman 1985: 299–300)

Letters to loved ones on the Wall communicate to them, to visitors, and thereby clarify for the author how she or he has come to terms with and dealt with their deaths:

> After you all died, I guess two boyfriends and several friends gone was a bit too much for me and I pretty much screwed up for ten years. Two boyfriends is just too much, too much, too much.
>
> Now I'm much better, more responsible. I learned that the pain and loss never go away. It just changes—
> I have had
> twenty years
> now
> to reflect on this
> madness
> and it is
> always the same. (VVMC, x1,416)

Many offerings from non-veterans as well as veterans tell stories about life since the war. They describe—and thus select and interpret—key events of the past 20 years; some are annual updates. Many attach pictures—"I'm 23 now!" "these are my children," "you'd be very proud of me"—as if to say "this is what I've become."

The process of telling a story can also define and constitute a relationship with someone on the Wall:

> My dearest friend of all my high school years—my college years. We grew up together—half way anyway. I'd hoped we could grow old together . . . Your death changed my life in a way I didn't even know until recently. I will always hold you in a special place in my heart. And you *will* grow old with me. (VVMC, x1,148)

Most messages simply, and often tenderly, say "I love you":

> In my mind I came
> to see the memorial
> to touch your sweet name.
> But in my heart, that
> reservoir that holds only
> cherished memories of you
> I longed to hold, to see,
> to touch, to feel you one
> more time.
> Dearly I do love you. (VVMC)

As non-verbal expressions of experience, material objects are also part of a performance at the Wall; they, too, embody a particular memory. Two pages from a 1966 desk calendar tell a story of Kathi and Bobby: scribbled all over the first page is "Bobby loves Kathi," "280 more days," "254 more days"; each day for 7 months is crossed off on the next page, but the x's do not make it to the date circled—presumably the end of his tour (VVMC, x1,015). A Hummel music box, a blue high heel, a plastic Christmas tree, a can of sardines, and an eight-track Carpenters tape are among the eclectic array of objects left at the memorial that make manifest some relationship.

While observers can only speculate on the intentions of the people who leave items here, as well as the extent to which the visit and offerings are truly therapeutic, it is clear that at the Vietnam Veterans Memorial people "author themselves" (Myerhoff 1986: 263). The act of telling a story—in a note, a letter, a poem, or non-verbal object—may not always heal or lead to deeper self-awareness, but it does express, define, and thereby construct an experience or a relationship. Many visitors do describe "feeling better," "getting this load off my mind," "getting it off my chest" after leaving something, telling a story, or breaking down in sobs at the Wall (cf. Palmer 1988). During a visit with a veterans' support group, one vet center counselor commented "this wall has done more for these guys than years of therapy."

The nature of this ritualistic secular healing cannot be fully understood without recognizing how catharsis, self-knowledge, and redemption are closely associated with western concepts of self and personhood. Anthropological literature on self and emotion has pointed out how emotions, feelings, and conceptions of self are not strictly personal, but culturally constructed, as Michelle Rosaldo has written: "Feelings are not substances to be discovered in our blood but social practices organized by stories we both enact and tell. They are structured by our forms of understanding" (Rosaldo 1984: 143; see also Geertz 1983; Lutz 1988).

The modern western distinction between an inner, feeling, private individual/self and the public persona adhering to rules, norms, and contexts is blurred at the memorial, a liminal zone betwixt and between the private and the public. The concept of catharsis here entails the release of private emotions in a specific public cultural setting; the public purging of an inner self's suppressed guilt by defining and symbolically leaving it at the memorial in a letter or poem or with a pair of combat boots is part of the Wall's redemptive power; and self-knowledge, long associated in western psychology with the notion of a "healthy individual," is gained through the public telling of an individual, personal story.

HISTORIES AND THE CONSTRUCTION OF HISTORY

Among the over 25,000 items left at the memorial that are now stored in a National Park Service warehouse is a large flag of the former Republic of South

Vietnam. The veteran who brought it home from the war asked a friend to take it to the Wall; a committee was formed to transport the flag to the memorial, and it made its way across the country, stopping at various veterans organizations where people signed it and attached to it whatever they wanted. The flag left at the Wall is covered with signatures, dates of service, messages to buddies on the Wall, unit insignias, patches, a combat infantry badge, a "Universal Death from Above" insignia, a six-inch patch inscribed with "Vietnam Hunting Club," a button of the Illinois State Vietnam Veterans Memorial, buttons that say "agent orange sitting duck" or "agent orange victim," and MIA/POW pins. It is a collage of experience, a bricolage of individual stories that together tell a larger story about the war and its aftermath.

Like the signatures, buttons, patches, and pins on the flag, the voices at the Wall tell individual histories that contribute to the construction and reconstruction of a public memory of the Vietnam era. Offerings left at the memorial connect personal biographies to national stories. There is a sense in which histories make history here; private experiences of the war collectively constitute the national experience.

Discussions of history at the memorial convey several understandings, conceptions, and uses of the term. Memory, both public and private, is closely associated and frequently equated with a notion of history as posterity in much of the memorial's discourse. Many of the items left at the Wall are part of a conscious construction of public memory in this sense. While the offerings during the first few years were clearly spontaneous, and many continue to be, the nature of the items left at the memorial has changed since their collection and cataloging by the National Park Service has been publicized through the media and popular literature on the memorial.[10] Often more carefully assembled for presentation and preservation, these offerings are intended for posterity. Attached to a set of jungle fatigues, for example, was the following note:

> Pants and shirt belonged to Chuck Louviere. Dedicated to the Vietnam Veterans Memorial as part of a future exhibit. (VVMC, x788)

People also want to be remembered in a particular way. Personal narratives, like published memoirs of public figures, detail what the author wants people to remember about him- or herself or about the person described in the story. The curators of the collection receive increasingly more inquiries from people who want to make sure their offering made it into the collection. Aiming to ensure their voice's position in future historical accounts, several persons have even tried to bypass leaving an object at the Wall and ask if they can send it directly to the warehouse.

This notion that memories can be collected to form a history implies a second conception of history as written, organized, or displayed. Such a history requires a historian, curator, or other agent to explain and interpret voices of the past. Diary entries or letters written in Vietnam and left at the Wall are individual stories from the war as well as documents for future historians. In fact, a network news special on the Vietnam Veterans Memorial Collection described it as containing "relics of a history that is yet to be written" (Koppel 1987). Offerings at the memorial consciously construct historical knowledge as well.

The voices at the Wall are thus demanding not only to be heard, but to be remembered, as one veteran on his way to a Veterans Day ceremony at the memorial explained:

> We're coming out. Out of our holes, and shells. Out of the closet, I guess. We have to talk and find out what happened to us. We're not going to find that in the history books.[11]

Lyrics to a song about the Wall similarly express this:

> We'll stand here at the Wall, our backs are braced,
> We're not going to have our history erased any more,
> No, we're not just going to forget that it happened this time. (Fish 1987: i)

Like many individual narratives, these lyrics convey a sense of personal memory as resistance to an official history. Although not always distinguishable from a history produced by historians, this type of history is imposed from above, most frequently by the state. "Memories fade, and only official history remains," Noam Chomsky has written (Hess 1987: 275). Individual offerings at the memorial may aim to ensure the perseverance of memory—or counter-memory—over official history by donating personal memories to a kind of history conceived of as posterity.

Historical knowledge is also produced and reproduced at the Wall as multiple voices struggle over the meaning of the war itself. Among these are voices of authority who attempt to impose a monologic interpretation of the memorial. President Reagan declared in a speech on Veterans Day 1988 at the memorial that "we have healed" and asked, "who can doubt that the cause for which our men fought was just?" Speeches at opening ceremonies for the Moving Wall (a half-scale replica of the Washington Vietnam Veterans Memorial that tours the United States) in Kokomo, Indiana, used the memorial for similar appropriation and re-interpretation of history: "The price of freedom is paid with young men's lives"; "the war was fought with honor but lost by people with less than honorable ends"; and "these men paid a price for our freedom."

Offerings at the Wall also interpret and impose mythical significance on the Vietnam War, forcing it to conform to narratives of other American wars fought for freedom and democracy—the dominant narrative of American military history prior to Vietnam. A framed drawing of the 199th Infantry Brigade insignia related this message:

> Comrades you gave your lives for a reason, so that we who remain can live in freedom. (VVMC)

A note from a 13-year-old girl reflected what she has been taught about the war:

> I feel like I owe you something because if it were not for you, I might not be living in a free country. You men sacrificed yourselves for my freedom. (VVMC, x1,617)

Lyrics to a song performed in a concert at the tenth anniversary of the Wall's dedication reflected a similar interpretation:

> He may be gone but not forgot
> We have our freedom because he fought.

Questionable as these claims about the war may be—there is a very tenuous relationship, if any, between the deaths of soldiers in Vietnam and American freedom—they represent attempts at the Wall to produce a mythologized history.

Contradictory voices contest these and similar interpretations. The following poem, entitled "A Tribute to Political Folly," was left typed and stapled to an American flag shortly after the Supreme Court's decision on flag burning and President Bush's subsequent call for a constitutional amendment prohibiting the desecration of the flag. It is an angry, bitter, and sarcastic retort to patriotic claims like those above:

> Please read me every Nigger's Name
> Please read me every Nigger's Name
> I really do not see too well, but my eyes are not to blame,
> So, Please read me every Nigger's Name.

> Most of us went over there thinking it was a game,
> Aspirin Tablet Monkeys trying to stake a claim,
> Eager to do their bidding each time they pulled the chain,
> Please read me every Nigger's name.

> The reasons they gave us were pretty
> much the same,
> That Princess-Whore called Freedom, that
> syphilitic dame,
> She feeds upon the flesh of young men
> she's killed and maimed,
> And never even bothers to learn a single
> Nigger's Name.

> So, they builded this black alter [sic] hoping to shift the blame,
> And then I traveled here to shed my rage and shame,
> Forgiving myself and others, it might tote out the same,
> First, I must hear every Nigger's Name.

> To make them all Immortal, you say, that's our single aim,
> They will rest in fields of grandeur beneath the eternal flame,
> The thing we have given them here is certain, lasting fame,
> You see, we've listed every hero's name.

> Moreover, we're sick of your crap, your
> whining, you exclaim,

Don't dwell on this; Don't remind us;
You're driving us insane,
Forget it; Get beyond it; What in hell
do you hope to gain?
Here's your monument listing every
Goddamn name,
they're still just as dead all the same.

Yet these listed here are more lucky—that one fact is plain,
Democratic Bands? They've cast off all their chains,
They really are the lucky ones; they don't live with the pain,
Still, read me every Nigger's Name.

Please read me every Nigger's name,
Please read me every Nigger's name,
I really do not see too well, but my
eyes are not to blame,
Let me light this flag as you read me
every Nigger's Name! (VVMC)

The reference to "nigger" in this poem is not a racist slur. It may refer to the fact that a disproportionate number of those who fought and died in Vietnam were black. Even more than that, however, it may represent a metaphor for everyone who died in Vietnam: "niggers"—oppressed, despised, and sacrificed to the ambitions of politicians who remained safe from the scourge of war.

Expressions of opposition to the war may also be subtle: a bush hat with a button from a veterans group that was part of the anti-war movement, a George McGovern campaign button, and protest poems written during the war. Rather than viewing the deaths in Vietnam as sacrifices for freedom, many voices stress the futility of the war. This note was addressed to Sharon Lane, the first nurse killed in Vietnam:

God Bless you Sharon for holding the hands of the dying for a war there was no need to fight. Bless us Lord, stop ALL the fighting. Amen. (VVMC, x1,448)

"What a waste" and "they died for nothing" are the most uttered comments at the memorial. "The main emotion I feel here is anger," one visitor remarked, "the way the war was fought, the senseless waste of the lives lost. I am thankful neither I nor my son had to serve." Many voices urge us to learn from the lessons of history, offering an assessment of the war as well as a reading of the memorial's message:

That war is gone now
and as years go by
some of these men
are still wondering why.

We work and raise families
through thick and through thin

> and still we remember
> lest it happen again. (VVMC, x1,369)

A sign carried at a Veterans Day ceremony at the Wall read:

> I am a Vietnam veteran. I like the memorial. And if it makes it difficult to send
> people into battle again . . .
> I'll like it even more. (Lopes 1987)

Several interpretations of the war voice a sentiment among veterans in particular that the war was lost due to lack of support at home. "How could we be expected to win a war that people here opposed?" a veteran from an MIA/POW[12] table near the memorial argued. A poem left at the Wall expresses a similar opinion:

> But we did not know that freedom's greatest foe
> was not the enemy we faced
> But a faction back in America
> composed of cowardice and disgrace.
> The media called us monsters
> the protesters did the same
> They made us out to be savages
> who would torture, kill and maim.
> And in the end, they sold out a nation
> and men who, for them, served
> For the sake of sniveling protesters
> masquerading their lack of nerve. (VVMC, x1,645)

This poem is part of a wider discourse produced at the Wall that constructs veterans as victims of the war and the silence that followed it. A letter from a veteran's mother expresses sympathy for the indifference to veterans following the war:

> We understand fully and are very bitter about the treatment of veterans. Please be
> kind to yourself—and try to stay with us. We need you. (VVMC, x1,136)

Similarly, a letter to a veteran who took his own life following the war argues that his name, too, belongs on the Wall:[13]

> I will see it each time I go to the Wall though others will not . . . Your death will go
> down as another suicide but it was murder by a nation. (VVMC, x333)

The memorial's discourse also defines friends and families of Vietnam casualties as victims of the war. Expressions of grief, pain, and rage individualize the memorial, attaching to each name engraved in the black granite the names of mothers, siblings, wives, and children whose lives were affected by the war. The open design of the memorial avoids the imposition of any fixed meaning upon the deaths inscribed on it (Foss 1986), and despite attempts to assert otherwise, the nature of the war itself prevents the Wall from representing sacrifices for a noble, successful cause. Utterances at the memorial attempt to give meaning to the deaths in Vietnam by focusing on the pain of individual loss. As one woman who has left over twenty letters to her son at the memorial explained, "people could look at the names, but none of them had any meaning. I wanted to bring something personal to the Wall" (Broyles 1986: 19). Veterans, families, and friends are represented as victims, and thus heroes:

> I say we have heros "Heros Extraordinar" [*sic*]
> Both those that have their names on the wall
> and those who still wonder if their loved ones [*sic*]
> name belongs on there. (VVMC, x971)

This focus on individual experience not only escapes the political controversy still generated by the Vietnam War, it has also produced another silence: the voices of the war's other victims, the Vietnamese, are conspicuously absent here. By stressing the sacrifice, personal loss, and heroism of American veterans, their families, and friends, the memorial's discourse neglects the unvoiced stories of destruction and atrocities committed by Americans during the war. Earlier stereotypes of veterans as baby killers and rapists have been successfully overcome since the memorial's dedication by including them in a discourse of victimization—"the media made us out to be monsters," for example—that fictionalizes the images, portraying them as unreal and unreasonable. However, separating the warriors from the war has also separated the American military from the destruction and atrocities that are also part of the "Vietnam experience" but now silenced at the memorial. The breaking of the silence that suppressed the voices of veterans and their loved ones has constrained other voices of the past.

Every remembrance can thus also be an act of forgetting. The silencing of Vietnamese voices and the suppression of discussion about the war's origin or the way it was fought and lost are products of the construction of history that takes place on several levels at the memorial, authored by multiple voices in a constant and simultaneous dialogue with each other. Like many commemorations, the struggle to build the memorial itself produced struggles over the control of historical knowledge. Unlike other memorials, however, the Vietnam Veterans Memorial continues to be a site where historical memory is in constant production, ever-changing, often ephemeral and contradictory. It has thus not produced a consensual memory of Vietnam now manipulated by some "administrative power," as Harry Haines has argued (Haines 1986).[14] Indeed, the multiplicity of opinions expressed during the tenth anniversary commemoration of the memorial in 1992 demonstrated that the Wall continues to evade monolithic interpretations. Comments during the Veterans Day ceremony ranged from the former football player Rocky Bleier's condemnation of U.S. policies during the war to Major General Edward Baca's triumphant assertion that the Vietnam War had been a "pivotal battle in the Cold War. You were part of a victory in a much larger war," he assured veterans. "Because of your sacrifices, Communism is dead, dead, dead!" Rather than producing a fixed consensual memory of Vietnam, individual histories and biographies collectively and often consciously construct and reconstruct public memory and history of the Vietnam War and its aftermath in the United States.

HISTORY AND NATIONAL IDENTITY

The relationship between memory, history, and national identity is a complex and debated issue. "Memory is certainly a prerequisite of identity, which rests on an awareness of continuity throughout time," the historian Charles Maier writes. "Memory . . . mingles private and public spheres . . . it conflates vast historical occurrences with the most interior consciousness" (Maier 1988: 149). Also essential for the construction of identity is history, as several German historians have argued in discussing German national identity in relation to the Holocaust: "Our identity is explained sufficiently only when our history is known: we are what we have become" (150).

My intention here is not to argue that history alone constitutes national identity, but to explore the way in which the past as commemorated and constructed at the Vietnam Veterans Memorial informs changing perceptions of Americans' identity as a nation. Questions of American national identity in particular have often centered around "American" values of freedom, democracy, and individualism expounded by the beliefs, symbols, and rituals of a civil religion (Bellah 1970). While history alone does not constitute national identity, a mythologized history is a crucial constituting force of this civil religion.

The iconography of the nation's capital illustrates how history as myth forms an element of national identity. A place where the past is conserved, recollected, honored, and practiced, the memorials in Washington, D.C., serve to "educate and edify" citizens through a cult of the hero about the "virtues of the past" (Griswold 1986: 691). At the Washington Monument, visitors learn about the father of the country and the virtue of American independence; the Jefferson Memorial enshrines the principles of enlightenment, reason, and rights of man; and the Lincoln Memorial commemorates the nation's savior and healer and affirms the values of national unity, peace, and equality. Public access and tours of the Capitol Building itself convey a general message underlying American political ideology that government exists solely for the protection, service, and encouragement of individual destiny.

The discourse of the Vietnam Veterans Memorial contests such unified, monolithic interpretations of American identity. At this memorial, visitors acknowledge a lost war whose aims and methods remain extremely controversial and divisive. Pilgrims and offerings also remind visitors that the cost of the war extends far beyond the names on the Wall. They read embittered, cynical, or disillusioned messages like the "Tribute to Political Folly" quoted above, or the following letter to a childhood friend:

> Jamie, I feel as if I'm getting out of control at times. All of the things that we were told that "America" is, all the things we believed in have been put on trial by one dip shit or another and we're losing. (VVMC)

Before visitors even see the memorial, MIA/POW groups situated on either end of the approaches to the memorial site tell them that their government lies about missing servicemen. Items related to the MIA/POW issue comprise a significant portion of the offerings left at the Wall: news clippings related to the issue, questionnaires and literature from organizations like the League of Families of Servicemen Missing in Action, aluminum bracelets inscribed with the name of an MIA, flags or stickers with the MIA/POW emblem, and letters to missing servicemen on the Wall:

> Dad,
>
> I am here once again reminding everyone I can of you and the POW's [*sic*] in Vietnam. We will not leave you wasting away in Vietnamese prison camp forever, we just have not figured a way to get you home yet. Hang in there dad, I'm trying everything I think that might work. (VVMC, x1,895)

The POW/MIA offerings are part of a larger effort by family members as well as the various organizations who have stands near the memorial to raise public awareness and support for their cause. But the issue is indicative of a deeper, more fundamental shift in national identity that occurred during the war. As many historians and sociologists have pointed out, Vietnam shattered America's long-standing illusion of invincibility, moral superiority, and broad national consensus: "the American Century foundered on the shoals of Vietnam," wrote Daniel Bell (Karnow 1983: 15).

Statements made at the memorial reflect this transformation in national identity by focusing on a severed relationship between the individual and the state. There is a sense here not only of a widespread distrust of the government, but also that the state abandoned its responsibility to the individual during Vietnam. "They even sold us out in Nam because of an election, a few people's jobs, as our guys were checking out," a veteran's letter lamented (VVMC). The MIA/POW groups' claims that the U.S. government has abandoned American servicemen in Vietnam mirrors, vocalizes, and contests this broader change in the individual's relation to the state.

The memorial is thus neither an "ideological artifact" (Ingersoll and Nickel 1987: 199) nor a site or ritual for the integration of diverse groups into a collective whole as other memorializations may be (Warner 1962). It is a contested site where memory, biography, and personal histories call attention to, challenge, and resist unified and traditional versions of American identity and government, thereby reflecting as well as constructing a diversified and skeptical sense of national identity.

REPRODUCING THE DISCOURSE: THE AMPLIFICATION OF VOICES

Popularization of the memorial in the media and in the tourist industry, as well as at other commemorations of Vietnam veterans, has multiplied and amplified the voices at the Wall. Over 143 state and local Vietnam veterans memorials have been erected since the dedication of the one in Washington. Inspired by the national memorial, most contain the names of local casualties inscribed on black granite (Strait and Strait 1988).[15] The Moving Wall, a half-scale replica of the Washington Vietnam Veterans Memorial that has toured the United States since 1984, elicits similar responses in visitors—many of whom are family members who cannot make the trip to Washington to see the original. As at the Washington Wall, veterans come dressed in combat fatigues, loved ones leave mementos, photographs, and handwritten notes, and people tell their stories. Since this mourning, commemoration, and "healing" take place in the context of the local community—next to a church, a city park, or school—visitors may reveal for the first time to their own community a connection with the war as a veteran, a nurse, or a grieving family member. A volunteer who has traveled extensively with the Moving Wall commented: "It's like dedication day 1982 of the Washington Vietnam Veterans memorial every time." Similar to the Moving Wall is the photo-mural, a half-scale photographic replica that must be displayed inside but may also evoke emotional responses and personal offerings. State and local Vietnam veterans memorials, half-scale replicas of the Wall, and ceremonies honoring Vietnam veterans like the Chicago parade attended by 250,000 veterans in June 1986 have created new forums from which the voices have multiplied, thereby expanding the process of constructing and making visible a national history through the personal histories and memories of those involved.

The media has furthered this process through the reproduction of the Wall's voices and images. Press coverage of the memorial has contributed significantly to its popularization: the Wall appeared on the covers of *Time* and *Newsweek* in honor of the tenth anniversary of the war's end; all major television news shows have done pieces on the memorial; and articles on the memorial as well as the collection of items left there continue to appear in national magazines and local newspapers. Like the media's reporting on the memorial's dedication, these stories reiterate and proliferate a discourse that focuses on the individual. The *Washington Post* coverage of Veterans Day 1989, for example, included an article on a Vietnam veteran's emotional response to a wreath-laying ceremony at the Tomb of the Unknowns, a story on inmate-veterans' memories of the war at a dedication of a Vietnam veterans memorial at a Maryland prison, and a feature on the war stories of Vietnam's first prisoner of war.[16]

The tourist industry has also publicized the memorial by replicating its image. Ranging from professional photographs of the Wall at sunrise to traditional tourist kitsch, souvenirs are decontextualized representations that may convey particular messages about the meaning of this national symbol. The memorial is pictured alongside Washington's other monuments on postcards, calendars, and shot glasses, for example, indicating that it is now a "must see" during one's visit to the capital. Other souvenirs superimpose an American flag or eagle over the memorial's image, thereby imposing a more patriotic message than is conveyed by the original Wall.

The film industry has similarly popularized the memorial and participated in the production of public memory through movies about the Wall. *To Heal a Nation,* an NBC "movie of the week" that aired in June 1988, was based on Scruggs and Swerdlow's book of the same title and told the story of the struggle to build the memorial from Scruggs's point of view. The final scene included footage from the 1982 dedication ceremonies. Another film, *In Country,* is based on Bobbie Ann Mason's novel about a teenager's struggle to understand a war in which her father was killed before she was born. She lives with her uncle, a Vietnam veteran, reads her father's diaries and letters, and even dates a Vietnam veteran twice her age hoping to find answers to questions nobody wants to talk about. The title refers to the slang used by U.S. soldiers to describe the combat zone, but Mason's "in country" is a small Kentucky town where the war's battles are played out in veterans' flashbacks, a dead father's diaries, and a teenager's inquisitiveness. Like the novel, the film culminates in a cathartic visit to the Vietnam Veterans Memorial in Washington, where each character's offering symbolizes a part of him- or herself left behind with the names on the Wall. The film thus reproduces and projects the memorial's discourse: seen through the eyes of a generation too young to remember the war, Vietnam becomes the story of a teenager who lost a father, a veteran who can't leave the war behind him until he visits the memorial, and a mother who continues to believe her son died for the freedom of his country.

This multiplication and amplification of voices has generated an echo that tends to script performances at the Wall. What began as spontaneous expressions of grief has been transformed into ritualized and routinized cultural practices. Although these performances vary in content, their form remains strikingly similar: offerings like letters, poems, service ribbons and medals, uniforms, combat boots, and photographs are unlike the wreaths or flags left at other war memorials but are unique as well as now traditional at the Wall. Letters left here are often predictable in both form and content, and many veterans tell the same stories about combat or postwar experiences.

Interaction at the Wall between its visitors is distinctive from other memorials and ritualized at this one. The embrace of two veterans in combat fatigues, for example, is now part of a scripted ritual at the memorial and is performed at the Moving Wall as well. The image is widely associated with the memorial through press stories about the Wall and in films like *To Heal a Nation,* as well as in several popular coffee-table photography books of the memorial (Lopes 1987; Ezell 1987; Katakis 1988). While the reproduction of this image is not solely responsible for the liturgical nature of such an embrace, it may help explain it.

The 1992 commemoration of the tenth anniversary of the memorial's dedication made especially evident the way in which certain practices have become structured at the Wall. In a re-enactment of the 1982 dedication, drawing often not from personal experience of the 1982 ceremonies but from representations of it, veterans donned not their original fatigues as they had in 1982 but ones purchased at an army surplus. In fact, this ritual dress at the memorial has become so popular that people come to the Wall masquerading as veterans, a phenomenon referred to as "fake vets." During the parade and ceremony, spectators and participants repeated phrases from 1982: "thanks," "welcome home," or "I wasn't there but I care." Most items left at the Wall had been prepared for preservation in plastic covers, frames, boxes, or containers. Multiple copies of the same letters and poems have been left at the base of each panel to ensure their visibility to the thousands of visitors.

To say that commemorations become standardized by popularization or that behavior at the memorial is increasingly structured is not to deny the authenticity of human interaction and emotion experienced here, however. Letters to someone on the Wall, poems written about a loved one lost in the war, or a tearful encounter between two veterans are undoubtedly sincere and heartfelt expressions of emotion; they are also now the accepted and expected thing to do. The fact that many veterans tell a common narrative about being spit on upon arriving in the states does not mean they are lying; one can doubt the accuracy of an account without doubting some sort of truth in it. Stories express an interpretation or sense of lived experience, not necessarily actual reality. They may also reflect how cultural narratives become internalized as part of individual memory and reproduced in performances at the site.

However, every reproduction of a cultural practice is also a variation of that practice (Sahlins 1981). A mother may read in her local newspaper that people leave letters to their sons at the memorial, but she may choose to type and frame her letter and leave it on a homemade stand for public display. Variations also occur in the content or form of common narratives told by veterans at the Wall. Rather than focusing on whether individual stories represent some authentic memory or predetermined emotional response, it may be more useful to explore a dialectical interaction between individual lived experience, cultural representations, and expressions of that experience.

CONCLUSION

My aim here has been to explore the relationship between public space, private histories, and the production of culture and historical memory. The Vietnam Veterans Memorial illustrates how actors invest their world with meaning through performances and that these enactments may evolve from spontaneous expressions of experience and emotions into recognizable and replicated cultural practices. The memorial provides a physical as well as discursive and cultural space where individually constituted histories accumulate to collectively construct and represent national history and public memory. As this history is defined and debated at the memorial, it reflects and informs changing perceptions of American identity as a nation. The memorial immediately became, and in many respects remains, a site of resistance. Multiple voices successfully resisted a national silence here; they continue to contest a sense of "official" history and national identity through personal stories, memories, and statements about the war.

Proliferation of the memorial's discourse in mass culture and media representations as well as at other Vietnam veterans memorials has created a dominant memory of Vietnam that focuses on individual experiences and tragedies of the war. In defining veterans and their families as victims of the war, however, the narrative has silenced other voices and histories from the past. This discourse of the individual, largely a result of the way in which the memorial and the cultural practices surrounding it have separated those who fought from the war itself, later informed public response and experience of the Persian Gulf War (cf. Wagner-Pacifici and Schwartz 1991: 416). The yellow ribbons and flags scattered at the base of the Wall signified a similar dialectic of remembering and forgetting in this conflict—a dialectic that could only exist in the context of, and in relation to, the dominant memory of Vietnam generated at the memorial. This is not to argue that the memorial has reached a fixed, consensual memory of the Vietnam War, but illustrates the way in which cultural practices and historical memory continue to evolve here through a multiplicity of social voices that have produced—and continue to generate—a discourse that is both dialogic and dialectical, a historical memory that is both public and private, and cultural practices that are both spontaneous and standardized.

PART TWO

KELLA

2 CONSUMER RITES

The Politics of Consumption in Re-Unified Germany

A YEAR AFTER THE BERLIN WALL FELL, residents of a former East German border village were treated to a sort of collective initiation ceremony into West German society. One of many such encounters between East and West in the early days of German re-unification,[1] this particular meeting entailed a "product promotion show" (*Werbeveranstaltung*) that was sponsored by a West German health products company. For 3 hours, the 150 villagers assembled in the community hall learned about health, nutrition, and the spirit of capitalism. According to a "renowned" nutritional society, the company's sales representative explained, one would have to drink over thirteen liters of milk each day to receive the necessary allowances of calcium, eat two kilos of beef for the requisite daily amounts of iron, and consume a jar of honey a day to build up one's immune system through bee pollen. "Our health and our bodies are also forms of capital," she informed her listeners, "in fact they may be the only form of capital we possess. We need to invest in them, like money in the bank."

To eliminate the need for such huge quantities of food, she was offering a "course of treatment" (*Kur*) of tablets, powders, and vitamins that would clear arteries and reduce cholesterol within 30 days. Although the "treatment" usually sold for 964 DM, she announced, the first ten buyers would receive it at half price. For those villagers who were unemployed or retired, the full price of the "treatment" nearly equaled a month's income.

Throughout the evening, this saleswoman used a variety of strategies to promote her products. Alluding to the mounting tensions and suspicions between East and West Germans throughout the country (ironically through people and practices like hers), she said: "Today I want to restore trust." Her tone was both paternalistic and patronizing as she presented herself as an educator, invested with authority as a self-proclaimed nutritionist and as a westerner. "Invest in yourself," she urged members of the audience, invoking the languages of production and consumption while privileging the values of western individualism. Her frequent references to the body as "capital" were a central aspect of her presentation's "educational" function. Like many other advertisers, she was selling belonging.[2] But by linking her products' purported benefits to certain rules and values of western capitalism and consumption, she was also selling access to, or entry into, the new society; her actions entailed the work of making citizen-subjects. By the end of the evening, she had sold ten "treatments" as well as numerous other products ranging from rugs and pillows to garlic pills.

I begin with this "promotional show" for it provides much food for thought: it not only reflects the construction of Otherness in East and West through particular discourses on the body, but also illustrates how consumption became a realm in which and through which many of the dynamics between East and West were experienced, expressed, negotiated, and contested. The acquisition of a certain "cultural competence" (Bourdieu 1977) in consumption, I argue, became a central initiation rite for eastern Germans into West German society. Although my focus is on re-unified Germany, the complex dynamic of consumption I examine here is part of a much larger dynamic present in the globalization of consumption-oriented market economies, particularly in postsocialist societies.[3] Indeed, in the context of postsocialist transitions in eastern Europe, we should be reminded of the degree to which the inability of eastern bloc political economies to either shield their populations from the consumption "triumphs" of the west or to in any way match them was one main cause of their collapse.[4]

As anthropological approaches to the study of consumption have shown,[5] cultural practices of consumption are far more complex than the simple competition involved in buying and selling. The consumption I examine here, for example, was deeply embedded in the asymmetrical power relations between East and West, demonstrating that consumption has important political and symbolic dimensions (Appadurai 1986; Ferguson 1988). It is a gendered and gendering activity (De Grazia 1996; Mills 1997). It became, and to some extent remains, a form of resistance or oppositional practice.[6] In the former GDR, it has entailed the construction and negotiation of memories and nostalgia for former lifeways that are in contest with emerging "all-German" lifeways. And, drawing from Arjun Appadurai's insight that "from a theoretical point of view human actors encode things with significance, [while] from a methodological point of view it is the things-in-motion that illuminate their social context" (Appadurai 1986: 5), it involves what people actually do with things. In sum, I view consumption here not as a distinct sphere of cultural or economic life, but as something that permeates, and is permeated by, complex negotiations of identity, gender, and memory within changing political and economic structures.

My aim in this paper is to explore transformations in cultural meanings and practices of consumption since the fall of the Berlin Wall. By focusing on both productive consumption and the consumption of production, I attempt to destabilize traditional binaries of consumption and production that have characterized many consumption studies both within and outside of anthropology. Studies of consumption have similarly emphasized polarities of resistance and domination (Löfgren n.d.; Miller 1995b), and in this paper I attempt to offer a more nuanced approach to the issue (see also Abu-Lughod 1990a; Ortner 1995). Further, my discussion of the politics of consumption both during and after socialist rule highlights certain continuities between socialism and post-socialism, thereby challenging, like other recent ethnographic studies of post-socialist transitions,[7] notions of total rupture (the "big bang" scenario [Verdery 1996]) present in many popular representations of socialism's collapse.

My study derives from a borderland situation, where the politics of consumption have been articulated in a variety of social spaces. Kella, the village where I conducted fieldwork between 1990 and 1992, is located directly on and is halfway encircled by the former border between East and West Germany. It was and, to some extent, remains a true borderland, both literally and metaphor-ically, a place where identities are especially articulated as well as a transitional zone, a place betwixt and between cultures.[8] At the time of my fieldwork, Kella was, as Gloria Anzaldúa wrote of her borderland, "a vague and undetermined place created by the emotional residue of an unnatural boundary. It is in a con-stant state of transition" (Anzaldúa 1987: 3).

Following the *Wende* in 1989 (the transition or turn, the term used to refer to the fall of the Wall and collapse of socialist rule), much of the daily interaction between Kella's 600 residents and its neighbors to the west occurred while shop-ping. It is thus no accident, perhaps, that consumption became a central meta-phor for East-West distinctions, a space where differences were most marked before and after the fall of the Wall.

CONSUMING PASSIONS

Long before the fall of the Wall, of course, power and wealth imbalances between East and West were reflected most visibly in the realm of consumption. The eastern bloc "economies of shortage" (Kornai 1992) contrasted sharply with the affluence and abundance of consumer goods in the west, and nowhere was this disparity more evident than in divided Germany. Anyone who visited Berlin before 1989 will recall the contrast between the Ku'damm and Unter den Linden. Local as well as state-level practices, including the exchange of people for western currency, West German state loans to the GDR, images on west-ern television (whose airwaves easily crossed the otherwise impermeable bor-der), and the coveted *Westpakete* (western packages) full of chocolates, coffee, and hand-me down clothing for eastern relatives, reflected this imbalance and confirmed an image of the "golden West" as a world where "everything shines" (*alles glänzt*), a paradise that, if attained, could solve most every problem.[9] As the Yugoslavian writer Slavenka Drakulić noted:

> Sometimes I think that the real Iron Curtain is made up of silky, shiny images . . . These images that cross the borders in magazines, movies, or videos are . . . more dangerous than any secret weapon, because they make one desire that "otherness"

badly enough to risk one's life by trying to escape. Many did. (Drakulić 1991: 27–28)

This observation also reflects why consumption under socialism was deeply politicized. The socialist "ideology of rational distribution" (Konrád and Szelényi 1979), which defined the centralized appropriation and distribution of surplus as being in the common interest of all citizens, depicted consumption in terms of the collective good rather than individual entitlement. The fact that the promise of redistribution was rarely met was a key factor in the "politicization of consumption" under socialism (Verdery 1996: 28). In Kella, for example, dust-free displays of rare crystal or the wearing of western jeans were not only markers of distinction (see Berdahl 1999a), they were also intensely political acts. A blue Aral Gasoline bumper sticker posted on the inside of a cupboard, or red and green adhesive packaging peeled from a West German wurst and stuck underneath the kitchen table, similarly entailed what Verdery has described as the forging of "resistant political identities" through consumption (1996: 29). Further, the Communist Party (SED) in the GDR (as elsewhere in socialist eastern Europe) frequently measured the regime's success in material terms, reflected especially in its well-known slogan referring to West German postwar progress and abundance: "outdistance without catching up."[10] Such measurements of success and frequent assurances of imminent improvements in the standard of living, combined with constant deprivations in daily life (especially during the last decades of socialist rule), not only politicized consumption but also stimulated consumer desire (Borneman 1991; Verdery 1996). As John Borneman has argued, this combination of deprivation and stimulation structured much of East Germans' behavior as consumers after the collapse of socialist rule: "socialism had trained them to desire. Capitalism stepped in to let them buy" (Borneman 1991: 81).

Immediately after the fall of the Wall, one of the most pervasive images was that of East Germans on a frenetic, collective shopping spree. Although, as noted above, these consumption practices were largely the product of a cultural order formed under an economy of scarcity, West German discourses hailed the triumph of capitalism and democracy as reflected and confirmed in the *Konsumrausch* (consuming frenzy) of the *Ossis* (East Germans). Local as well as national newspapers carried numerous photos of East Germans gawking at western products; a typical newspaper headline, for example, read: "Waiting, Marveling, Buying." The 100 DM *Begrüßungsgeld* (welcome money) handed to all first-time visitors from the GDR by the West German state as well as spontaneous gifts of cash from individual West Germans not only helped finance the easterners' spending spree, but also accentuated the discrepancies between East and West by placing westerners in the dominant position of gift giver. As one villager recalled: "I found the 'welcome money' embarrassing. It made me feel like a beggar. And when a *Westler* tried to hand me twenty Marks, telling me to buy something nice with it, I tried to give it back. I was so ashamed."

Consumption not only became an important symbolic marker of this histor-ical moment (represented most tangibly in what people chose to purchase with their "welcome money"), but became constitutive of the meaning of the transi-tion (Wende) itself: state socialism collapsed not merely because of a political failure, but because of its failure, quite literally, "to deliver the goods" (Borneman 1991: 252). The drab and clumsy East German products that embodied this fail-ure were quickly collected as "camp"[11] by West Germans as they were resound-ingly rejected by the easterners who had made them. Museum displays of GDR products similarly affirmed and constructed an image of socialist backwardness as reflected in and constituted by its quaint and outdated products. As one cata-log from a museum exhibit in Frankfurt shortly after the Wende read:

> East Germany has unwittingly preserved fossils of articles which, twenty to thirty years ago, were near and dear to us . . . [It is] high time then to embark upon a light-ning archeological excursion into the world of consumer goods before this distinc-tive quality is submerged beneath the tide of western goods. (Bertsch 1990: 7)[12]

More than any other product, the East German Trabant (Trabi) quickly be-came a key symbol not only of the GDR but of socialist inefficiency, backward-ness, and inferiority. A small, boxy car made of fiberglass and pressed cotton, the Trabi with its two-stroke engine contrasted sharply with the fast West German Mercedes, Porsches, and BMWs. Indeed, as Robert Darnton observed, this con-trast in cars could not help but embody "the two Germanys: one super-modern, hard-driving, serious, and fast; the other archaic, inefficient, absurd, and slow, but with a lot of heart" (Darnton 1991: 155). In the GDR, East Germans often waited 15 years and paid the equivalent of two annual salaries to obtain one. With the fall of the Wall, the Trabi was not only rendered valueless in monetary terms but was at first affectionately, and then as relations between East and West Germans grew increasingly hostile, antagonistically ridiculed in West German jokes as well as in everyday interactions.[13]

This consumption metaphor became increasingly prevalent as the hopes for a "third way" of the 1989 protest movements were lost in the rush to German unity. Leftist critics in the GDR lamented their country's "sell-out" to capital-ism, for example, while West Germans derided the consumerism of their Ossi neighbors. East Germans themselves described being "bought" by the West, as the following letter written just days after the fall of the Wall by a young man from Kella reflects:

> Maybe [the West Germans] will destroy the GDR this way [through the "welcome money"]. It's like an investment. They buy the GDR citizens . . . and then they won't want to remain GDR citizens anymore.

Indeed, "Deutschmark nationalism," a term coined by Jürgen Habermas to de-scribe what he saw (and feared) as a rise in nationalist sentiments based on the promise of a consumer-oriented market economy supported by the almighty Deutschmark,[14] is widely viewed as having been the driving force behind the landslide victory of the coalition parties associated with Helmut Kohl's Christian Democratic Party in the East German elections of March 1990.[15]

CONSUMER RITES

Consumption was not only a metaphor for East-West distinctions before and immediately following the fall of the Wall, however. It was also a means of preserving and re-constructing them. Indeed, consumption was part of a process through which the former political boundary that once divided East and West Germany was replaced by the maintenance, indeed invention, of a cultural one. In the taxonomies of classification—of identifying who was an Ossi and who was a *Wessi*—that became part of the construction of Otherness on both sides of the former border after the fall of the Wall,[16] the lack of a certain cultural fluency in consumption quickly emerged as a key marker of an Ossi. In the first years after the Wende, for example, the stereotypical insecure Ossi walked with her head down and asked the store clerk not "where" a specific item was, but "do you have it?"[17] Whereas West Germans could refer to certain products by their brand names—such as "Tempo" for a tissue or "Uhu" for glue—East Germans would describe their function. When people described differences between East and West Germans, they frequently pointed only to consumption practices. "Ossis compare prices," I was often told. "Wessis always know what they want to buy." It was usually during shopping trips in an adjacent western town that people would recriminate themselves for behaving like an Ossi. "Now she probably knows I'm an Ossi," one woman whispered to me about the bakery clerk. "I didn't know what that bread was called."

The perceived backwardness of East German products was often projected onto the bodies of East Germans themselves. In the first years after the fall of the Wall, clothing, grooming, makeup, even smell were identifying markers of Ossis. According to a discourse of Otherness in the West, Ossis could be identified by their pale faces, oily hair, washed-out formless jeans, generic gray shoes, and acrylic shopping bags. They smelled of body odor, cheap perfume, or "that peculiar disinfectant." Wessis, on the other hand, were recognizable by their stylish outfits, chic haircuts, Gucci shoes, tan complexions, and ecologically correct burlap shopping bags. They smelled of Estée Lauder or Polo for men. In describing eastern German women, for example, a West German friend of mine commented: "You can recognize Ossis because they like things that have been out of fashion here for a long time." Similarly, a young woman from Kella explained:

> Women are most easily recognized [as Ossis]. You see the differences immediately. Especially with older and middle-aged women. Women in the West still wear makeup. Their hair is stylish. But here, women aren't confident enough of themselves to even speak over there. They have these unstylish, frizzy perms and no makeup.

Although different in content, these comments reflect both how the inability to read complex and "ever-shifting fashion messages" (Appadurai 1996: 82) was perceived as a marker of an Ossi. They also illustrate how distinctions between East and West were often structured in gendered terms: in the reading of bod-ies[18] that became part of the construction of Otherness on both sides of the for-mer border, it was women's bodies that were especially read.

As tensions between East and West mounted on both sides of the former border, insults and complaints directed at easterners frequently focused on a stereotype of the materialistic Ossi ignorant of western consumption practices: "Stupid Ossis! They don't know how to shop!" "See the packs of Zonis that are shopping again today?" or "Look at them! They're shopping again! Don't they have anything better to do?" After the currency union in July of 1990, when east-erners overwhelmingly opted to buy western products with their newly acquired Deutschmarks, Ossis were projected as ignorant and foolish by West German dis-courses for being seduced by the fancy packaging of western goods. East Germans were eagerly and naively buying western milk, explained many westerners, while farmers in the East were forced to dump out the milk they were unable to sell.

Easterners' ignorance of western consumption practices was not only ridi-culed and berated, it was also exploited. As throughout the former GDR, nu-merous villagers in Kella were the objects, and occasionally victims, of various mail order gimmicks, door-to-door charlatans, and company-sponsored shows and trips (similar to the health products "show" described earlier). Some villag-ers sent in money after receiving notice in the mail they had "won" a house; oth-ers purchased items from door-to-door salesmen that were never delivered.

Just as unfamiliarity with western consumption practices was a key marker of an Ossi, then, learning how to consume became a central initiation rite into the new society. Eastern Germans not only had to learn how to navigate their way through new structures of consumer credit, domestic finance, and money management, they also simply had to learn where and how to shop after having only experienced an economy of scarcity with standardized products and prices. If, as Arjun Appadurai has suggested, we view consumption as the "principal work of late industrial society" (Appadurai 1996: 82), Ossis, it could be said, had a lot of work to do.

Through personal experience and collective negotiation, and even through more formal instruction, easterners soon became well versed in product names, prices, advertising strategies, and fashion messages. Women would talk for hours at a dinner party about the quality and prices of everything from coffee to bed mattresses. Children could recite the price of a loaf of bread from three different bakeries. Even the new grade school textbooks, read by children and parents alike, contained lessons on the aims and functions of advertising. "Advertisements lie," a 10-year-old child told me, "we've now learned that." These lessons, discussions, and collective negotiations of new consumption practices also became part of a new discourse of solidarity that often replaced the "them" of the state with the foreignness of a market economy, a notion that "we" need to be savvy about this new power just as we had to be savvy about the power of the socialist regime.[19]

People thus came to understand why the same margarine was cheaper at the discount store Aldi than at the more expensive Edeka market; they discovered the fine print in mail-order gimmicks, and they learned to ask "where" a certain product was located rather than "whether" the store had it. And as Ossis learned to differentiate Nikes from Reeboks,[20] they also began to uncover the cultural meanings of certain consumption practices. Several villagers with well-paying jobs in the West abandoned Aldi for the more prestigious grocery stores frequented primarily by West Germans. Others began paying careful attention to brand names of electronics, appliances, and clothing. Taste, an important manner in which consumption expresses distinction (as Bourdieu has argued [1984]), thus began to enter into the construction, experience, and expression of difference in Kella.[21]

DESIGNING WOMEN

In the early years after the fall of the Wall, the realm of consumption—and the effort to acquire a cultural fluency in it—did not merely provide a new source of activity, entertainment, and labor. Consumption also became a site for the negotiation of gender, a central means through which certain gender ideologies were conveyed and contested. As feminist scholars of eastern Europe pointed out, the transitions or "revolutions" of 1989 have been deeply gendered.[22] In the GDR, for example, state policies and ideology aimed to involve women directly in the process of socialist nation building through participation in the labor force, required norms for women's involvement in local politics, and pro-natalist policies like state-sponsored child care and generous maternity benefits. After German re-unification, however, women were disproportionately affected by rising unemployment, the abolition of socialist gender quotas for political involvement, and the replacement of the socialist state welfare policies with the Federal Republic's social policies that direct women toward the family, motherhood, and part-time work (DeSoto 1994; Rosenberg 1991). As throughout eastern Europe, the disappearance of an active second economy, informal networks, and alternative groups after the collapse of state socialism resulted in a "newly valorized" public that, as Susan Gal has pointed out, is often conceptually defined as male while the private is defined as naturally female (Gal 1994). In the former GDR (as elsewhere), these changes were accompanied by a rapid influx of western images and ideologies of womanhood that challenged 40 years of East German women's experience under socialism as workers and mothers, or worker-mothers. Like many aspects of the Wende, the implications of these changes for women were reflected and, to a large extent, constituted in the realm of consumption. Anthropologists have widely recognized that commodities can carry with them particular cultural doctrines. Frequently, I would add, these doctrines can be highly gendered.

To illustrate, I turn to a Tupperware party held in Kella around the same time as the health products presentation. Following in its decades-old tradition of home marketing, Tupperware apparently saw a market niche in the former GDR. The enthusiastic salesperson at the gathering I attended, Sabine Schneider, was a native villager (in contrast to the health products representative from West Germany). Her marketing skills acquired at a training seminar for Tupperware representatives, combined with her own creative asides, provided Sabine with a story for nearly every plastic container she presented: "this one is perfect for keeping dinners warm while the men are away at *Frühschoppen*,"[23] or "I always send this one to school with the kids." Her audience of seven women marveled at the range of offerings and possibilities: "An onion would fit in here"; "This would be good for leftover ground pork"; and "This is just right for milk," Sabine informed them.

Not only was consumption presented as a social and gendered activity, but the products themselves were laden with explicit and implicit gender ideologies. Above all, the plastic containers conveyed a certain cult of domesticity, something that resonated with the unemployment of women and upgrading of motherhood and femininity after re-unification (Nickel 1993). A woman's domain, as the marketing's setting itself indicated (we were seated around the kitchen table), was naturally in the private sphere of the family home, caring for her husband while he partakes in traditionally male activities, or for her children as they enter the outside world. The large offering and diversity of plastic Tupperware containers seemed to represent the triumph of capitalist abundance and the new possibilities it offered for women to be better nurturers and homemakers. By the end of the evening, her audience had apparently been converted: Sabine sold over 500 DM of Tupperware products.

The transformation from a communist to a kind of consumption regime was perhaps best exemplified by the seminar offerings of the regional office for women's affairs, or *Gleichstellungsstelle* (women's equality office). Introduced after re-unification to address the unique needs and interests of women in the "New Federal States," this office provided financial support to women's groups and funded educational programs throughout the former GDR.[24] Its lecture and seminar topics conveyed a message about what women had to learn in the new system. Often co-sponsored by the prominent West German Sparkasse bank, seminar topics included "Wishing, Planning, Buying"; "Fashioning One's Life and Consumption Behavior"; and "Shopping to Your Advantage."

Shopping, then, which for women under socialism had meant hours in long lines, bartering, or dealing with tensions among shoppers competing for scarce consumer goods, became a form of recreation. "I feel freer now," one woman told me, citing the liberating effects of frozen dinners and the availability of a range of consumer goods. "I can do what *I* want. I go shopping, not necessarily to buy things, but to look." In addition to the Tupperware parties, village women gathered in each other's homes to learn about the latest line in Avon cosmetics or to peruse the most recent catalogues from Otto or Quelle.

For women in Kella, as elsewhere in the former GDR, acquiring a cultural fluency in consumption not only entailed a lot of work, it was also a highly gendered and gendering activity.

OSTALGIA FOR THE PRESENT

Much of what I have just described would seem to support a thesis that eastern Germans passively accepted and internalized the hegemony of the West—an image that was prevalent in both eastern and West German discourses in the first years after the fall of the Wall. At the same time easterners would strive to imitate the West, however, they also resisted it. This paradox is not inconsistent; rather it reflects the complex and contradictory aspects of identity in the borderland (Rosaldo 1989). Like the construction, experience, and expression of East-West distinctions, this dynamic of imitation and resistance frequently occurred in the realm of consumption.

In the effort to "catch up" and "blend in" with the Wessis, for example, many villagers discarded their East German clothes, abandoned their Trabis for secondhand West German cars, changed their hairstyles, and undertook extensive home renovation projects. On the other hand, however, they also began using East German products as a means of asserting an emerging consciousness or counter-identity as eastern Germans, or Ossis. As Steven Sampson has noted, "Unification wiped out East Germany, but created an East German consciousness" (Sampson 1991: 19).

A conversation in 1991 with two women in their late twenties, Ingrid and Anna, about their smocks (*Kittel*) first brought this to my attention. The common attire of female factory workers under socialism, the smock had been a symbol of working women in the GDR both before but especially after 1989. At a church gathering where middle-aged women were wearing their smocks while serving tables, Ingrid remarked to me: "You know, I never wear my smock anymore. I used to run around the house all day in one, but not anymore since the Wende. It's because of them [women] over there (*drüben*). Nobody there wears a smock anymore. It's not modern." During the course of her comment I noticed Ingrid becoming more interested in this topic, which she then pursued with a mutual friend, Anna, when she joined our conversation not having heard Ingrid's first remark:

Ingrid: "Anna, do you still wear a smock?"
Anna: "No."
Ingrid: "Since when?"
Anna: "Since the Wende."

Several weeks later, I ran into both women independently wearing their smocks again. Because I saw both women almost daily, I knew this was a practice they had only recently renewed. When I commented about this to Ingrid, she grinned and said, "I guess after we talked I realized I could wear it again." When I asked Anna, she explained: "The wearing of smocks subsided in the first years after the Wende, but somewhere it's a part of us."

The smock incident was similar to other assertions of identity as East Germans I witnessed during the course of my fieldwork. In another instance, a family chose to drive the Trabi instead of their western Opel to a dinner with West German relatives, thus consciously highlighting, indeed magnifying, the distinctions between them. "We took the Trabi," they proudly told me, "and parked it next to their 68,000 DM Mercedes." Similarly, a group of men decided to drink East German beer after it had been nearly taboo to serve it socially; women resumed buying the eastern German laundry detergent Spee.

During the mid-1990s, however, such subtle tactics of symbolic resistance became widespread cultural practices throughout eastern Germany. Often referred to as the "renaissance of a GDR *Heimatgefühl*" (feeling of belonging or GDR identity), these practices were part of a discourse of nostalgia and mourning—a "hazy beautification of the past" (Huyssen 1995: 47)—that has contested a general (and often systematic) devaluation of the East German past by dominant West German legal and discursive practices. Such practices included the selling of East German factories to western companies by the *Treuhand,* the agency headed by West Germans that was charged with privatizing the former GDR economy, occasionally for next to nothing; the discrediting of the GDR educational system, particularly the *Abwicklung*[25] of the universities; the renaming of schools, streets, and other public buildings; the trial of Berlin border guards that for many eastern Germans represented a sort of victors' justice; debates over what to do with and about East Germany's Stasi (state security police) heritage that often compared the GDR to the Third Reich; and, to return to the Trabi again, discourses that ridiculed the backwardness of East Germany while ignoring the social and historical contexts that may have produced it. As the eastern German psychotherapist Hans Joachim Maaz remarked: "People here saved for half a lifetime for a spluttering Trabant. Then along comes the smooth Mercedes society and makes our whole existence, our dreams and our identity, laughable" (in McElvoy 1992: 219).

As a challenge to this undermining of some of the very foundations of easterners' identity and personhood, a number of cultural practices emerged that recalled GDR times (also referred to as "our time"): P . . . , a disco in East Berlin, for example, seeking to reconstruct the GDR period with East German drinks, music, and the old cover charge; a cinema or regional television station showing old GDR films that were watched by more people than during the socialist period; a self-described "nostalgia café" called the Wallflower (*Mauerblümchen*) decorated with artifacts from the socialist period serving "traditional" GDR fare; several supermarkets specializing in or at least carrying East German products, including one in eastern Berlin whose name seems to reflect a now common sentiment, typical of "nostalgia's stubborn implications of loss and desire" (Ivy 1995: 56): Back to the Future.[26]

In this business of Ostalgia (*Ostalgie*), East German products have taken on new symbolic meaning when used the second time around. These recuperations are both gestures of defiance toward and an ironic play with images and stereotypes of Ossis. And they entail the manipulation of culturally provided forms of resistance (Abu-Lughod 1990a) within the context of a market economy: consumer choice. Contrary to one of Kella's initial lessons in western consumption, then, Ossis investing in themselves or their "bodies as capital" has not entailed consuming pills, powders, and vitamins; it has involved the acquisition of a certain amount of cultural competence in knowing how to consume.

However, now stripped of their original historical context of an economy of scarcity or oppressive regime, these products also recall an East Germany that never existed. Thus while there may be nothing new in the strategic use of consumption as oppositional practice, what is unique in this context is the way in which memory shapes, and is being shaped by, the consumption and re-appropriation of things. These products have, in a sense, become mnemonics, signifiers of a period of time that differentiates Ossis. They illustrate not only the way in which memory is an interactive, malleable, and highly contested phenomenon, but also the process through which things become informed with a remembering—and forgetting—capacity. There is not merely a tension, but a dynamic interplay between nostalgia and memory here, and one of the key links is consumption.

This dynamic of remembering and forgetting also represents a different twist in the important but, in many studies of consumption, often overlooked relation between consumption and production.[27] Ostalgic and similar practices do not merely reflect a form of "structural nostalgia" (Herzfeld 1997a)[28] or a longing for a glorified past; they also reveal a certain mourning for production. However counterproductive socialist production rituals may have been in generating workers' loyalty to the state (Burawoy and Lukács 1992; Verdery 1996), they appear to have inculcated, to some extent at least, an identification with production.[29] People in Kella often recalled with pride, for example, the products of their labor in the local toy factory. Similarly, during a village parade in honor of German re-unification in October 1990, women replicated a sign that once hung on the walls of their workplace: "My hand for my product." In a society where productive labor was a key aspect of state ideology and where the workplace was a central site for social life, the high incidence of unemployment throughout eastern Germany has undermined profoundly many people's sense of self and identity. The resurgence of eastern German products must thus be viewed in the larger context of the shift in the balance between production and consumption in the former GDR that has occurred through rapid deindustrialization.[30] Consuming products of Ostalgia may not merely be an assertion of identity as eastern Germans, then; it also may recall an identity as producers that was lost in this transition.

Finally, this re-memorization of trivialities has also been part of a process through which consumption practices and the meaning of things have contributed to the creation and reification of a temporal and spatial boundary. Ostalgic practices are not only part of a dynamic of boundary maintenance and invention between East and West, they have also helped to create a division between before and after "the Fall." The items purchased with the "welcome money" connect personal biographies to a nationally (indeed, internationally) shared historical moment (the fall of the Wall). Yet they are also what Susan Stewart has called "souvenirs of individual experience" (Stewart 1993) in connection to a rite of passage. The inexpensive cassette recorders that broke within months after their purchase or the gold jewelry that turned one's skin green became, in a sense, material signs of many easterners' first lesson in western consumption. They came to represent not only easterners' transformation into more knowledgeable consumers, but also symbolized the loss of an illusion of the "golden West." And the loss of this illusion has been one of the most devastating aspects of re-unification.

CONCLUSION: INGRID'S COLLAR

In a 1993 newsmagazine article identifying the emergence of such oppositional practices throughout the former GDR, the former East German writer Monika Maron is quoted as ridiculing the notion that anyone who buys "Bautzener mustard or Thüringer wurst is a resistance fighter."[31] Indeed, the marketing and consumption of Ostalgia represents a certain commodification of resistance, particularly when several of the supposedly eastern German products are now produced and distributed by western firms. This framing of resistance to West German dominance in terms of product choices and mass merchandising entails a sort of Ostalgia for the present[32]—practices that both contest and affirm the new order of a market economy.

On the other hand, however, these practices also reflect an ongoing politicization of consumption, different in context but similar in form to the socialist period. Rather than using coveted western goods to construct and express resistant political identities, as under socialism, eastern Germans turned to old GDR products—an inversion of what John Borneman termed the "mirror imaging process" that contributed to the construction of two German states and identities during the Cold War (1992). These consumption practices thus not only highlighted continuities between socialism and postsocialism, but underlined the dynamic of agency in consumption as well (Orlove and Rutz 1989). Above all, they both reflected and constituted important identity transformations and negotiations in a period of intense social discord. They also point to the complexities, ambiguities, and contradictions of resistance (Ortner 1995: 184).

To illustrate, I turn to a final story involving Ingrid, who asked me one day how women in America wear their shirt collars. I told her I didn't really know. Somewhat taken aback and almost irritated by my ignorance, she said: "Well, now it's modern to wear your collar up. That's how women do it in the West. Here [in the former GDR] women wear their collars down." Ingrid seemed not only to be struggling to figure out current fashion etiquette on shirt collars, but also where she, as an Ossi who both mimicked and resisted what she perceived to be Wessi standards, fit in. For weeks after our conversation, I couldn't help noticing that on some days she was wearing her collar up, on other days down. Then, one night at a dinner party, I looked across the table and saw that her collar was askew—a rare occurrence for someone as concerned with her appearance as Ingrid: one corner of her collar was up, the other one was down.

To me, this probably fortuitous position of Ingrid's collar was loaded with meaning, symbolizing the interstitiality of the borderland, the way in which its residents are somehow betwixt and between East and West, the constructed and gendered nature of these distinctions, as well as the role of consumption in this dynamic. I imagine the uneven collar was most likely the result of Ingrid's indecision over how to dress for the dinner party; she probably had spent some time in front of a mirror switching the collar back and forth until she had to leave, when she apparently was unable to check it one last time. As in the preceding weeks, her tampering with the collar entailed a gendered negotiation of and play with identity—a metaphor for identity in the borderland; indeed, for identity itself.

Thus the Trabi's move from the jokebooks of 1989 to the "cult automobile" (*Kultauto*) of the 1990s and beyond,[33] the resurrection of the women's smocks (*Kittel*), or the simple craving for a glass of East German Rotkäppchen champagne are products of complex and often contradictory processes of identity formation, re-evaluation, and negotiation in the former GDR. These processes are part of an ongoing dialectic of remembering and forgetting as well as a dynamic and often subtle interplay of imitation and resistance, both of which are closely linked to the power and social life of things (Appadurai 1986).

EPILOGUE

In the years since my initial fieldwork, I have visited Kella many times; my most recent visit was in 2003. Although there have been many changes in the village—home renovations, freshly painted facades, new construction, furniture, and clothing—the invisible boundary between East and West remains. Indeed, even the generation too young to have any memory of the GDR still identify themselves as "Ossis." Many young people have either remained in the village or returned to Kella after living in the West. According to church records through 2003, all marriages except one were between easterners, and the one exception was to a descendant of a family from Kella who fled in 1952. During a brief visit in 2002, Kai Niemann's widely popular (among eastern Germans) song, "Im

Osten" (in the East), often hailed throughout the former GDR as "our national anthem,"[34] could be heard booming loudly from young residents' cars. Despite the radical decline in tensions and antagonisms between people on both sides of the former border, there continues to be a strong identification as "Ossis" among most villagers. Indeed, I would still argue that Kella remains a borderland in the metaphorical sense of the term: although the literal border of the fence has long disappeared, there is still a heightened consciousness of being betwixt and between East and West.

In terms of consumption practices, the rituals of initiation are a distant memory; Kellans, like other eastern Germans, are very "competent" consumers. Taste and style—in clothing, home decor, automobiles, vacation travel—while determined by economic opportunities, have also increasingly become a means of social distinction and expressions of identity. And as Kella has been absorbed into a consumer market economy, many villagers who experienced socialism will offer clear and articulate critiques of global capitalism. In discussing proposed reforms to the German welfare state, for example, one man in his mid-forties, recalling the benefits of full employment and healthcare under socialism, angrily exclaimed, "Now it's all about money. Jobs go to people who will work for the least amount of money, especially in eastern Europe. We have to pay so much for healthcare now that it's unbelievable. But that's capitalism." This comment does not reflect a desire to return to socialist rule, but like other forms of postsocialist nostalgia, prevalent in most central and east European societies, represents not only a critique of capitalism but also, perhaps, a longing for an alternative moral order.

3
"(N)OSTALGIE" FOR THE PRESENT
Memory, Longing, and East German Things

ON THE WEEKEND OF OCTOBER 3, 1997, a national holiday in honor of the re-unification of Germany in 1990, many eastern Germans gathered throughout the former GDR in various forms of counter-commemorations. While politicians in the West claimed and applauded progress toward unity, "GDR weekends" at local pubs in the East served East German beer at GDR prices to guests dressed in socialist youth group (FDJ) outfits or people's militia (*Kampfgruppe*) uniforms. Even more extreme were the wilder and self-parodying "*Ossi* parties," "*Ostivals*," and "*Ossi* discos"[1] (held not only on this holiday) featuring East German rock music, party propaganda songs (frequently remixed to a techno beat), and a double of the former Communist Party leader Erich Honecker complete with drab gray suit and stiff wave of the hand. Although most eastern Germans were more likely to stay at home and, like their neighbors in the West, joke—or lament—that there was little to celebrate on this seventh anniversary of German re-unification, such gatherings did represent one end of a spectrum of growing practices in the former GDR commonly referred to as *Ostalgie* (Ostalgia, or nostalgia for the East).[2] Indeed, the last several years have witnessed the birth and boom of a nostalgia industry in the former East Germany that has entailed the revival, reproduction, and commercialization of GDR products as well as the "museumification" of GDR everyday life.

Embarrassing, irritating, puzzling, or laughable to many western and eastern Germans alike, such practices are readily dismissed in popular, political, and academic discourses as "mere" nostalgia—as the questionable products of "GDR romantics," former Communist Party loyalists (PDS), and clever entrepreneurs. In a similar vein, Ostalgie is consistently and pointedly distinguished from more "historical" (i.e., "authentic") practices of collecting, displaying, or cataloguing "GDR everyday life" in public and private commemorative contexts. As potentially disruptive practices that emanate from the margins to challenge certain nation-building agendas of the new Germany, Ostalgie is at the center of what Michael Herzfeld has called a "politics of mereness" (Herzfeld 1997a).

One of my principal aims in this paper is to interrogate the politics of this distinction between "mere" nostalgia and socially sanctioned commemorative practices by tracing the social lives of East German things, including their paths, diversions, and recuperations. Following Appadurai's insight that "from a *theoretical* point of view human actors encode things with significance, [while] from a *methodological* point of view it is the things-in-motion that illuminate their social context" (Appadurai 1986: 5; emphasis in original), I seek to elucidate not only the social conditions that have produced the recent explosion of Ostalgie in the former GDR, but an interplay between hegemonic and oppositional memories as well.[3] In this sense, I attempt to offer a more nuanced notion of the complexities, ambiguities, and contradictions of resistance practices more generally (Ortner 1995). Ostalgie, I suggest, both contests and affirms a new order.

PRODUCTION AND COLLAPSE

In order to examine the decontextualization of East German objects, I begin with a few points on the contexts from which they became dislodged. In the heavily industrialized society that was East Germany, the pursuit of prosperity was intricately connected to an ideology of production. Indeed, one of the definitive features of socialist citizenship was production, a worker's identity that was inculcated through 40 years of state ideology, factory production rituals, and physical, industrial labor. The factory brigade, for example, was also an important social unit; factory-sponsored field trips often provided the only opportunities for travel away from home; and socialist production rituals aimed to engender loyalty to the state as well as an identification with the products of production. Many East German factories housed a daycare center, a general store, and even a doctor's office on factory grounds. Such policies and practices were not only a way of making it easier for women to enter the workforce, they were also part of a process through which the state attempted to supplant certain roles and functions of the private sphere—child rearing, family meals, and so forth— with the public sphere of the socialist workplace. In the GDR, the workplace was thus not only the center of everyday sociality, it was also a symbolic space of community and national belonging.

In the logic of centralized planning, socialism's locus of competition made success dependent upon socialist firms' ability to bargain for and procure materials rather than their ability to sell them. Although East Germany witnessed its own "economic miracle" of sorts in the 1960s, in which product design and marketing were important features (see NGBK 1996), most everyday East German products remained largely unchanged in the last decades of the GDR. For many people on both sides of the inter-German border, this lack of product innovation and consumer choice, more than any political difference, constituted the principal distinction between East and West. As one woman told me: "We saw on western TV that every year they [West Germans] had a new model of car, while our Trabi remained the same." Or, as another young man joked: "We always used to say that Marxism could have worked if it hadn't been for cars."

Such sentiments were echoed and amplified in the discourses of capitalist "triumphalism" following the fall of the Berlin Wall. The drab and clumsy East German products that embodied socialism's failure to "deliver the goods" were quickly collected as "camp"[4] by West Germans as they were resoundingly rejected by the easterners who had made them. After the currency union in July of 1990, when easterners overwhelmingly opted to buy western products with their newly acquired Deutschmarks, Ossis were projected as ignorant and foolish by West German discourses for being seduced by the fancy packaging of western goods. Although there was a certain element of truth in the images of East Germans on a frenetic, collective shopping spree following the conversion of their eastern marks into western currency,[5] eastern products had also disappeared, nearly overnight, from the store shelves as West German distributors assumed control of the East German market. "All of a sudden the products from the East vanished," one woman told me, "it wasn't just that we all only wanted to have the nice western products. Rather there were no eastern products to buy."

THE POLITICS OF VALUE

In the immediate aftermath of socialism's collapse, many everyday East German products entered a new phase of their "careers" (Appadurai 1986). Relegated to storage warehouses, the depths of domestic closets, and even waste dumps,[6] GDR goods often came to stand for the meaning of the transition itself. More than any other product, the East German Trabant (Trabi) quickly became a key symbol not only of the GDR but of socialist inefficiency, backwardness, and inferiority. A small, boxy car made of fiberglass and pressed cotton, the Trabi with its two-stroke engine contrasted sharply with the fast West German Mercedes, Porsches, and BMWs. Indeed, as Robert Darnton observed, this contrast in cars couldn't help but embody "the two Germanys: one super-modern, hard-driving, serious, and fast; the other archaic, inefficient, absurd, and slow, but with a lot of heart" (Darnton 1991: 155). In the GDR, East Germans often waited 15 years and paid the equivalent of two annual salaries to obtain one. With the fall of the Wall, the Trabi was not only rendered valueless in monetary terms, but was at first affectionately, and then as relations between East and West Germans grew increasingly hostile, antagonistically ridiculed in West German jokes as well as in everyday interactions.[7]

Museum displays of GDR products similarly affirmed and constructed an image of socialist backwardness as reflected in and constituted by its quaint and outdated products. As one catalog from a museum exhibit in Frankfurt shortly after the fall of the Wall read:

> East Germany has unwittingly preserved fossils of articles which, twenty to thirty years ago, were near and dear to us . . . [It is] high time then to embark upon a lightning archeological excursion into the world of consumer goods before this distinctive quality is submerged beneath the tide of western goods. (Bertsch 1990: 7)

These devaluations of East German things have taken place in the context of a more general and often systematic devaluing of the GDR past since German re-unification. Such practices have included the selling of East German factories to western companies, occasionally for next to nothing; the discrediting of the GDR educational system, particularly the *Abwicklung*[8] (restructuring) of the universities; the renaming of schools, streets, and other public buildings; the toppling of socialist memorials and monuments; the trial of Berlin border guards that for many eastern Germans represented a sort of victors' justice; debates over what to do with and about East Germany's Stasi (state security police) heritage that often compared the GDR to the Third Reich; and to return to the Trabi again, discourses that ridiculed the backwardness of East Germany while ignoring the social and historical contexts that may have produced it. Although generated and experienced differently in form and content (*Abwicklung* was viewed as an affront and degradation by eastern German academics, for example, whereas the toppling of socialist monuments and memorials was divisive and often done by GDR anti-communists), such practices have generally been grouped together in an eastern German discourse of oppositional solidarity against western hegemony. As the eastern German psychotherapist Hans Joachim Maaz remarked: "People here saved for half a lifetime for a spluttering Trabant. Then along comes the smooth Mercedes society and makes our whole existence, our dreams and our identity, laughable" (in McElvoy 1992: 219).

As a challenge to this undermining of some of the very foundations of easterners' identity and personhood, shortly after the fall of the Wall many eastern Germans began asserting an emerging consciousness and identification as eastern Germans, or Ossis. During the course of my fieldwork in an East German border village between 1990 and 1992, for example, women pulled their East German *Kittel* (smocks), an important symbol of working women in the GDR, out of the backs of their closets after not having worn them for nearly 2 years because they were not considered "modern" in the West; a family chose to drive the Trabi instead of their western Opel to a dinner with West German relatives, thus consciously highlighting, indeed magnifying, the distinctions between them: "We took the Trabi," they proudly told me, "and parked it next to their 68,000 DM Mercedes." Similarly, a group of men chose to drink East German beer after it had been nearly taboo to serve it socially; women resumed buying the eastern German laundry detergent, Spee; teenagers sought out the East German Vita Cola. As my friend Anna explained, when I asked her about her resuscitated smock: "The wearing of smocks subsided in the first years after the *Wende*, but somewhere it's a part of us."

BACK TO THE FUTURE

By the mid-1990s, however, such tactics of symbolic resistance had become widespread, and to some extent, routinized cultural practices throughout eastern Germany. Often referred to as a "GDR revival" or the "renaissance of a GDR *Heimatgefühl*," these practices include, for example, a disco in East Berlin that seeks to reconstruct GDR times with East German drinks, music, and the old cover charge; a local cinema that shows old GDR films; a self-described "nostalgia café" called the Wallflower (*Mauerblümchen*) that is decorated with artifacts from the socialist period and serves "traditional" GDR fare; and several supermarkets that specialize in East German products, including one whose name seems to reflect a now common sentiment: Back to the Future.

Ostalgie has also become an increasingly profitable industry. One product of and catalyst for the current Ostalgie boom is a card game, designed by two university students in East Berlin, consisting of forty-six different GDR food brand labels—all but three of which are now obsolete. Entitled Kost the Ost (Taste the East), a clever retort to the "Test the West" slogan of West cigarettes that proliferated on billboards throughout East Germany following the Wende,[9] over ten thousand games were sold during its first week on the market in late 1996. Since then, numerous other Ostalgie products have made their way into eastern German stores. One board game, Überholen ohne Einzuholen (outdistance without catching up, a well-known SED party slogan promising to exceed West German prosperity on East German terms), has as its goal Wandlitz, the elite compound of party leaders in the GDR; players must collect a Trabi, a phone, and party membership along the way. Ferner Osten (Far East) is another board game in which teams of "collectives" are asked to answer trivia questions about details of daily life under socialist rule, ranging from the product names of East German non-alcoholic drinks to the texts of party songs to the price of a chocolate bar in the GDR. Similarly, a memory/matching game whose packaging recalls the East German scouring powder ATA includes pairs of GDR products and icons. Postcards of Trabis or GDR products, collections of GDR jokes, replicas of SED party merit certificates, and numerous books about GDR products, including a *Small Encyclopedia of Eastern Products,* fill store windows in many eastern German cities. During my fieldwork in the summer of 1998, sales clerks in Leipzig consistently reported rapid sales of these items.

In this business of Ostalgie, East German products have taken on new meaning when used the second time around. Now stripped of their original context of an economy of scarcity or an oppressive regime, these products largely recall an East Germany that never existed. They thus illustrate not only the way in which memory is an interactive, malleable, and highly contested phenomenon, but also the processes through which things become informed with a remembering— and forgetting—capacity.

These recuperations also reveal a certain mourning for production. However counterproductive socialist production rituals may have been in generating workers' loyalty to the state (Buroway and Lukács 1992; Verdery 1996), they appear to have inculcated, to some extent at least, an identification with production.[10] During the time of my fieldwork in an East German border village, people often recalled with pride, for example, the products of their labor in the local toy factory. Similarly, during a village parade in honor of German re-unification in October 1990, women replicated the familiar GDR placard that once hung on the walls of their workplace: "My hand for my product." More recently, a former steel-girder construction worker in Leipzig explained to me: "I can't tell you how painful it was for me to see the products of my labor simply dismissed after the Wende."

In a society where productive labor was a key aspect of state ideology and where the workplace was a central site for social life, the high incidence of unemployment throughout eastern Germany has undermined profoundly many peoples' sense of self and identity. "Unemployment," explained one woman, "is for our understanding the worst thing there is. We were all raised to be socialists, and we were taught that work is what separates humans from animals. That is what we learned. Suddenly to be without work is unthinkable for us." The resurgence of eastern German products must thus be viewed within the larger context of the shift in the balance between production and consumption in the former GDR that has occurred through rapid deindustrialization[11]—a process that took decades in most advanced industrial societies that eastern Germany has undergone in just a few years (Geyer 1994). Consuming products of Ostalgie is not merely an assertion of identity as eastern Germans, then; it also recalls an identity as producers that has been lost in this transition.

An effort to refashion an identification with production and to capitalize on an increasingly defiant eastern German identity is also reflected in a different trajectory of East German things: the production and marketing of former GDR products in new packaging and contexts. Many supermarkets throughout eastern Germany will note next to a particular product if it has been produced in the "Five New Federal States." Konsum Leipzig, a regional supermarket chain in Leipzig and one of the few surviving East German enterprises in a landscape dominated by western discount stores, has based much of its business, reputation, and advertising on this very premise. "We're sticking together and shop in Konsum" reads one of its marketing slogans; "We're from *here*" declares another in an advertising supplement whose heading includes the five coats of arms of the New Federal States; and most of its storefronts proudly proclaim, "Konsum Leipzig: One of *Us*." Still functioning as a cooperative, Konsum stores specialize in products produced in the former GDR, often by re-privatized firms, including many "trusted old brand-names."

One aim of the company's advertising efforts is to educate citizens about the workings of a market economy and the relationship between employment and consumer choices: "Our recommendation: Purchase products that are produced here [former GDR]," says one advertisement. "In this way you strengthen our economy and create jobs." Another objective, however, is to tap into widespread resentments toward large western retail chains and discount stores that quickly entered the eastern German market after the currency union in 1990, driving many local shops out of business. "Give priority to shop in the stores of your Konsum Leipzig. After all, enough has been 'liquidated' [*abgwickelt*]!" states one promotional pamphlet, whose choice of the term *abwickeln* alludes to the general restructuring and dismantling of GDR institutions after the collapse of socialism. Similarly, a Konsum employee is quoted in another brochure: "It's too bad that so much has been liquidated [abgewickelt] and only a few businesses here have survived. Among those survivors is our Konsum Leipzig, which has held its own against the powerful West German retail chains. Konsum is for us a part of our identity that has been preserved. We are proud of this."

Such efforts to specialize in and market former GDR products have been largely successful. The chairman of the board of directors of Konsum explained that people buy such products

> out of disappointment, out of pride, out of definition and demarcation [from western Germany], and finally, but very important, out of remembrance. These [eastern] products were on the market, then they were gone, and suddenly they are back again. People have really fallen for them, and there are a lot of success stories now for these companies producing them.

When given a choice, I was routinely told, people choose to buy eastern products. As one woman in Leipzig explained:

> After the Wall fell we all threw ourselves at the western things...In the first months after the Wall I gained 25 pounds! I had to try out every chocolate bar—Toblerone, Rittersport. And the nice large rolls! But then we saw that they were only made out of air and we wanted our Ossi rolls back. Our Spee laundry detergent, our mustard, our spices. We all search until we find these things. Eastern products are back.

In addition to the re-invention, re-production, and mass merchandising of East German products, this "GDR revival" has also included the collecting, cataloging, and "museumification" of "GDR everyday life." Voluntary associations dedicated to the "documentation and preservation of everyday life," for example, allocate responsibilities among members for collecting everything from East German packaging materials to work brigade medals. Informal museums, galleries, and displays in community centers or people's homes similarly contain various objects of the vanished state (see especially Ten Dyke 2000). Museum exhibits of "GDR culture" in eastern Germany,[12] including a recent show in Erfurt entitled Deutsche Demokratische Restbestände (German Democratic Remainders), strive to preserve, instruct, and dignify. One exhibition, for example, aims explicitly to counter the dominant images of the GDR as an economy of scarcity; another categorically contrasts its collection of "historical" objects from widespread nostalgia for an "allegedly better past." The widespread popularity of these exhibits—a Berlin exhibit on GDR consumer culture and product design was described in one newspaper account as having unleashed a "cult event"—reflects a dynamic interplay between "official" and "unofficial" forms of remembering, linked by nostalgia.

NOSTALGIA AS A WEAPON

Such practices of recuperation—in the museums, discos, and board games—entail what Marilyn Ivy has called "the vanishing": that which "(dis)embodies in its gerund form the movement of something passing away, gone but not quite, suspended between presence and absence" (Ivy 1995: 20). As with most forms of nostalgia, recovery of a lost past is not the object or objective of desire, as Susan Stewart has noted in theorizing nostalgic desire more generally:

> Hostile to history and its invisible origins, and yet longing for an impossibly pure context of lived experience at a place of origin, nostalgia wears a distinctly utopian face, a face that turns toward a future-past, a past which has only ideological reality . . . nostalgia is the desire for desire (S. Stewart 1993: 23)

As elsewhere, nostalgia here is, as Kathleen Stewart has argued, "a cultural practice, not a given content . . . In positing a 'once was' in relation to a 'now,' it creates a frame for meaning, a means of dramatizing aspects of an increasingly fluid and unnamed social life" (K. Stewart 1988: 227). In this sense, nostalgia is about the production of a present rather than the reproduction of a past. Although certainly a form of "structural nostalgia" (Herzfeld 1997a),[13] these recuperations are also culturally specific practices that are connected to social, political, and economic processes of late capitalism more generally (cf. Ivy 1995; S. Stewart 1993; K. Stewart 1988) and to postsocialist eastern Germany more specifically.[14] In the context of profound displacement following re-unification, reflected in the popular saying that we have "emigrated without leaving [home]," Ostalgie can be an attempt to reclaim a kind of *Heimat* (home or homeland), albeit a romanticized and hazily glorified one (Huyssen 1995).

In the asymmetrical context of remembering in the new Germany, Ostalgic practices reflect and constitute the construction and expression of a kind of counter-memory. These resuscitated products have, in a sense, become mnemonics, sometimes explicitly so, as one exhibit catalog suggested: "Each object [in the exhibit] carries with it its own meaning, is connected to everyday experiences, and can serve as an occasion for remembering." Similarly, the designers of the Kost the Ost card game, whose rules require fairly extensive and detailed knowledge of GDR everyday life, described their product as a kind of mneumonic device (*Errinerungsstifter*). Indeed, many of these Ostalgie products seem to fulfill this purpose. After a small group of friends finished playing the Überholen ohne Einzuholen board game, for example, their two hosts, Andrea and Volker, brought out of storage boxes of GDR identity cards, Junge Pioneere and FDJ membership books,[15] and other personal artifacts from the vanished state. The group spent another hour poring over these items together, recalling the various state-sponsored activities and groups they had participated in, poking fun at Andrea for dutifully pasting the tiny monthly membership stamps into her membership books, and reminiscing about the shortages of goods and materials that had dominated much of daily life in the GDR. In perusing the passport-size photos contained in identity cards and nearly every membership book, people also commented on how Volker and Andrea had changed, and aged, over the years. In a similar instance, I witnessed people digging old GDR goods—often slated for disposal—out of the backs of cupboards and closets after seeing them featured in some of the recent catalogues, photo collections, or "encyclopedias" of eastern products. "These plastic ice cream bowls were wedding presents," one man recalled, "and we were going to toss them. But after seeing them in this book, we decided to keep them after all." The products of Ostalgie, then, offer a means of remembering the GDR as well as of connecting personal biographies to the passing of time and a state.

In contrast to the kind of "imperialist nostalgia" (defined by Rosaldo [1989] as a nostalgia for that which one has destroyed) reflected in the earlier Frankfurt exhibit, these recent commemorative and instructional efforts represent an attempt to recuperate, validate, and anchor a collective memory of a shared past. "It's not only the music," said one customer at an "Ost-disco," "it's the shared memory. When the music is playing, people look at each other and just know, without having to say anything."[16] The popular board and card games are viewed in a similar vein. "The games are like pieces of memory," one woman told me. "Those were, after all, our times." Or, as a sales clerk explained when asked about the reasons for the Ostalgie products' commercial success: "Some people can't quite let go of those times, you know. For others, it's a kind of fun joke. Many view it as a kind of remembrance game and buy it for their children to show them how things used to be."

This woman's explanation reflects the multiple meanings of Ostalgie and the uses of memory in the former GDR. For many, these nostalgia games and products are camp, proving Marx's dictum true that history repeats itself as farce. For others embittered by the disappointments of re-unification, Ostalgie represents loss, belonging, solidarity, and a time that differentiates Ossis. Still others find the products of Ostalgie appealing as reminders of the daily hardships they have overcome through the collapse of socialism. Ostalgie, then, does not entail an identification with the former GDR state, but rather an identification with different forms of oppositional solidarity and collective memory. It can evoke feelings of longing, mourning, resentment, anger, relief, redemption, and satisfaction—sometimes within the same individuals.

To illustrate, I turn to another Ostalgie game, Ferner Osten (Far East), played at a birthday gathering of about twenty friends. Most of the game consists of answering trivia questions pertaining to everyday life in the GDR, and participants were asked, among other tasks, to list GDR actors, sing GDR rock group songs, and remember brand names of cigarettes, wine, beer, food, and other products available during socialist rule. Because all those in attendance were new to the game, the first round began with one player reading aloud the instructions, written in a tongue-in-cheek style that employed much socialist lingo:

> In the last years, a large percentage of our population has suffered due to the fact that around 50 percent of the knowledge they acquired during the course of a lifetime was rendered useless through sudden and unforeseen events. The well-planned introduction of this board game will end this untenable situation! No one will laugh at you anymore, if you can grab the price of a Schlager chocolate bar out of a hat, if you can tie a *Pioneer* (scarf) knot at lightning speed, or if you can name ten DEFA[17] western films.

"That's right, that's absolutely right!" several people agreed. One woman added: "So much of what we knew back then suddenly didn't matter anymore and much of it we have forgotten. Our children don't know it at all."

The group became increasingly absorbed in the game as it got under way. When one team had won, the group started a new round. By the end of the evening and over 3 hours later, we had nearly made it through all of the trivia questions. Laughter and groans of recognition greeted details long forgotten. "What were our candies called?" "Who were our movie stars?" "What were some of our magazines?" The frequent use of the term "our" to denote certain boundaries of identification, inclusion, and exclusion was reflected in the structure of the game itself: the requisite detailed knowledge of GDR everyday life would have precluded any western German from participating. Indeed, when players didn't agree with an answer provided at the bottom of a game card, they would half-jokingly assert, "A *Wessi* must have written that!" Amidst the fun and joking, there were also moments when a particular trivia fact prompted more intense discussion and reflection. After a multiple-choice question concerning the price of a color television in the GDR (5,575 Marks), for example, one woman grew very animated and passionate when she recalled how much they had paid for theirs. "We paid 6,000 marks. It was a huge sacrifice back then and that was if you could actually get one! We've forgotten this and even take the way things are now for granted. And the children, they don't even know about this and think they can have anything. That's not good!" The game thus provided an opportunity for amusement, remembering, the venting of resentments, as well as the expression of identification and affirmation of distinction as eastern Germans.

As I mentioned at the outset of this paper, many western Germans and eastern Germans alike have been quick to dismiss such practices as "mere" nostalgia, "pseudo" nostalgia, or "just" another instance of German regionalism. What such allegations overlook, however, are the asymmetrical power relations in which these practices are embedded. Further, I would suggest, those who dismiss Ostalgie as trivial or inconsequential are similarly entangled in a "politics of significance"; accusations of "mereness" are often leveled at anthropology (Herzfeld 1997b). As I have argued elsewhere (Berdahl 1999a), moments and processes of transition are not to be measured solely by their political outcomes. Ostalgic and similar practices reveal and contest official master narratives of a united Germany by proposing an alternative vision of "Germanness"—of eastern German particularism and *Eigen-Sinn*.[18]

My aim here in probing and questioning a distinction between history, memory, and nostalgia is not to equate Honecker doubles with carefully documented and often richly sophisticated museum displays (like the Berlin *Wunderwirtschaft* exhibit). Certainly there are important distinctions to be made between choosing to drive a Trabi, purchasing an eastern German product, visiting a museum, and playing a board game. Rather, I am arguing for the need to examine an interplay among these various forms of remembering as well as the contextual deployment of terms and categories that dismiss some of these practices as "mere" while validating others as "history." Such deployments are an important part of the processes through which, and the social domains in which, history and memory are produced.

Indeed, one of the principal criticisms of Ostalgie is that it provides a means of eliding questions of complicity, responsibility, and accountability in relation to a burdened GDR past—it "neglects," as one newspaper account put it, "the necessary *Vergangenheitsbewältigung.*"[19] Underlying such accusations (which are admittedly not totally unfounded) are notions of the GDR past as something that must and can be mastered rather than an understanding of historical memory as an ongoing process of understanding, negotiation, and contestation. Indeed, dismissals and attempts to belittle Ostalgie may be viewed as part of a larger hegemonic project to devalue eastern German critiques of the politics of re-unification. More generally, the allegations of "mereness" and accusations of neglect, as well as the culturally specific practices of Ostalgie, both reflect and constitute struggles over the control and appropriation of historical knowledge, shared memories, and personal recollections—all of which interact in highly complicated ways (cf. Lass 1994).

Following Foucault, Lila Abu-Lughod has advocated looking to resistance as a "diagnostic of power" (1990a). Resistance, she points out, signals sites of struggle, and a focus on these sites may illuminate important structures, practices, and relations of power. I am making a similar case here for exploring the details of oppositional modes of memory: a focus on oppositional memories not only offers possibilities for reconceptualizing the domains in which history and memory are constructed and deployed, as Matti Bunzl (1998) has pointed out, but can reveal the specific workings of hegemonic forms of memory and "official" historical knowledge. The re-memorization, re-appropriation, and ideological re-assertation[20] of trivialities in the former GDR—ranging from the resuscitation of women's smocks during my fieldwork in the early 1990s to the "cult-like" museum exhibits to the recent trivia games of recent years—unveil the workings of hegemonic memory making in the new Germany. Or as Tobias Stregel, co-designer of the Kost the Ost card game, explained: "The East was not only about Stasi files and barbed wire."[21]

CONCLUSION: OSTALGIE FOR THE PRESENT

In a 1995 *Der Spiegel* cover story identifying the emergence of such oppositional practices throughout the former GDR, the former East German
writer Monika Maron is quoted as ridiculing the notion that anyone who "buys
Bautzener mustard or Thüringer wurst is a resistance fighter." Indeed, the marketing and consumption of Ostalgie represents a certain commodification of resistance, particularly when several of the supposedly eastern German products
are now produced and distributed by western German firms. This framing of
eastern German identities and of resistance to western German dominance in
terms of product choices and mass merchandising entails a sort of Ostalgie for
the present (to transform a phrase of Fredric Jameson's [1989]): practices that
both contest and affirm the new order of a consumer market economy. In other
words, to paraphrase de Certeau, consumers of Ostalgie may escape the dominant order without leaving it.

The archival practices of collection and display can have a similar, if unin-
tended, implication. Imagine what it must be like for many eastern Germans to
walk into a museum and be surrounded by the things in their own living rooms.
The effect of such historicizations of the present is uncanny (in the sense of a
"strangeness of that which is most familiar" [Ivy 1995: 23]). The past is connected to the present by distancing it in space and time. In the context of the museum as well as the Ostalgie games, East German objects—and, by metonymic
association, the GDR itself—are things of the past, consigned to an officially
sanctioned realm of obsolescence, memory, and amnesia (cf. Huyssen 1995).

Like other forms of re-membering, then, Ostalgie tells us more about the
present than the past. The social lives of East German things, as Appadurai argues
more generally in advocating a processual approach to commodities, illuminate
long-term shifts in value and demand—broadly defined: shifts in the value of
objects that are linked to re-valuations of a contested past, shifts in the demand
for products that are connected to demands for visibility and recognition. In
using available materials and languages for constructing defiance, identity, and
solidarity, Ostalgic practices reveal a highly complicated relationship between
personal histories, disadvantage, dispossession, the betrayal of promises, and the
social worlds of production and consumption. These practices thus not only
both reflect and constitute important identity transformations in a period of
intense social discord, they also reveal the politics, ambiguities, and paradoxes
of memory, nostalgia, and resistance, all of which are linked to paths, diversions,
and multiple meanings of East German things.

—ᴍ—

4
"GO, TRABI, GO!"
Reflections on a Car and Its Symbolization over Time

THIS IS A PAPER ABOUT A LITTLE CAR made of fiberglass and pressed cotton that is sometimes called a "Saxon Porsche," "racing cardboard" (*Rennpappe*), or an "asphalt bubble" (*Asphaltblase*). Although these images alone might benefit from some an-trope-ological analysis, that is not my intent here. Instead, I am interested here in the "changing symbolism over time" of the East German Trabant, or Trabi, and what its place in an "argument of images" (Fernandez 1986) can tell us about the politics of memory and German re-unification more generally.[1] Drawing on James Fernandez's more recent work on the symbolic *longue durée* (e.g., 1990), as well as his well-known contributions to metaphor theory and studies of expressive culture, my focus here is on the symbolic conjuncture, a shorter time span that began with the fall of the Berlin Wall. I am interested, in other words (Fernandez's, actually) in the "conditions that make practical artifacts into evocative symbols with some historic resonance . . . the historical problem of how things become resonant, pass into history and out of it, and go through phases in doing so" (1990: 95). The Trabi's resonance as a symbol and emblem of identity is linked to and makes manifest certain large-scale social and political processes, I argue, and its transformation and revitalization over time reveals much about the internal dynamics of post-Wall Germany. More specifically, the Trabi's place in the recent *Ostalgie* boom not only represents particular cultural practices of re-membering (and forgetting), but also reflects a certain "politics of significance" (Herzfeld 1997b) surrounding the production of memory in the new Germany: discourses that dismiss certain practices as "mere" Ostalgie or "cult-like" while valorizing others as legitimate forms of nostalgia and commemoration. I am thus interested as well in the politics of this distinction and how it both reflects and constitutes ongoing struggles over the meanings and effects of 1989—all of which, I believe, can be explored by tracing the symbolism of a little car over time.[2]

TRABITIONS

In order to understand the multiple meanings of the Trabi as a symbol after the fall of the Wall, it is important to note its practical and symbolic place in social and economic life under socialist rule. Produced in the city of Zwickau, the Trabi, with its two-stroke motorcycle-size engine, oily blue exhaust, and distinctive splutter, remained largely unchanged in its boxy form and pug-nose design until the last car rolled off the production line in 1991. The Trabi thus embodied the lack of product innovation and consumer choice seen by many to be the principal distinction—more than any political difference—between the socialist East and capitalist West. As one woman told me when I asked her to describe East-West differences: "We saw on western TV that every year they [West Germans] had a new model of car, while our Trabi remained the same." Or, as another young man joked: "We always used to say that Marxism could have worked if it hadn't been for cars."

In the GDR, the Trabi was a highly prized luxury possession. East Germans often waited 15 years and paid the equivalent of two annual salaries to obtain one; some even sold their valuable place on the waiting list. Secondhand Trabis were usually more expensive than new cars because they could be obtained right away, and people spent much time and energy hunting for and hoarding new and used Trabi parts. Furthermore, a shortage of Trabi mechanics throughout East Germany placed the Trabi repairman in an important position within the barter economy of the GDR. "You always remembered the Trabi repairman's birthday," one woman told me, smiling, "and we usually tried to bring him home-made sausage after we had slaughtered." The Trabi thus occupied a critical place in and represented an important aspect of everyday life in a socialist "economy of shortages": a second economy in which social relations and access to goods and services were based upon connections, barter, and bribes.

As a luxury object, the Trabi occupied a distinctive place in GDR social life as well. Parties were held to celebrate its arrival, and washing it could be a regular family activity. Eastern Germans often developed a highly sophisticated sense of sound in relation to their automobiles. In the former East German border village where I did fieldwork, not only could people recognize the difference between a Trabi, Wartburg, or a Lada (the principal automobile choices in the GDR), but they could also make distinctions among them and thus identify individual cars. Furthermore, the sound of a spluttering Trabant, which could be heard from afar, would give most villagers enough time to make it to a window, peer behind lace curtains, and ascertain, as well as comment on, its driver and passengers. People throughout the GDR filled their Trabis with various knickknacks, stroked and coaxed it lovingly (there was a particular way of talking to a Trabi), and devoted much time and money to the upkeep of this notoriously unreliable car. Owners learned to improvise basic repairs with highly coveted and hoarded

Trabi components or with everyday items (women's stockings were a favorite ersatz part), and it was not uncommon for mechanics to perform dazzling feats of Trabi transplant or amputation surgery ("out of two make one") (Darnton 1991). As Slavenka Drakulić has written of domestic living spaces in socialist societies (Drakulić 1991), Trabi interiors had a "strange ability" to divide, multiply, and contract upon demand. Seats would be removed to fill it up with the latest hoarding purchase (*Hamsterkauf*) of scarce goods, or to accommodate more family members on a long drive, and special pup tents could be mounted on the roof for camping vacations. The object of both affection and scorn in the GDR, East Germans sometimes used a special word—*hasslieben* (love-hate)—in referring to their car (see also Darnton 1991).

TRABULATIONS

With the fall of the Berlin Wall, the Trabi was, as Fernandez has written of symbol formation and transformation more generally, "removed from its normal routine and associations" (1990: 99). In the days following November 9, West Germans lined border crossings all along the inter-German border to greet Trabis and their occupants; the verb *Trabiklopfen* (Trabi patting/slapping) stems from this period and alludes to the act of patting or slapping the roof of a Trabi as a gesture of welcome. Indeed, images of Trabis crossing the once impermeable border into an atmosphere of what Victor Turner called spontaneous communitas proliferated in the national and international media as the car quickly came to be hailed as a symbol of newfound freedom and mobility; its distinctive fuel mix of gas and oil produced what some media accounts called "the smell of freedom." The Trabi was celebrated as the "car of the year" and was even given favorable and (fairly generous) reviews in automobile magazines.[3] A major national newspaper (*Frankfurter Allegemeine Zeitung*) even compared the Trabant with the Porsche Carrera, praising both as "useful as getaway cars" but noting that the Trabi had twice the Carrera's trunk space.[4] The association of the Trabi with the GDR and the fall of the Wall was so widespread, in fact, that the car had a starring role in the first major motion picture about German re-unification, a 1991 comedy entitled *Go, Trabi, Go!* that filled movie theaters throughout Germany.

The Trabant also quickly became a key symbol of socialist inefficiency, industrial backwardness, and inferiority. Its two-stroke engine contrasted sharply with the fast West German Mercedes, Porsches, and BMWs as it took a distant third place behind old VWs and Opels in the class warfare of the German autobahn. Indeed, as Robert Darnton observed, the contrast in cars couldn't help but embody "the two Germanys: one super-modern, hard-driving, serious, and fast; the other archaic, inefficient, absurd, and slow, but with a lot of heart" (Darnton 1991: 155). The Trabi thus became a central metaphor in an argument of images about the "failures" of socialism and "triumphs" of capitalism. Socialism failed, in other words, because of its inability, quite literally, "to deliver the goods." In a discourse that linked "democratization" to the freedom to consume, the transitions of 1989 were not about demands for political or human rights, but for consumer rights (e.g., Bauman 1992; Borneman 1991; Drakulić 1991). The widespread use of the Trabi image (and often the actual car) in post-Wall advertising both reflected and constituted this discourse of a consumer democracy; it also was part of a more general production of new citizen consumers in the former GDR (Berdahl 1999c).

After the fall of the Wall, Trabi jokes—long a tradition in the GDR—became a national pastime in West Germany.[5] Although largely affectionate, some of these reflected projections of socialist backwardness and technological inferiority:

> How many workers does it take to make a Trabi?
> Two: One folds and one pastes.

Other jokes focused on the Trabi's speed and power, particularly compared to West German cars:

> What has happened if a Trabi doesn't go when the light turns green?
> It has gotten stuck in gum.

With the fall of the Wall and currency union, the market value of Trabis plummeted as easterners flocked to secondhand car dealers in the West—a particularly painful situation for people who had purchased a Trabi shortly before November 1989. The following jokes reflect this trend:

> How do you double the value of a Trabi?
> Fill it up with gas.

> OR

> Customer: I need a pair of windshield wipers for my Trabi.
> Salesperson: That seems like a fair exchange.

The monetary devaluations of the Trabi, however, were symptomatic (and symbolic) of a more general and often systematic devaluation of the East German past by dominant West German legal and discursive practices, including the selling of East German factories to western companies, occasionally for next to nothing; the discrediting of the GDR educational system, particularly the *Abwicklung*[6] of the universities; the renaming of schools, streets, and other public buildings; the trial of Berlin border guards that for many eastern Germans represented a sort of victors' justice; debates over what to do with and about East Germany's Stasi (state security police) heritage that often compared the GDR to the Third Reich; and to return to the Trabi's place in an argument of images again, discourses that ridiculed the backwardness of East Germany while ignoring the social and historical contexts that may have produced it.[7] As the eastern German psychotherapist Hans Joachim Maaz remarked: "People here saved for half a lifetime for a spluttering Trabant. Then along comes the smooth Mercedes society and makes our whole existence, our dreams and our identity, laughable" (in McElvoy 1992: 219).

As relations between East and West Germans grew increasingly antagonistic, the Trabi was ridiculed in hostile jokes and everyday interactions. West Germans living in border regions complained about the smelly polluting exhaust, endless streams of Trabi traffic jams, and the lack of parking spaces at local shopping centers. Indeed, the Trabi also became associated with the "consuming frenzy" of the *Ossis* (eastern Germans) as cars full of western goods purchased with newly acquired Deutschmarks filled the streets of western border towns. Demonstrating how symbols not only reflect but also influence attitudes and behavior, Trabis were reportedly set on fire, their tires were slashed, dog feces were spread on windshields, and angry messages ("Go Home Ossis!") were left under wipers.

RETRABITULATIONS

Not surprisingly, the Trabi has also been useful in fighting back. In an ongoing and evolving argument of images, it has been deployed in contesting western projections of the GDR and its former citizens as inferior and in asserting an identity as eastern Germans, or "Ossis." This first came to my attention in a "revelatory incident" (Fernandez 1986) during fieldwork in 1991, when friends chose to drive their Trabi instead of their western Opel to a dinner with West German relatives, thus consciously highlighting, indeed magnifying, the distinctions between them. "We took the Trabi," they proudly told me, "and parked it next to their 68,000 DM Mercedes." Similarly, a group of men decided to drink East German beer after it had been nearly taboo to serve it socially; women resumed buying the eastern German laundry detergent, Spee.

By the mid-1990s, however, such tactics of symbolic resistance had become widespread, routinized cultural practices throughout eastern Germany generally referred to as Ostalgie (nostalgia for the East). This "GDR revival" has taken many forms: a self-described "nostalgia café" called the Wallflower (*Mauerblümchen*) that is decorated with artifacts from the socialist period and serves "traditional" GDR fare; dance parties (*"Ostivals"* or "Ostalgie Nights") featuring East German rock music, a double of Erich Honecker, and, occasionally, a Trabi or two ("two-stroke techno parties"); numerous publications and trivia games recalling life in the GDR; supermarkets and an annual "OstPro" trade fair that specialize in East German products, including one store whose name seems to reflect a now common sentiment: Back to the Future. Demand for products through an "Ossi mail order" (*OssiVersand*) website that opened in 1998 far exceeded supply, and the 1999 release and phenomenal box-office success of two "Ostalgie films" (*Sonnenallee* and *Helden Wie Wir*) marks the culmination of Ostalgie as a truly mass cultural phenomenon.

As a symbol of the former GDR, the Trabi image has been at the forefront of this Ostalgie trend. Trabis or Trabi parts decorate Ostalgie discos, bars, or cafés, and images of Trabis abound in Ostalgie games and books. More significant are Trabi fan clubs located throughout the former GDR[8] that gather to exchange stories, memories, ideas, and spare parts. Like many automobile clubs, discussions often focus on technical matters of Trabi repair and maintenance; unlike many such fan clubs, however, members are also often interested in creative reconfigurations and design (a cultural transformation, perhaps, of the "out of two make one" Trabi repair jobs under socialism): Trabis transformed into stretch limos, innovative and outlandish Trabi paint jobs, Trabis as race cars, Trabis as luxury vehicles ("Trabillacs"). Now frequently described as a "cult automobile," the Trabi, as several accounts put it,[9] is the "ultimate object of Ostalgie." Very recently, two eastern German art students, stressing the car's status as a "cult object,"[10] built a "Trabi Stonehenge" as an advertisement for their "Trabi Shop."

As I have argued about Ostalgie more generally (Berdahl 1999b), such practices must be seen in the context of feelings of profound displacement and disillusionment following re-unification, reflected in the popular saying that we have "emigrated without leaving home." Ostalgia can thus be an attempt to reclaim a kind of *Heimat* (home or homeland), albeit a romanticized and hazily glorified one (Huyssen 1995). It is also a way of using available languages and images for constructing defiance, identity, value, and solidarity as eastern Germans. As one of the organizers of the "Ostpro Messe" (an annual trade fair for East German products) recently commented: "These are our old products. They are actually not so bad as is always asserted, and we are also not so bad as we are often depicted."[11] In this sense, Ostalgie is also about reclaiming a devalued self. Contrary to many interpretations and representations of this phenomenon in popular discourses, Ostalgie does not usually represent an identification with the GDR state or a desire to recover the old socialist political system. Instead, it can (among many other things) be an effort to affirm a sense of personal worth and dignity, to see one's past life and present self as meaningful and worthy in the context of a devalued and ridiculed past. Or, as one Trabi fan book put it, "Cars of paper need drivers of steel" (Kämper and Ulbrich 1995).

The revitalized Trabi is also symptomatic of what I have called "Ostalgie for the present"(transforming a phrase of Fredric Jameson's) (Berdahl 1999b): practices that both contest and affirm the new order of a market economy by expressing politicized identities in terms of product choices and mass merchandizing. In other words, to paraphrase de Certeau, consumers of Ostalgie and drivers of Trabis may escape the dominant order without leaving it. Indeed, the "ironic awareness" (Fernandez 1986: 268) that is contained in many of the Ostalgic practices—including Trabillacs, "two-stroke techno parties," and Trabi cafés— may even reflect a certain consciousness of this.

The frequent description of the Trabi as a "cult automobile," however, echoes popular discourses about Ostalgie more generally as a "cult" phenomenon and raises important questions, I think, about the politics of labeling in post-unification Germany. Descriptions and discussions of Ostalgie were featured prominently in many German as well as American accounts of the 10-year anniversary of 1989 and have been heightened by the recent release of the film *Sonnenallee,* a coming-of-age comedy about a group of teenagers living in the shadow of the Berlin Wall, on what would have been the fiftieth anniversary of the GDR (October 7); at its premiere guests passed through a reconstructed border control checkpoint into the movie theater. In these recent popular discourses, Ostalgie is described, often with a certain degree of suspicion, as something that turns the GDR into a "cult object," "a joke," a phantasm. "There is a specter haunting Bonn and Berlin," concludes one *Der Spiegel* article, invoking the famous line of Marx's. "Only it is not socialism but the GDR that won't die."[12] A review of the Ostalgie films in the leading weekly newspaper *Die Zeit* similarly commented (although this time invoking the language of postmodernism): "Now the [GDR] appears as a fake . . . the copy triumphs over the original . . . Ten years after its demise, the GDR is living a second life as a cult object."[13]

But what does it mean to speak of Ostalgie, and more generally, representations of the GDR, in this way? Like the Ostalgic practices that they describe, the discourses that depict Ostalgie as cult-like entail particular strategies of representation.[14] They are part of a politics of labeling that is located, in other words, in "specific contested histories" (Rofel 1999) and political projects. To call something cult-like evokes images of eccentricity, ephemerality, irrationality—it designates whatever is being labeled as marginal. This may be part of a discursive strategy when the eastern German PDS (Party of Democratic Socialism—the renamed former Communist Party of East Germany) is accused, for example, of exploiting Ostalgie in its recent electoral success. Indeed, while criticisms of Ostalgie as a means of eliding issues of complicity, responsibility, and accountability in relation to a burdened GDR past need to be taken seriously, and while distinctions need to be made among Ostalgic practices themselves (something I have attempted to do elsewhere [Berdahl 1999b]), I would also suggest that dismissals and attempts to belittle Ostalgie as a cultural phenomenon in the former GDR may be viewed as part of a larger hegemonic project to devalue eastern German critiques of the politics and disappointments of re-unification.

The Trabi's move from the car of the year to the jokebooks and junkyards of 1989 to the "cult automobile" of the late 1990s thus tells us much about the politics of identity and memory in united Germany. Its "property of contrast" (Fernandez 1990: 97) as an object, and the actions—indeed performances—the Trabi enables have been part of boundary-maintaining practices on both sides of the former East-West divide. Indeed, to conclude with another (although non-

Trabi) joke, the revitalized Trabi reflects the transposition of a popular joke told shortly after the *Wende* that revealed at that time much about boundary maintenance and power dynamics from the western side. Now the joke goes:

Wessi says to Ossi (recalling the slogans of 1989): We are one people!
Ossi to Wessi: So are we.

5
MIXED DEVOTIONS
Religion, Friendship, and Fieldwork
in Postsocialist East Germany

MOST ETHNOGRAPHIC FIELDWORK IS punctuated by distancing moments, instances when the ethnographer's dual and paradoxical insider/outsider status becomes highlighted in particularly bold relief. Often these moments seem to confirm what we, as ethnographers, already know and feel: that we are the (uninvited) guests of those we study, our work made possible by the tolerance, patience, and cooperation of our hosts. At other times these moments may come as a complete shock, suddenly jolting us out of our feelings of satisfaction at having been approved by those around us and challenging our sense of competence in the culture (cf. Dubisch 1996: 115; Kondo 1990). When these incidents are shocking, they are also revelatory. We may come away with a sense of self-revelation, having gained insights into our personal and ethnographic selves (Bruner 1993), and we may experience a "revelatory incident" in the ethnographic sense (Fernandez 1986), emerging with a better understanding of our relationship to and with the people we study, with an improved sense of the relation between the processes and products of our research, and above all, with a richer perspective on the subject of our study itself.

This essay tells three stories. It is a chronicle of a friendship, describing my struggle to come to terms with the terminal illness of a close friend, whom I met in the field, and with her decisions about treatment. It is an account of the dilemmas of doing research as a "westerner" in a postsocialist setting, particularly in relation to the "halfie" or "hybrid" status of anthropologists working in European societies (Dubisch 1996; see also DeSoto 2000a). And it is an exploration of transformations in religion, popular faith, and the Catholic Church after the collapse of socialist rule in East Germany. All of these stories converged around a single distancing moment during fieldwork, to which I shall later return. I begin, however, by describing the events and relationships that provided the context for the incident.

OF FRIENDS AND FIELDWORK

Anthropologists have rarely written about "friends," for to do so would blur and thereby threaten the discipline's classically coveted boundary between observer and observed, between "self" and "other."[1] In the authoritative voice of traditional ethnography (Clifford 1983), friendships formed and cultivated during the course of research were transformed in the course of writing through distancing concepts like "informants" or "interlocutors."[2] Yet it is inevitable that meaningful friendships develop after living intensively with people over an extended period of time, as ethnographic fieldwork requires us to do. Thus I may be guilty of certain professional transgressions when I call Johanna my friend, but to describe her in any other terms would not only be dishonest, it would "do violence" (Bruner 1993) to our shared experience.

I first met Johanna, a petite woman in her late twenties, on a dark December afternoon while she was working late as a secretary in the village mayor's office. I was hurriedly searching for a new fieldsite after the one I had arranged the previous summer had fallen through, and she immediately sensed my feelings of urgency and desperation as I entered the office to inquire about possible housing in the village. Because my research focused on issues of borders, boundaries, and identities in relation to the rapid transformations in everyday life after the fall of the Berlin Wall, it was important to me to live and work in a village along the former inner-German border. After careful thought and effort, she was able to convince a local family with a vacant apartment to take me and my husband in. Johanna, then, was essentially responsible for my presence in the former East German border village of Kella between 1990 and 1992.

Because her position at the mayor's office gave her access and insights into material on everyday life before and after socialism, Johanna was also what anthropologists have often called a "key informant." She patiently guided me through the confusion of the disorganized village archives, kept me abreast of the employment status of nearly all of the village's 600 residents, and attentively informed me of community building projects, local factory closings, and administrative restructurings. Together we spent long hours taping conversations, often while sunning ourselves on her balcony, about the pressures and pleasures of being a working mother in the GDR, about her perceptions of West German notions of femininity and womanhood, about the church and state during socialist rule, about her recollections of the border fortifications during the 1970s. We periodically took long walks at dusk, after she was finished with her office job and domestic chores but while it was still light, to survey the most recent renovations of local homes, new construction projects, and changes in village public space. Often our discussions lasted into the early hours of the morning, long after her husband and two children were in bed and she could speak uninterrupted by the demands of being a wife and a mother.

Throughout our interactions in which I sought insights and information, that is, "data," for my study, I came to value, indeed at times cherish, her companionship, sense of humor, and humanity. And I believe she sought from me not only a friend and confidante, but also a certain validation of her life experience that my interest in her as a friend and inquiring anthropologist naturally provided. After our difficult good-byes when I left the field, she later told me, she would drink every morning out of a travel mug I had brought her from the states as if to keep my memory and presence alive. Back at home, I placed a gift from her, a glitter-encrusted cat sculpture that reflected her tastes more than mine, on my window sill and looked at it longingly as I grappled with the dilemma of the returning anthropologist attempting to turn the particulars of fieldwork into a more general and coherent ethnographic account (cf. Dubisch 1996).

DEVOUT STRUGGLES

Many of my conversations with Johanna during fieldwork focused on the topic of religion, a mutual interest that was the result of my research as well as Johanna's own spiritual concerns. Born and raised in a village that remained devoutly Catholic despite the socialist state's attempts to root out religion in the GDR,[3] Johanna became increasingly involved in the church during early adulthood after the arrival in 1982 of a new priest in the village, Father Münster, a small yet domineering man in his mid-forties who was a member and avid promoter of the charismatic *Focolare* ecclesiastical movement. Based on an ideal of world unity and universal love preached by its founder and leader, Chiara Lubich, around whom the movement's personality cult is centered, Focolare is one of the more powerful of the newer ecclesiastical movements within the Catholic Church.[4] Its notion of piety is also strongly connected to a glorification of suffering, reflected in and inculcated through censured testimonial narratives told and retold at frequent Focolare gatherings. For Johanna, however, the movement's emphasis on tolerance and Christian love was the logical extension in practice of religious teachings that had been central to her upbringing. She was willing to devote the substantial time and energy required by the movement of its adherents and quickly became part of the priest's inner circle composed of the handful of villagers involved in Focolare activities. Together with Father Münster and these followers, Johanna attended local and regional Focolare meetings in the GDR; after the Wall fell, she traveled to western Germany, Italy, and Poland on behalf of the movement.

Father Münster's passionate involvement in the Focolare movement was greeted with much skepticism and controversy by the majority of the village's Catholics, however, who viewed many of the priest's religious practices as unconventional ("cult-like") and outside the realm of institutionalized religion. They complained that his Focolare commitments divided the congregation[5] and detracted from his responsibilities as a priest to the community, which, many parishioners felt, primarily entailed presiding over local masses and pilgrimages. Frustrated by his failure to garner widespread support for the movement within the village, Father Münster often confessed to his most devoted followers that he viewed many of his duties as a Catholic priest as secondary to his vision of the ideals of Focolare.

Local sentiment surrounding the priest and the Focolare movement was complicated by the changing role of the church—and by extension, of the priest—after the collapse of socialism. During the period of socialist rule, religion in this border village, as in other areas of the GDR and Poland, had been both a reason for and expression of resistance to the regime (Berdahl 1999a; cf. Kubik 1994 and Nagengast 1991).[6] Having one's child baptized, sending a child to communion, or attending a local pilgrimage were both religious and overtly political acts. In a gesture of religious commitment, political opposition, and dedication to local tradition, for example, during the period of socialist rule village residents defiantly sent their children to the Catholic kindergarten housed in the *Schwesternhaus,* a church-owned facility staffed by three nuns who lived in the house, instead of the state-run daycare located in the community center. Many of the pilgrimage sites in the surrounding regions, including the most sacred and popular one, were located in the highly restricted border zone of the GDR and were thus accessible only with special passes; yet pilgrimage attendance here was always high during the socialist period.

Since German re-unification, however, the church has lost much of its appeal and interest as an alternative institution preaching against the official values of the socialist regime. As in the rest of the former GDR (as well as in many other postsocialist societies), there has been a dramatic decline in religious activity here. Church attendance has decreased, contributions to the collection plate on Sundays are half of what they were in the GDR, and participation in pilgrimages is far below what it used to be when special passes were required. Concomitantly, the priest's influence and role in the community has also declined. Villagers have increasingly sought out clergy in other churches for confession,[7] thus severely limiting Father Münster's access to and control of local and often privileged knowledge. People have also begun attending Saturday evening masses in a nearby western German village, once inaccessible before the fall of the Wall, so they could sleep late on Sundays. The priest's declining influence and involvement in community affairs, it should be noted, were also the product of the dramatic change in circumstances since the fall of the Wall, in which all community members have had less access to shared information.

These changes in circumstances include, above all, the end of the community's geographic isolation as a border village in the "high security zone" (*Schutzstreifen*). Under socialism, villagers were able to keep track of one another's comings and goings as well as the occasional outside visitors because only residents and relatives with special passes were permitted to enter the village. Now, with the freedom to travel and receive visitors, keeping track of such details is impossible. This process of isolation was accelerated with the closing of regional factories in the early1990s, where local information was exchanged and shared.

Father Münster responded to these challenges by attempting to cling to his control, occasionally through methods and strategies of manipulation. During the time of my fieldwork, for example, he would occasionally test the loyalty of his most dedicated followers (primarily women) by planning Bible study groups that conflicted with other scheduled public gatherings in the village. Similarly, viewing every stranger to the village as a possible recruit for the Focolare movement, he frequently attempted to schedule social events involving outside visitors at his own home. My husband and I both benefited from and were challenged by his actions. On the one hand, Father Münster had helped integrate us into village life by his introduction and stamp of approval during a Christmas Eve mass several weeks after our arrival (see Berdahl 1999a). On the other hand, however, it was evident that he viewed us as a foreign and potentially disruptive presence in the village. We soon gathered that he was closely monitoring our activities, and we were often surprised, and dismayed, to hear him misrepresenting things we had said about the community, village residents, or the Focolare movement to promote his own perspective.[8] As educated outsiders, I believe he felt his association with us might grant his ideas a certain degree of legitimacy, and he often guarded that association jealously.

Johanna grew to be deeply troubled by what she, among others, viewed to be hypocritical and contradictory behavior on the part of the priest toward us and other members of the community. She was confused and alarmed by his comments about jettisoning friends who hadn't been persuaded "to believe,"[9] and she was particularly disturbed by what she knew to be misrepresentations of me and John, my husband. Johanna's ambivalence toward the priest did not affect her own deeply held religious convictions; as Riegelhaupt (1984) has noted, anticlericalism does not necessarily imply a rejection of religion. However, it did entail a difficult and emotional personal struggle.

The amount of space in my fieldnotes devoted to this issue attests to its presence as a dilemma I found myself frequently negotiating throughout fieldwork. I felt a personal obligation to balance honesty about my own religious views and background with my professional needs as an anthropologist to observe the changing relationship between the priest and parishioners. Having been baptized in the Methodist church as a child but raised with little religious instruction in a family whose observances of Christmas and Easter were largely secular, I had developed my own sense of spirituality that had little connection to any organized religion. When asked by people in the village, however, I told them I came from a Protestant background. Although deeply skeptical of the charismatic, anti-intellectual nature of the Focolare movement and clear in my refusal to become involved, I also appreciated that its ecumenism was partially responsible for our warm welcome into the village's traditional Catholic Church. I further recognized that, although Father Münster was a fairly controversial figure in the community, he still retained a certain measure of authority invested in him as a priest that needed to be acknowledged and respected if I were to remain in good standing in the community. So it was with delicate diplomacy, particularly in regard to Johanna, that I struggled to negotiate these contradictions, and I was not always successful.

ILLNESS AND POWER

Johanna was diagnosed with an inoperable brain tumor the day I left Germany after a brief visit in 1994. She didn't tell me then, typically setting her own concerns aside to help me prepare for what promised to be a stressful drive to the Frankfurt airport with my feverish infant daughter. In fact, it was Father Münster who called me, once I was back in the States, to break the news. "It's very serious," I remember him telling me, "[some of the doctors] can't believe she's even still alive." He went on to explain that he was calling because Johanna would be reluctant to convey the severity of her situation to me. Blaming the messenger for the message, perhaps, I hung up the phone angry at Father Münster and questioning his motivations for the call.

Without fully considering the implications or consequences of my actions, I immediately went to work to try and help Johanna. A friend who had visited me in the field and who had thus met Johanna put me in touch with a friend of hers with close contacts to leading neurologists throughout the United States and Europe. Assuring me he knew the best person in Germany to handle the case, he referred me to a brain specialist in Hamburg who graciously agreed to take on Johanna as her primary doctor or as a second opinion. Johanna was a bit overwhelmed by all this attention, but agreed to send her test results to Hamburg, where the specialist confirmed the diagnosis and recommended against a biopsy until there was some indication of the tumor's growth. Much to everyone's relief, a second set of tests 6 months later revealed no significant change.

A year later, however, a CAT scan revealed that the tumor had grown, and Johanna's doctors in Göttingen were offering seemingly inconclusive advice about treatment. They informed Johanna that the risks of doing a biopsy of the tumor, a necessary precursor to treatment, included the slight possibility of total paralysis due to the tumor's location and size; yet allowing the tumor to go untreated, they said, could be fatal. On the other hand, there was the remote possibility that the tumor would stop growing and merely continue to be the source of Johanna's severely piercing headaches. At my request, she forwarded her test results to the Hamburg specialist who, after consulting with several colleagues, quickly responded with a conclusive recommendation in favor of a biopsy followed by appropriate treatment. To me, Johanna's options, while painful and full of risk, seemed clear: the "leading specialists" had concurred that the danger of allowing the tumor to go untreated was greater than the risks of a biopsy. Johanna, however, fearing the risks of the biopsy more than death, opted to wait.

Concerned that she was making a potentially fatal mistake, I set out to ensure her decision would be fully informed. I drafted a list of questions to ask of both the Hamburg specialist as well as her doctors in Göttingen. I talked to her husband about the importance of his presence during meetings with the doctors to relieve her of the burden of dealing with this alone. I initiated a series of phone calls and e-mails in order to convey through my contact in the United States to the doctor in Hamburg that Johanna was receiving mixed messages about treatment; I even discussed, but ultimately decided against, the possibility of a conference call with the German-American contact of my friend in order to answer Johanna's questions and, possibly, to persuade her of the Hamburg doctor's expertise and experience.

I soon realized that I was also competing with the priest for a voice in providing Johanna with medical advice and personal support. I had easily sensed over the past year Johanna's growing closeness to Father Münster. The occasional criticism and ambivalence she had once felt comfortable sharing with me had ceased, and I began hearing through others in the village of her increased activity within the church. Father Münster, it appeared, had become Johanna's closest confidante. Knowing Johanna to be deeply faithful, I attributed this to a sense of spiritual security and companionship the priest was able to provide her as she faced a potentially imminent death. My experience of the priest, however, made me suspicious that he was acting out of both altruism and self-interest. I could imagine him genuinely wanting to help one of his most devout parishioners at the same time that I could imagine him striving to validate a religious authority and social identity as the village priest.

Father Münster, it turns out, had his own medical contact, an eastern German doctor actively involved in the Focolare movement, to whom Johanna was also sending her test results. According to this doctor, it was a "miracle" that she was still alive, which all three—the priest, the doctor, and Johanna—interpreted more literally, I believe, than the usual figure of speech. I knew Johanna to be a strong believer in destiny (she refused to wear a seatbelt for this very reason), and upon hearing her repeat the eastern German doctor's words (attributed in that first phone call by the priest to all "the doctors" caring for Johanna), I realized that she had decided to place her confidence in divine fate rather than in medical experts, at least for the time being. I had no choice but to accept, albeit regretfully, her decision.

Implicit in my actions and reactions, but unrecognizable to me at the time, was an assumption that my elite western contacts were superior to the care and advice she was receiving from the less renowned doctors in Göttingen or especially in the former GDR, and that I knew best how to negotiate the western medical system. My efforts also revealed an unquestioned confidence that medical science was more likely to help Johanna in fighting the tumor than any religious faith or belief in miracles. In retrospect, I was surprisingly unconcerned about appearing and acting like a *Besserwessi,* the term East Germans use to describe West Germans who act like "they know everything better." As DeSoto points out, the term also alludes to a more general power imbalance between East and West following the collapse of socialist rule in East Germany (2000a). Often described by eastern Germans as a process of "colonization," the hegemony of the West was reflected in nearly all realms of social and political life, ranging from the dismantling of East German legal and educational institutions to the perceived victors' justice of the border guard trials to the dominance of western media. The power dynamics resulting from my positioning as an educated "westerner" in this asymmetrical postsocialist context were of little concern to me; at the time, I was focused on trying to save my friend.

DISTANCE AND DISPLACEMENTS

An anthropologist's positioning, Jill Dubisch points out, is never static (1996: 107). Shortly before I returned to Germany for fieldwork in the spring of 1996, my mother was diagnosed with breast cancer. I had spent the month before my departure keeping her company during the awkward and frightening days before surgery, alternating nightly hospital shifts with my father after her double mastectomy, and educating myself about the various forms and treatments of breast cancer. As an academic, perhaps I found particular comfort and refuge in the assortment of books and articles on breast cancer that I collected immediately upon learning of my mother's diagnosis. By the time I arrived in Germany, I was exhausted, but also admittedly relieved by the opportunity to direct my energies elsewhere, at least for the moment. I soon discovered, however, that my own positioning as an anthropologist had been transformed by my experience of my mother's illness.

I also returned to the village as a mother. Although my daughter Audrey had accompanied me as an infant during a brief visit in 1994, this was the first time I would be doing fieldwork with offspring. Like many childless couples in the field, John and I had been the object of some curiosity and village gossip due to our decision to postpone childbearing; I was curious to see how Audrey's presence would affect the dynamics of field research.

Finally, I returned to Germany knowing this might be my last visit with Johanna. Because I recognized the topic's potential divisiveness, I had resolved to avoid discussions with her about the priest. Indeed, although I intended to pursue in my research questions about the changing role of the church and religion, I hoped to distance myself from the personal dynamics surrounding the priest and his relationship to parishioners that had consumed so much time and energy during my initial research.

When I arrived to find photographs of Audrey prominently displayed across the priest's kitchen cupboard, however, I quickly discovered that this would be difficult. The pictures had been enclosed with Christmas cards that I had sent to Father Münster, along with many other villagers, since I had left the field;

they were the only photographs in his kitchen. I was both amused and angered by what I perceived to be the use of my daughter in the priest's attempts to legitimate both his threatened position in the community and his religious views through an association with me and John. But I also sensed genuine affection for me and John and our child in the display of the photographs, and I was even slightly touched by the gesture and consequently embarrassed at my suspicion of his ulterior motives. The location of the pictures in the semi-private space of the kitchen,[10] rather than in the priest's more public office, I believed, was both an expression and performance of a certain intimacy he felt toward us that was quite different from his relationship to parishioners.[11]

A conversation over lunch with Father Münster confirmed this perception. At his initiative, we began talking about Johanna's illness in a manner that would have been unusual with other members of the community. Just days before, she had received the results of her semi-annual tests that revealed further growth in the tumor; her doctors in Göttingen, although astonished at Johanna's relatively good health considering the tumor's size and location, were now recommending a biopsy, as the Hamburg specialist had a year earlier. Father Münster, who had once reportedly told a dying villager that he envied him "for he would soon be with Christ," was deeply skeptical of any form of treatment. "I know two priests who have died of cancer," he told me, "and all they [the doctors] do is prolong your suffering." Growing increasingly passionate, he went on to castigate Johanna's husband and family, arguing that they failed to take seriously her illness or her religious faith. "[Johanna] has accepted and embraced this illness," he said, echoing the Focolare movement's glorification of suffering that encourages a passive and non-interventionist approach (Urquhart 1995: 62), "and her family must do the same."

During the course of this conversation, Johanna's recent behavior became increasingly understandable to me. If the priest was saying similar things to Johanna—and I had good reasons to believe he was and that she was listening—it was little wonder if she feared medical treatment more than death itself. In accusing her husband and family of indifference,[12] it appeared the priest had successfully positioned himself as Johanna's most trusted and caring confidant. It was also little wonder, then, that she was devoting much of her time and energy to the church. Johanna was one of several village women who had voluntarily assumed many of the duties and responsibilities once held by three nuns who had lived in the community until 1993. These included, above all, preparing the sanctuary and ringing the church bells for services, keeping church records updated, and, frequently, cooking and cleaning for the priest. As elsewhere in Europe, women here are often regarded as "the guardians of their family's spiritual health" and their religious involvement as "religious activities on the family's behalf" rather than a "neglecting of their duties as wives and mothers" (Dubisch 1996: 210–211); however, several of these women, including Johanna, had crossed the boundary of appropriate behavior in the minds of many villagers.

I, too, began to view Johanna's religious activities as rather extreme and found myself growing increasingly irritated by her seemingly blind devotion to the priest. Her daily church attendance entailed arriving 30 minutes before services in order to ring the bells; afterward she would frequently stay to clean up and talk with Father Münster. She regularly took over his religion classes for grade-school children, and could frequently be found running an errand or taking care of something at the rectory on his behalf. What disturbed me, however, was her apparent uncritical acceptance of the priest's attitudes toward suffering, illness, and death. Indeed, I found myself at times enraged by this, angry at Johanna because I felt she wasn't fighting the disease and furious at the priest, whom I (perhaps unjustly) blamed.

One Sunday that spring, as I was sitting among the congregation waiting for the morning mass to begin, I watched Johanna emerge from the sacristy where she had been helping the priest and altar boys prepare for services. After gently closing the sacristy door, she proceeded to the base of the altar stairs and delicately genuflected to the ornate altarpiece containing a dark oil painting of the crucifixion. Johanna then carefully ascended the stairs to light several candles on the marble altar and place an open Bible on the wooden pulpit. At the bottom of the stairs she genuflected again and then, with hands folded piously below her breast and eyes cast humbly to the ground, she tiptoed to her seat in order to avoid disturbing the silence of the waiting congregation. Upon reaching her seat she crossed herself, said a silent prayer, and sat down. Her actions and demeanor revealed an intensity of faith and purpose that I suddenly almost envied, and at that moment it occurred to me that her deep religious faith—and her devout practice, indeed embodiment, of it—just might be keeping her alive. Why hadn't I thought of this before? What was the source of my anger at Johanna? Would I have been so frustrated by her decision not to seek traditional medical treatment if I were doing research in a "non-western" context—if she had been consulting a shaman, for example? Few experiences in fieldwork are perhaps as revealing of cultural differences as are divergent understandings of health and illness, for implicit in these understandings are deeply held cultural conceptions of the body, science, and religion. I knew that moral dilemmas surrounding conflicting cultural concepts of illness were nothing new for anthropologists; as Keith Brown points out, these kinds of dilemmas are variants of the old problem of "cultural relativism" in anthropology. However, I had not expected to encounter this in my own research in Europe (Brown 2000).[13]

The complex and contradictory nature of my "halfie" status (Abu-Lughod 1991), "in which the 'other' is at least partly the 'self'" (Dubisch 1996: 15), thus became painfully clear. Of course to some extent anthropologists are always "halfies," positioned as insiders and outsiders in one sense or another. Indeed, as Narayan has pointed out, they are more than this, for "two halves cannot account for the complexity of an identity in which multiple countries, regions, religions, and classes may come together" (Narayan 1993: 673). Fieldwork in any society entails shifting identifications, in which particular aspects of one's positioning become salient. Working in a "less alien" society (cf. Jaffe 1993),[14] particularly within the context of a similar religious tradition that I had chosen only moderately to accept, had carried with it a set of expectations, theirs and my own, about my involvement, responsibilities, and behavior as an anthropologist in the field and as a member of the community.[15] Further, the postsocialist context of my fieldwork, I later realized, had been almost dangerously deceptive: the apparent cultural similarities between the new eastern Germany and my "western" experience—capitalist market economy, democratic political structures, familiar consumer products, and common mass cultural references—had the potential to conceal the profound cultural, political, and economic differences and life experiences that had separated us just years ago. Or, as Jill Dubisch, drawing from an observation of Ernestine Friedl, has written about ethnographic fieldwork in Europe in general: "Europe presents the anthropologist with an anomaly, for it offers the unfamiliar in the deceptive guise of the familiar" (1995: 35). Observing Johanna that day forced me to acknowledge and respect both the distinct value of her experience as well as the cultural distance between us.

"Anthropology," Ruth Behar has written, "is frequently about displacements" (Behar 1991: 351).[16] My anger at Johanna and the priest and the way they were dealing with her illness was, I believe, also the product of displaced emotions compounded by my hybrid (Narayan 1993) positioning. To some extent at least, I had displaced my rage at the cancer that had invaded my mother's body, and displaced my fear at the possibility of losing her, onto Johanna and her illness. I vehemently rejected the priest's insistence on accepting death because this was not an option I was willing to accept for my mother. I needed for Johanna to fight the illness not only because I cared deeply for her, but because I wanted so desperately for my own mother to survive. The fact that I had been asking Johanna to fight the illness in terms that I understood—by educating herself about the illness and treatment options, by asking critical questions of her doctors, by seeking the best medical advice and treatment available—highlighted for me my distance and displacement.

That Sunday after mass, with tears in my eyes and hands trembling, I lit a votive candle for my mother.

POPULAR FAITH, INSTITUTIONALIZED RELIGION, AND POWER

This revelatory moment of distancing and recognition of inter-cultural subjectivity, as well as Johanna's relationship to the priest that had to some extent prompted my reaction, all occurred within the context of transformations in religion, popular faith, and the Catholic Church after the collapse of socialist rule.[17] The priest's involvement with Johanna's illness was in part, I believe, an attempt to sustain some sense of purpose and authority that had been diminished by divisions within the congregation surrounding the Focolare movement as well as by the declining influence of the Catholic Church and changes in religious practices since the fall of the Wall.

A week after this incident, on Easter, Father Münster announced to the congregation that the bishop had ordered him transferred out of the village. In 3 months he would take over a larger congregation located 30 km away, Father Münster explained, and a new priest in a neighboring village would assume responsibility for this congregation in addition to two other nearby parishes. The village would thus not only be losing Father Münster, but a resident priest as well; the future of the parish rectory, which had recently undergone extensive renovations, was yet to be determined. The news came as a surprise to everyone, even to Johanna and others among the priest's closest parishioners.

Although there was little visible reaction among the congregation that morning, villagers soon began expressing a range of opinions and speculations surrounding the reasons for and ramifications of Father Münster's departure. Many parishioners welcomed the change; others were indifferent. Many were saddened and angered at the loss of a resident priest, and several lamented a waste of time and money spent renovating the local rectory only to have it stand vacant 2 years later. Those parishioners close to Father Münster understandably felt a deep personal loss.

Further, having been given no concrete reason by the priest or the bishop for the transfer, particularly after Father Münster insisted to inquiring parishioners that he had not requested a change, people were left to speculate. For many, it was merely a normal course of events; 10 years was a normal tenure for a priest in any community, they argued, and this one had already exceeded his. Others pointed to the widespread shortage of priests in the Catholic Church and explained the transfer as a product of diocese reorganization and consolidation. Soon, however, rumors began circulating that the bishop had received letters of complaint from several villagers. According to local gossip, one letter was critical of Father Münster's involvement in Focolare and claimed he was responsible for creating troublesome factions within the congregation. Another letter allegedly accused the priest of improper conduct in relation to several of his closest female parishioners. There were reportedly no charges in the letter, nor were there rumors in the village, of sexual involvement; rather the priest was blamed for having created divisions within families and between spouses as a result of his frequent activities and close relationships with several women in the village. Sensing a problematic and potentially disruptive situation, it was speculated, the bishop had determined it was time for the controversial priest to move on.

Most significant about the local gossip were the changes it reflected in perceptions and attitudes toward the church as an institution. The church had not merely lost the appeal it had under socialism as an alternative institution and forum for opposition to the regime; it had now itself become a power that had to be interpreted, negotiated, and contested. Echoing similar comments I heard from several villagers, a letter to the bishop protesting Father Münster's transfer stated: "Many [of us] working in the West have learned that those in power care little about the human effects of their decisions ... Is this true in this case as well?" Of the approximately four letters written to the bishop, three mentioned the painful loss of the Schwesternhaus, a visible landmark within the village because of its size, unusual yellow exterior, and hillside location. The building now stands empty, slowly showing signs of abandonment and decay with its crumbling facade and broken windows. The three nuns who once lived in the house, along with the elderly residents of its small nursing home, left in 1994 because of the financial pressures of their parent house, and its Catholic kindergarten is now housed in the former GDR daycare facility. What was once an important symbol of religious presence and resistance under socialism, particularly in the context of the community's status as a village in the high security border zone (*Schutzstreifengemeinde*),[18] has thus now become for many residents a symbol of loss and betrayal. As one woman told me, "it makes me ill even to look up there at the Schwesternhaus." Similarly, in a letter to the bishop protesting Father Münster's transfer a resident wrote: "The Schwesternhaus overlooks [the village] like a memorial, empty and yawning ... Must our rectory also stand empty and unused?"

The priest's transfer and villagers' reactions to it thus also reflected an increasing divergence between popular faith and institutionalized religion (e.g., Badone 1990), religious traditions whose interests had remained largely congruent during the period of socialist rule when both popular religious expressions (local legends, superstitions, or religious symbols) united with institutionally sanctioned practices (baptisms, communions, church marriages) in opposition to the regime.[19] With the loss of a shared understanding of the meaning of religious survival after the collapse of socialism, the interests of unofficial and official religion have, to some extent, diverged, resulting in renegotiations and redefinitions of religious identities and practice. Whereas the clergy has been quick to preach about the dangers of consumerism and deplore the decline in church attendance, parishioners have initiated new forms and expressions of religious devotion. Rather than attending Sunday mass in the village, for example, once an important means of social control and measure of religious commitment because of the lack of alternatives to the village church during the period of socialist rule, villagers may now choose to go to Saturday evening mass in a neighboring village. Similarly, others may simply visit a famous pilgrimage site on a day trip in lieu of Sunday mass.

Reactions within the village to the priest's transfer reflect this increasing divergence. Recalling their allegiance to the church during socialism, for which many villagers paid a price through increased surveillance by the state or by being denied passes to visit western relatives, for example,[20] parishioners described feeling abandoned and betrayed by the church. As one letter to the bishop argued: "We have defended our faith over the past years ... And what has it brought us? We feel abandoned, especially because along with Father Münster we are losing a permanent resident priest." Several parishioners, similarly reflecting a split between official and unofficial religion, threatened to leave the church, as conveyed in another letter to the bishop: "Some [people] have even indicated their intention to leave the church. They claim they don't need to pay church taxes in order to believe [in God]."

The bishop responded to parishioners' complaints with a single letter from a suffragan bishop addressed to Father Münster, which the priest shared with the congregation during a Sunday morning mass. Although the bishop appreciated the community's concerns, the letter read, "there are other points of view that must be considered." There was no explanation following this assertion, nor has one been forthcoming in response to an additional inquiry by a small group of parishioners. Many villagers were angered by the dismissive tone of the letter; for several, it confirmed their view of the ecclesiastical hierarchy as men in power indifferent to human and community concerns. "You'd think you could expect more compassion from the church," one woman told me, adding, "It's not necessarily the church that's bad but the individuals who are in power there."

ETHNOGRAPHIC INVERSIONS, ATTACHMENTS, AND POSITIONING: SOME CONCLUDING THOUGHTS

Quite predictably, Johanna has been at the forefront of efforts to keep Father Münster in the community. Not only does she foresee the loss of a close confidante, but with the absence of a resident priest and subsequent decline in religious activities in the village, Johanna anticipates no longer being able to partake in the many church activities and responsibilities through which she finds deep spiritual and personal meaning. After watching her before mass that Sunday, I, too, became concerned about the latter possibility. As a mutual friend said to me, "I'm concerned that with the priest gone, it [her illness] could go rapidly downhill."

Johanna and I continued to be in telephone contact after my return from Germany that spring.[21] During one conversation in which she shared her anger and frustration at the bishop's reply to parishioners, I expressed my curiosity about the reasons for the transfer and wondered aloud if a letter for my own research purposes would be answered similarly, if at all. Immediately upon uttering the thought I regretted it. "Oh Daphne!" Johanna exclaimed. "You would do that? I'm sure a letter from you, an outsider with some experience of living in the community, would help. The bishop wouldn't be able to dismiss it as being from us 'simple people,' as he has the other letters." Hoping to avoid becoming more involved than I suddenly already was, I explained that *if* I were to write such a letter, I would refrain from expressing any opinion about the transfer itself; my aim merely would be to learn the reasons behind the decision. I would think about it, I told her.

Johanna's enthusiasm and expectations for a letter from me revealed her own recognition and acknowledgment of my dual insider/outsider status; in her mind, I was also a "hybrid." For me, this "hybrid" status in relation to Johanna was compounded by my recent experience with my mother's cancer: studying "the other" was, in this case, also a personal and emotional study of the "self." My initial frustration with and subsequent compassion for Johanna, deriving in part from my experience with my mother, forced me to recognize and accept my own helplessness in relation to both women. Despite my attempts to secure the best medical advice for Johanna, and despite all the books I could read about breast cancer for my mother, I was ultimately, and painfully, powerless. Our different approaches to a life-threatening illness—indeed, our different fears—had both bridged and highlighted a cultural distance; the coevalness of the experiences made them mutually illuminating.[22] Lighting the candle for my mother that Sunday was thus a peace offering, a sign of hope, and a prayer. Together, the experiences have given me an unexpected awareness and understanding of what Ruth Behar has called "the paradoxes of attachment and displacement" (Behar 1991: 374), all reflected and united in the flame of a votive candle.

The conversation with Johanna and her argument in favor of my involvement, with its implications of her perception of the persuasiveness of my institutional letterhead and title, also reflected a shift in my professional status and positioning as an anthropologist. To my surprise, I would invoke that status several days later when Johanna called to suggest that if I did intend to write such a letter, it would be most helpful if I did it sooner rather than later while there was still time for the bishop to reverse his decision. In a gesture of inverted distancing, I chose to point to my own need as a researcher to avoid becoming entangled in local politics. "It might position me within the community in ways that I might find difficult later," I explained to Johanna, "and I doubt if I would get an answer from the bishop's office, anyway." Her obvious disappointment only complicated my conflicting emotions of guilt and responsibility. Had I invoked a notion of "objectivity" that I myself found highly questionable, indeed fictional, to protect my own (selfish) research interests? Was I putting those interests ahead of the needs and desires of my friend? Or was I being a "responsible anthropologist" by avoiding potentially troublesome partisanship? On the other hand, was I being truly partisan because of my own suspicions of and, at times, difficult interactions with, the priest?

My affirmative answers to all of these questions reveals the "multiple and sometimes contradictory and inconsistent ways" in which all observers are positioned (Dubisch 1996: 107). This shifting and hybrid identification (Narayan 1993) may be especially highlighted by a distancing moment emerging out of the contexts and accidents of fieldwork, or, as described above, by an inverted distancing initiated by the anthropologist; it may also be accompanied, and complicated, by conflicting allegiances and emotions. In this essay, as in fieldwork, my positioning has included friend, "westerner," anthropologist, professional scholar, mother, daughter. My emotions surrounding Johanna, the priest, my role and identity as an anthropologist and friend, faith and illness, and the writing of this paper have been similarly mixed and contradictory—feelings that were only compounded by eerily coincidental messages on my answering machine from both Johanna and Father Münster just days before completing an initial draft of this paper. Although the specifics are unique to my situation, many of the issues raised here concerning the politics and practices of ethnography will be quite familiar to anthropologists. What is different, here, however, is the postsocialist context of my fieldwork, which at times appeared deceptively similar to historically capitalist "western" societies. The transformations in and negotiations of local and extra-local power dynamics as well as changes in a dynamic interplay between organized and unorganized religion were products of the collapse of socialist rule; they were also processes that affected the social relations among, and my own relationships to, the people with whom I lived and worked. It was the convergence of these various processes around the specifics of a single distancing moment during fieldwork that highlighted for me particular dilemmas of research in a postsocialist context.

Anthropologists have long been committed to exploring the intersection of the large and the small; indeed, we may consider it one of the fundamental tasks of anthropology to explore how larger social, political, and economic processes are manifested and negotiated locally and specifically. More recently, anthropologists have devoted much attention to the separate issue of the poetics and politics of ethnography (e.g., Clifford and Marcus 1986), both through a re-evaluation of anthropology and the colonial encounter (e.g., Asad 1973), as well as through more reflexive explications of the fieldwork encounter itself. My point here is simply that these are all related: that the specific politics, struggles, and paradoxes of our ethnographic research and writing are situated within these larger contexts. Not only are the processes of production that shape the direction and outcome of our research the product of daily events, personal interactions and even struggles in fieldwork,[23] they may also be the product of the very political, economic, and social processes that we intend to study. Indeed, there can be a dynamic interplay between the two. These dynamics are difficult, but, I think, important to write about. For me, as an anthropologist and friend, this particular attempt has been an exercise in mixed devotions.

—ɯ—

PART THREE

LEIPZIG

6
THE SPIRIT OF CAPITALISM
AND THE BOUNDARIES
OF CITIZENSHIP
IN POST-WALL GERMANY

IMMEDIATELY AFTER THE FALL OF THE Berlin Wall in November 1989, one of the most pervasive media images consisted of East Germans on a frenetic, collective shopping spree. For many western Germans, as well as for much of the world, the "triumph" of capitalism and democracy seemed to be reflected and confirmed in the "consuming frenzy" (*Konsumrausch*) of the *Ossis* (East Germans). Although these images of consumption following the collapse of socialism were new, they were structured by and contributed to a dominant narrative of "democratization" and national legitimacy in which access to consumer goods and consumer choice are defined as fundamental rights and democratic expressions of individualism. Indeed, many observers have since suggested that the transitions of 1989 were not about demands for political or human rights, but for consumer rights (e.g., Bauman 1992; Borneman 1992; Drakulić 1991). They were also, I would add, about consumer *rites*—about the making of citizen-consumers.

My aim in this paper is to interrogate visions, meanings, and the boundaries of citizenship in the context of East Germany's transition from state socialism to a consumer market economy. My argument is that these transformations are suggestive of a more general phenomenon concerning the relationship between citizenship and late or "millennial capitalism" (Comaroff and Comaroff 2000). I am thus proposing an alternative ethnography of the nation-state that focuses not on state practices, bureaucracies, or institutions but on performances and practices of citizenship and national belonging. Drawing on fieldwork conducted in the eastern German city of Leipzig, I explore an emerging and transformative relationship between citizenship and mass consumption especially visible in the radically deindustrialized former GDR. The nation-state and national belonging are forged not only through neoliberal ideologies of consumer democracy and the "freedom to choose" as in market life, I argue, but also through the activities, places, and objects of consumption.[1] Transnational processes may nationalize (Verdery 1998) through the creation of new categories of inclusion and exclusion—by redefining what practices and people count as national (cf. Berlant 1997).

DELIVERING THE GOODS: CITIZENSHIP, CONSUMPTION, AND NATIONAL LEGITIMACY

A "defining mark of modernity," argue James Holston and Arjun Appadurai, is the association between citizenship and nationality as definitive of "the meaning of full membership in society" (Holston and Appadurai 1996: 187). As renewed discussions of citizenship within public and academic discussions have revealed, however, liberal notions of citizenship and citizenship rights have been transformed in the face of large-scale movements of people and goods, the globalization of production, the consolidation of supranational institutions like the European Union, and an increasingly complex and interconnected system of global capitalism. In contrast to an emphasis on civil or political rights in earlier modes and ideals of citizenship, and unlike the notion of social rights that is at the center of T. H. Marshall's classic formulation (1992),[2] recent studies and critiques of citizenship have moved beyond a notion of the state as arbiter of citizenship to examine its "de-territorialized," "post-national," "pluralistic," "cultural," "privatized," or "global" dimensions (e.g., Berlant 1997; Falk 1994; T. Miller 1993; Rosaldo 1994; Sommers 1993; Soysal 1994; B. Turner 1994). As Holston and Appadurai have noted:

> Citizenship concerns more than rights to participate in politics. It also includes other kinds of rights in the public sphere, namely, civil, socio-economic, and cultural. Moreover, in addition to the legal, it concerns the moral and imperative dimensions of membership which define the meanings and practices of belonging in society. (1996: 200)

Citizenship may thus be understood as an ongoing process, a social practice, and a cultural performance rather than a static category. It entails complex and often contradictory struggles over the definition of social membership, over categories and practices of inclusion and exclusion, and over different forms of participation in public life. "Citizenship," writes Gershon Shafir, is not "just a bundle of formal rights but the entire mode of incorporation of a particular individual or group into society" (1998: 23).

In the context of contemporary debates over globalization and the future of the nation-state, a move beyond traditional conceptions of citizenship must also include, among other areas of inquiry, a focus on consumption and the marketplace. The relationship between citizenship and capitalism, and theorizing about this dynamic, has a long history in social theory, including Marx's discussion of modern citizenship rights in his critique of the liberal state in "On the Jewish Question" (Marx 1972), as well as Marshall's penetrating description of citizenship as the "instrument of social stratification" (1992: 39). Along similar lines, scholars have more recently observed that access to consumer goods and the concept of choice in relation to consumption emerged in the middle of the twentieth century as a fundamental political right in western industrialized societies (Bauman 1992, 1998; De Grazia 1996; McGovern 1998; L. Cohen 1998). This transformation, argue Jean and John Comaroff, is one critical aspect of the "culture of neoliberalism": "a culture that . . . re-visions persons not as producers from a particular community, but as consumers in a planetary marketplace" (2000: 304). The most explicit connection between citizenship and consumption is made in a recent study by Néstor García Canclini, who points out that "redefining citizenship in connection with consumption and political strategy requires a conceptual framework for examining cultural consumption as an ensemble of practices that shape the sphere of citizenship" (Canclini 2001: 22).

The analytical utility of the category citizenship, in contradistinction to an analytics of nationality (although the two are obviously closely related), lies in its focus on the public sphere, the role of the state, as well as on questions of the rights, duties, and obligations of national membership, all of which have been transformed by the cultural and economic dominance of consumption and the market.

The consequences of this relation between consumption, citizenship, and political rights have been profound, resulting, for example, in the emergence of the female "citizen consumer" empowered politically through consumption (De Grazia 1996; B. Davis 1996), as well as a redefinition of the rights and obligations of citizenship itself. As De Grazia argues, the latter change has resulted in a new kind of "post-political citizenship" in which an individual's "presence in the public sphere is defined not so much by the transformation of the political system as by a notion of the self, of collective identity, and of entitlement associated with the diffusion of mass consumption" (1996: 356).

This redefinition extends to the duties and obligations of citizenship as well. Because mass consumption is linked to economic prosperity,[3] responsibilities of citizenship also include the duty to consume—a nation of shoppers. It has also significantly transformed the role of the state in providing a framework for private consumption. Indeed, as the collapse of socialism throughout eastern Europe to a large extent demonstrated, the ability of national regimes to guarantee access to consumer products—"to deliver the goods"—has become, as Terence Turner has pointed out, "their essential basis of legitimation" (1997).[4]

This relationship between consumption and national legitimacy has particular relevance in the German context. The postwar economic miracle in West Germany, for example, was largely based upon the promise, and premise, of entitlement and prosperity as the products of democratic freedoms, as Ludwig Erhard, its architect, suggested: "Every citizen must be conscious of consumer freedom and the freedom of economic enterprise as basic and inalienable rights" (quoted in De Grazia 1996: 283). Further, as Erica Carter (1997) has argued in a provocative study of consumption and gender in postwar West Germany, economic prosperity became an important element in a developing West German national identity, with women as consumers playing a major role as active agents in economic integration. In the search for a new, unencumbered national narrative, Carter suggests, ideas of German nationhood were transposed throughout the 1950s onto a flourishing social market economy. This notion of the economy as a focus of national sentiment attained renewed visibility immediately after the fall of the Berlin Wall. Indeed, "Deutschmark nationalism," a term coined by Habermas to describe what he saw (and feared) as a rise in nationalist sentiments based on the promise of a consumer-oriented market economy supported by the "almighty" Deutschmark, is widely viewed as having been the driving force behind the landslide victory of the coalition parties associated with Helmut Kohl's Christian Democratic Party in the East German elections of March 1990.

CONSUMING METAPHORS

The fall of the Berlin Wall thus quickly came to be a key symbol affirming the relationship between national legitimacy and mass consumption. The eastern bloc "economies of shortage" (Kornai 1992) contrasted sharply with the affluence and abundance of consumer goods in the west, and nowhere was this disparity more evident than in divided Germany. Local and state-level practices, including the exchange of political prisoners and dissidents for western currency, West German state loans to the GDR, images on western television (whose airwaves easily crossed the otherwise impermeable border), and the coveted *Westpakete* (western packages) full of chocolates, coffee, and hand-me-down clothing for eastern relatives, reflected this imbalance and confirmed an image of the prosperous "golden West," a paradise that, if attained, could solve most every problem.[5] As Slavenka Drakulić once wrote:

> Sometimes I think the real Iron Curtain is made up of silky, shiny, images.... These images that cross the borders in magazines, movies, or videos are ... more dangerous than any secret weapon, because they make one desire that "otherness" badly enough to risk one's life by trying to escape. Many did. (1991: 27–28)

After the fall of the Wall, images and metaphors of prosperity and consumption continued to define distinctions between East and West. West German triumphalist discourses hailed the end of the Cold War, while newspapers featured photos of East Germans gawking at western products (a typical headline, for example, read: "Waiting, Marveling, Buying"). The 100 DM *Begrüßungsgeld* (welcome money) handed to all first-time visitors from the GDR by the West German state as well as spontaneous gifts of cash from individual West Germans not only helped finance the easterners' spending spree, but also helped define consumption as the organizing metaphor for the collapse of socialist rule. Consumption thus not only became an important symbolic marker of this historic moment (represented most tangibly in what people chose to purchase with their "welcome money"), but became constitutive of the meaning of the transition (*Wende*) itself: state socialism collapsed not merely because of a political failure, but because of its failure, quite literally, "to deliver the goods" (Borneman 1992: 252). As the historian Ina Merkel has observed: "The struggle between the systems did not take the form of armed conflict, but was rather shifted to the marketplace. And it was here, in the sphere of consumerism, that the battle was won" (1998: 282).

CITIZENSCAPES

Since German re-unification,[6] consumption has continued to be a particularly important means of defining East-West distinctions as well as membership in a national community. As I have argued and described elsewhere (Berdahl 1999a), the acquisition of a cultural competence in consumption—not unlike Baudrillard's notion of consumer society as "the society of learning how to consume, of social training in consumption" (1988: 81)—became a central initiation rite for eastern Germans into West German society. In the first years after the fall of the Wall, the lack of a cultural fluency in western consumption practices was a key marker of an Ossi. Eastern Germans not only had to learn how to navigate their way through new structures of consumer credit, domestic finance, and money management, they also had to learn simply where and how to shop after having only experienced an economy of shortages. During the course of my fieldwork in a former East German border village between 1990 and 1992, for example, eastern Germans received both formal and informal instruction on the rules and values of a consumer market economy. New grade school textbooks, read by children and parents alike, contained lessons on the aims and functions of advertising. A prominent West German bank sponsored learning seminars whose topics included "Wishing, Planning, Buying," "Fashioning One's Life and Consumption Behavior," and "Shopping to Your Advantage." Such lessons in consumption following the fall of the Wall resonate with Bryan Turner's definition of citizenship as a "set of practices which constitute individuals as competent members of a community" (1994: 159).

More recently, many efforts have been devoted to educating eastern German consumers about the consequences and implications of their purchasing choices after the radical decline in demand for and production of eastern German products following re-unification. Explained the head of the supermarket chain *Konsum,* the East German consumer cooperative and one of the few surviving remnants of socialist commerce:

> When the Wall fell people didn't want to hear about products made here [in the former GDR]. Everyone clamored for the things that you couldn't get here, like Coca Cola, and that hurt our regional industry.... Since 1992 we have been working to make people aware that they strengthen their economy when they buy local products.

Many supermarkets throughout eastern Germany will note next to a particular product if it has been produced in the "Five New Federal States"; others specifically specialize in eastern German products.[7] Says one advertisement: "Our recommendation: Purchase products that are produced here [former GDR]. In this way you strengthen our economy and create jobs." What is significant about these and other attempts to advertise, inform, and instruct is that the rights and duties of consumer-citizens entail national belonging in the former GDR, not western or re-unified Germany. They reflect multiple and competing citizenship discourses (Shafir 1998), affirm narratives of national belonging based on consumption and economic prosperity, and constitute the citizen as an active and informed consumer.

In the new Germany, then, consumption has entailed the work of making citizen-subjects. The emergence of such "citizenscapes"[8] has occurred in the context of East Germany's rapid transition from a heavily industrialized production-driven society to inclusion in a late industrial society in which self, identity, and labor are defined primarily in relation to consumption (Appadurai 1996; Bauman 1992)—an "epochal shift in the constitutive relationship of production to consumption" (Comaroff and Comaroff 2000) that took decades in most advanced industrial countries but which eastern Germany has undergone in just a few years (Geyer 1994). Under the "rational redistributive" economy of state socialism (Konrád and Szelényi 1979), consumption was framed in terms of the collective good rather than in terms of individual entitlement. As recent work of cultural historians has shown (Kaminsky 2001; Merkel 1998, 1999; Pence 2001; Stitziel 2003), the notion of "scarcity" is a relative one, and the GDR indeed experienced a distinctive (although certainly not isolated) consumer culture. The milk-and-honey promises of the regime that frustrated consumer desires, combined with the constant and inevitable comparisons to the West, ultimately laid the foundations not only for 1989, but also for the constitutive relationship between political legitimacy and mass consumption. As Paul Betts has noted, "The irony is that the people apparently took these dreams of a better and more prosperous world more seriously than the state ever expected, so much so that the government was ultimately sued for false advertising" (2000: 765).[9]

Thus, although the pursuit of material prosperity was a critical feature of nation-building on both sides of the inter-German border (Borneman 1992; Carter 1997; Merkel 1999),[10] on the eastern side it was more explicitly connected to an ideology of production. Indeed, one of the definitive features of socialist citizenship was production, a worker's identity that was inculcated through 40 years of state ideology, production rituals, and physical, industrial labor (cf. Molyneux 2000). The slogans contained on party posters or workplace banners conveyed this emphasis on production, often stressing its relationship to consumption: "work today, live tomorrow" (in Merkel 1998), "high work productivity secures a high standard of living," or "I work at something, I can afford something."[11] The factory brigade was also an important social unit; factory-sponsored fieldtrips often provided the only opportunities for travel away from home; and socialist production rituals aimed to engender loyalty to the state as well as an identification with the products of production (another workplace banner: "My hand for my product"). Many East German factories housed a day-care center, a general store, and even a doctor's office on factory grounds. In the GDR, the workplace was thus not only the center of everyday sociality, it was also a symbolic space of social membership and national belonging. Like socialism's other transformations of phenomena associated with liberal polities (Verdery 1998), citizenship was associated with notions of collective entitlement, a mass of people as a community of equals, and a distinct philosophy of labor. The guaran-tee of full employment meant that everyone (or nearly everyone) was included.

ACTUALLY EXISTING CITIZENSHIP

The radical deindustrialization of the former GDR and the absorption of East Germany into a West German model of nationhood based on a consumer democracy have reconfigured the symbolic spaces of citizenship and created new boundaries of belonging. Visible in the industrial ruins and strip malls that surround most urban centers, this shift in balance is mapped onto the cultural landscape.

Leipzig, for example, where over 90 percent of manufacturing jobs have been eliminated since 1989 and unemployment remains steady at around 17 percent,[12] is a city of contrasts. On the outskirts of town, just near the freeway exit, are colorful shopping malls that contain both international and national re-tail chains—McDonald's, Burger King, Footlocker, the Swedish IKEA discount furniture store, and a ToysRUs (among many others). Erected on farmland pur-chased cheaply immediately after 1989, these enterprises have been perceived as serious threats to businesses located in downtown Leipzig, where real estate is often more expensive and difficult to obtain due to unresolved property dis-putes.[13] In the areas between the discount outlets on the outskirts of the city and the now thriving city center are the empty, dilapidated ruins of socialist in-dustrial production. At the city center, newly renovated buildings and Leipzig's famous nineteenth-century arcades, once showcases for socialist industrial de-sign during the city's famous biannual trade fair, now house elite boutiques and specialty shops. Leipzig's immense railway terminal, erected before World War I, and one of Europe's largest train stations, has similarly been transformed into one of Europe's largest shopping malls.

These projects reflect the heavy investment of western capital in Leipzig, more than in any other city in the former GDR besides East Berlin. Long a cen-ter of international trade because of its centuries-old trade fair, Leipzig is strug-gling to reclaim its status as the financial capital of eastern Germany.[14] The city's growth strategy has been based largely upon expediency, rapid turnover, and quick fulfillment of consumer demands and desires. The peripheral strip-mall sprawl is frequently the topic of local conversations and debates. "The western enterprises came in right after '89," one man explained. "All this construction took place before people really had an idea about what was going on. Everyone has called us dumb Ossis for letting this happen, but we didn't know or understand this new system." Construction cranes towering over the city in the first decade after re-unification came to symbolize Leipzig as a "boomtown" supported by western ideas and capital; they also represent for many residents economic growth and prosperity from which they have been excluded.

A 1998 conversation with a woman in her mid-forties, still employed as a librarian at the national library, first brought this to my attention.

> "Have you seen our downtown?" she inquired. I didn't realize it was a leading question. "Well, Leipzig does not consist of this glittering downtown alone. Beyond these colorful façades there is much depression. People can't participate in this prosperity. In fact, the different degrees to which people are excluded from this new prosperity is a source of depression, tension, and difficulty. We have a middle class and an unemployed class here, but neither group can truly afford to participate in the luxuries offered downtown."

She paused, and then continued, her voice growing increasingly adamant as she spoke:

> In a sense, we don't really experience these changes as being real. It all comes from outside, from the West. Everything is pumped in from the West. The fact that all the renovations, construction, up-scaling of the downtown are not the product of people's labor here but of western investment capital makes people feel alienated from their own city. . . . There is much resentment toward the people who shop at these stores (although I don't know anyone who can actually afford to). This is a model from the West that was imported here and many Leipzig citizens are having an allergic reaction to this model, in part because it is not theirs, in part because they are excluded.

New categories of inclusion and exclusion—*Wendegewinner* and *Wendeverlierer* (winners and losers of the "transition")—designate who is in and who is out in the new society. "My uncle and cousin are Wendegewinner," one young man told me. "He purchased the state store he had worked in after 1989. He has done very well and now drives the biggest BMW available!" Another man, a musician in the state orchestra, also characterized himself as belonging to this category: "I'm an exception. You could say I have profited from the transition. Look, we live well," he said, gesturing to his new house full of modern furnishings including a leather sofa, solid wood wall cabinets, and brand-name electronics.

At the other end of the spectrum are the "transition losers"—the unemployed, the underemployed, the homeless, the poor. These are the people whose presence in the new society is unsettling, for they are reminders not only of the human costs of a capitalist market economy, but also of the new nation-state's failure "to produce convincing fantasies of the commensurability of its citizens" (Holston and Appadurai 1996: 202). Often these transition losers rarely venture into the new symbolic spaces of social membership, knowing they make others uncomfortable and feeling deeply ashamed of their situation. As one woman who had been unemployed for 3 years after re-unification told me: "Unemployment is for our understanding the worst thing that there is. We were all raised to be socialists, and we were taught that labor is what separates humans from animals. That is what we learned. Suddenly to be without work is unthinkable for us. It makes us feel subhuman." Lacking the resources to consume, they are excluded from the rights and responsibilities of participation in the public sphere of a consumer democracy. "We used to all belong to the bottom half [of society]," I was frequently told, "now we are third-class German citizens." Although granted formal social, political, and civil rights, these people are outsiders in a (West) German nation-state founded and forged through an ideology of prosperity and entitlement associated with mass consumption. As one worker at a debt-counseling center—an increasingly expanding social service in the eastern German states—observed: "It doesn't matter how the debts were acquired, the consequences are all the same. It affects people's sense of self-worth to be perceived as losers and to be increasingly relegated to the margins of society in their daily lives. In other words, people lose access to the criteria that define modern life." In a context where citizenship "is measured increasingly by the capacity to transact and consume" (Comaroff and Comaroff 2000: 306), the presence of "transition losers" throws into sharp relief the contrast between what several scholars have called "formative" and "substantive" citizenship, or the difference between citizenship as an institution and citizenship as lived. It also reflects what Zygmunt Bauman has identified as a redefinition of poverty in a consumer society:

> having no access to a happy or merely normal life means to be consumers *man-quées*, or flawed consumers. And so the poor of a consumer society are socially defined, and self-defined, first and foremost as blemished, defective, faulty and deficient—in other words, inadequate—consumers. (1998: 38)

Somewhere in between the transition winners and losers are the majority of eastern Germans.[15] Many feel as if they are, as one woman put it, "caught up in a constant fight for their own survival." Often deeply ambivalent about the new nation and workings of a market economy, they view the glittering downtown as other-worldly, almost as unreachable as the West had been before the fall of the Wall, and they eagerly await the weekly advertising supplements for the discount outlets on the outskirts of town. With the prospect of unemployment always a threat, they struggle to make ends meet; many indulge only occasionally in the luxury of a restaurant meal or brand-name goods. Others accumulate substantial debts with newly available consumer credit. In a sense, these are people like the librarian quoted above, in that their limited economic means, combined with a cultural competence in consumption, have made them aware of their own partial exclusion from full membership in a national society based on consumer entitlements and economic prosperity. Still others, however, take substantial pride in the city's facelift, regardless of their ability to participate as consumers or producers.

URBAN OUTFITTERS

Over a decade after the collapse of socialism, eastern Germans are still receiving formal instruction about consumption, the spirit of capitalism, and their rights and obligations as citizen-consumers. To illustrate, I turn now to a "motivational seminar for women" held in the summer of 1998 and sponsored by the Leipzig Center for the Unemployed, a non-profit organization with major funding from the state. Although not advertised as such, the seminar was led by a Mary Kay Cosmetics consultant, Anita Mueller, who works extensively with women who are unemployed or are being retrained in another profession after losing their jobs. Many of her seminars are thus held at technical colleges and schools shortly before students enter the job market. Attended by a handful of women ranging in age from their late twenties to late forties, the presentation began with Anita introducing herself as an empathetic fellow Ossi. A steel worker in the GDR, Anita had spent several years on unemployment after 1989. "I faced a lot of despair and depression after the Wende," she told her small audience, "and I want to help others pull themselves out of the resignation that comes with being unemployed. It was so painful for me to see the products of my hard labor dismissed. I had no self-confidence left. Learning how to present myself was critical in helping me develop a new sense of self." She then pulled out laminated paper containing in large bold print the English words "Image" and "Outfit." "Learning about self-presentation and body language means understanding these two terms," she continued. "Outward appearances are very important; they are not only a façade. In order to cultivate this you will need to learn certain techniques that I will begin to introduce today."

For the next 3 hours, Anita demonstrated these techniques using Mary Kay products on two volunteers. Throughout the procedure she would pause to lecture on color combinations, the importance of appearing neat and clean, and the implicit messages of body language. Her presentation was lively and animated, often eliciting smiles and laughter from her audience. Sitting back with her arms across her chest or leaning forward with her cheek slumped into her hand, for example, she asked: "What kind of image does that convey to you? Not a very positive one." Similarly, she passed around a notebook with before and after photos of Mary Kay makeovers. "Which woman will find work?" she asked, "the one with the pale face and stringy hair or the same person with a neat, cultivated appearance?"

Such "image seminars" have become a standard component of job-retraining programs and company-sponsored educational seminars. "Image and identity consulting" is a relatively booming entrepreneurial business in Leipzig, with individual business names like "Style and Image Consultation," "Outfit Angelika Schneider," "Image Identity" [in English], and "Personality Consultation, Training, and Coaching." Its practitioners work in a variety of institutional contexts as well as with individual clients, and the local *Volkshochschule* (community education) offerings in the subject are unparalleled in comparable western German contexts. While the seminars and consultations may represent the most extreme form of socialization into the norms of mass consumption, they do throw into sharp relief Canclini's positing of consumption as a "means of thinking" that "creates new ways of being citizens" (2001, quoted in Yudice 1995).

The starting point for most seminars, and the selling point for individual consultations, is a promise of "success" based on culturally competent consumption practices. "That is the way society is today," one consultant began, "people don't say, 'what can this person contribute' but 'how does he or she look?'" Another session with a different consultant was more gender-specific. Noting the importance of self-presentation, Antje explained to a group of trainees: "This is especially so with women. People will consider whether they want to do business by whether the woman is attractive—but not erotic. It is important to learn how to manipulate not only your clothing, but to use [your clothing] to manipulate people." Underlying these promises of success is a notion of consumption as a learning process in contrast to the experience of consumption under socialism, as one woman explained to me: "So many former GDR citizens will say to me: 'Why do I have to present myself this way? This was never necessary earlier in the GDR.' But of course this is never a topic in the old federal states [West Germany]."

A typical seminar at a job-training program, then, begins by noting the importance of first impressions ("You never get a second chance to make a first impression"), and focuses largely on color coordination and fashion styles. "Compare what happens to her face with this color," one consultant told a group of trainees as she draped an olive-green scarf across the unsuspecting volunteer's chest, "you see the pores, pimples, and blemishes." She contrasted this with a softer blue, "more flattering for her skin tone and type." Body types and practices are also commonly covered as an important topic, with tips for dealing with the "plus and minus points" of proportions, eyes, noses, foreheads, legs, and so forth. Indeed, body habitus frequently plays a critical role in personality assessments and estimations. Consultants often ask to observe the walking strides and bodily mannerisms of clients in order to determine "personality types," the terms for which are either drawn from a culturally shared vocabulary ("natural, romantic, dramatic") or from a practitioner's specific training ("raffiné, tonique, sophistique"). Images and ideals of femininity are conveyed through magazine illustrations, makeup tips, and fashion choices. Despite the fact that it has been over a decade since the collapse of socialist rule, the need for such lessons is still explained in terms of the past, as one consultant explained to me in the spring of 2001:

> In the West femininity is encouraged differently. . . . They were always competing with each other for men, for a man who could earn enough money, and for that you had to present yourself well, you had to sell yourself. Whereas the East German

women said, "I earn my own money. I don't have to present myself like this.". . . The majority of women [in the GDR] didn't really take care of themselves, and didn't really know what it meant to be a woman. Didn't know how to live this on the outside. . . . Not everyone has learned this yet, so I still have work to do!

At the core of these consultation practices is a discourse of individual fulfillment, self-discovery, and even healing through consumption. The narratives told in seminars, echoed in all of my conversations with image consultants, reveal a notion of an inner self that both defines and is defined by an outer "image" or "identity" realized through consumption. "People don't understand the critical relationship between who you are and what you wear," one consultant told me. Another consultant promised her audience, "Today I am going to help you bring out the things that you keep inside, to show you how to make the best of your personality. I will show you how to harmonize what is inside with what you wear on the outside through styles and colors, so you will be able to answer the question: what kind of person is this?"

At issue in this work is the body of the consuming citizen; what is communicated is not only the performative aspect of citizenship in a consumer democracy, but also the notion, described recently by Patton and Caserio (2000: 6), of the good citizen as an "all-consuming agent of late capitalist production." Like fashion magazines and media images, such image seminars and consultations "contribute directly to transmuting the idea of political freedom into that of self-realization through consumer choice" (Gal and Kligman 2000: 107). In this sense, they are one instance of a much larger convergence of the consumer with the democratic citizen.

Yet the postsocialist context gives these practices particular meaning, reflecting important linkages between production and consumption both here and elsewhere.[16] A history of production and an identity as workers appear repeatedly in seminar presentations and individual narratives. (Recall the Mary Kay Cosmetics representative's empathetic story about the products of her labor being dismissed.) This tradition is perhaps best exemplified in one practitioner's trademark slogan *Produktivfaktor Image* (productive factor image), the frequent title of her seminar presentations as well as of an article in a newsletter for local entrepreneurs. "Productive factor image means knowing how to sell yourself," she explained, "and this has been a learning process." Indeed, discourses about "selling yourself" dominate consultations: consumption is productive—one must consume in order to produce (and vice versa).

Rather than thinking of such practices and performances as indicative of the "postmodern citizen consumer" inhabiting a space beyond the purview of the nation, however, I am suggesting that in the context of the "triumph" of capitalism and democracy associated with the new Germany—including notions of the nation-state as a locus of distribution, an arbiter of economic prosperity, and a champion of consumer choice contrasted with the material failures of state socialism—these and similar practices could be construed as local, global, as well as national. Anita Mueller, the industrial worker turned Mary Kay Cosmetics representative, embodied, indeed epitomized, the larger shift in balance from socialist production to late capitalist consumption and its implications for citizenship. Participation in the public sphere and membership in the new society depend not on what you produce but on what, how, and where you consume. My discussions with debt counselors and social workers in Leipzig, for example, revealed one particular indication of this shift: whereas in the first years after the Wende clients would name unemployment as their chief reason for seeking assistance, more recently people cite a mounting consumer debt as a primary concern.

CONCLUSION

In a provocative essay about Asian immigrants in the United States, Aihwa Ong defines citizenship as "a cultural process of 'subject-ification,' in the Foucauldian sense of self-making and being-made by power relations that produce consent through schemes of surveillance, discipline, control, and administration" (1996: 738). Concerned with how criteria of belonging are established, Ong is careful to point to disciplinary schemes outside of the state that nevertheless can have national effects. I am suggesting here that consumption be viewed as one such disciplinary scheme, as a cultural process of subject making that defines categories and criteria of belonging. In the context of a nation-state built in large part upon the promise of economic prosperity and the freedom to consume, global commodity flows may be re-appropriated in forging the nation and defining its citizens.

This relationship between national citizenship and mass consumption is, however, not unique to the German context, even though it may be especially visible there. Indeed, in the wake of September 11th, we have witnessed an intensification of this dynamic in the United States: whereas the patriotic response in World War II was to enlist in the army or cultivate a victory garden, we were urged as a nation to go shopping. In New York, banners streamed the streets saying: "Fight Back New York: Go Shopping";[17] in the San Francisco Bay Area, the organized local response was represented by a poster, displayed prominently in many store windows, of the American flag as a shopping bag with the slogan: "America: Open for Business." While at one level these discourses represent a recasting of "global citizenship as an anti-terrorist stance" (Creed 2002), they also conflate consumption with national allegiance and civic duty.

The dramatic transitions from socialism in eastern Europe, as Katherine Verdery has noted, provide a unique opportunity "to broaden a critique of western economic and political forms by seeing them through the eyes of those experiencing their construction" (1996: 11). As one debt counselor told me at the conclusion of our 2-hour conversation: "People have called this into question . . . thinking perhaps that it is not so ideal, this economic system. But it can't be questioned anymore. It's been decided worldwide." Indeed, it is in such moments of transition as that in post-Wall Germany that the relationship between economic systems, political entities, and culture—"cosmologies of capitalism" (Sahlins 1988)—may be observed in particularly bold relief. The work of consumption in postsocialist eastern Germany has reflected and constituted certain boundaries of national belonging, even as it simultaneously situates Germany and its "social market economy" within a neoliberal global order. Citizenship and the nation-state have become linked to consumer rights—and rites.

7

LOCAL HERO, NATIONAL CROOK
"Doc" Schneider and the Spectacle of Finance Capital

THIS IS THE STORY OF THE RISE AND FALL of a German property tycoon who, it is said, single-handedly "reduced Germany's powerful banks into cash machines."[1] It is the story of a man characterized by superlatives: the "largest builder and real-estate investor in German history," a "construction giant," "Germany's biggest property sector bankruptcy ever," the "greatest case of corporate deceit," and the "most spectacular economic scandal" in postwar history. For some, it is the legend of a Robin Hood, of a man who stole billions from the banks for the benefit of German cities and historical landmarks; for others, it is the chronicle of a trickster and imposter who duped the country's largest banks out of billions at the expense of innocent workers. Among other things, this is the story of a media legend, whose tale came to be viewed as a cautionary one—a "parable for our society," as the presiding trial judge wrote in his verdict, "that in social life and with the banks, appearances matter more than substance" (*schein vor sein*) (Schneider 1999: 336).

This is also a story that provides an example of what Anna Tsing has called "the economy of appearances." Noting that entrepreneurs often engage in "economic" and "dramatic performance" to succeed in raising capital, she points to "the self-conscious making of a spectacle" as an aspect of international finance. Tsing demonstrates how entrepreneurs "must dramatize their dreams in order to attract the capital they need to operate and to expand" (2000: 118). Thus, there is always the creation of an illusion, the conjuring of a project of such a scale as to fire the imagination of investors. It is, however, not only entrepreneurs who engage in such economic and dramatic performances. In order to attract investment in their communities, cities, regions, and even countries "must dramatize their potential as places for investment." "Dramatic performance," Tsing writes, "is the prerequisite of their economic performance" (118). The projects of real-estate tycoon Jürgen ("Doc") Schneider involved such dramatic performances to win the support of investment banks at the same time as they dramatically inspired dreams of revitalizing a depressed region of eastern Germany.

Furthermore, Schneider's performances drew upon, were enabled, and were legitimized by nationally recognized narratives as well as upon nationally shared cultural references.

At another level, therefore, this is a uniquely German story. The reception and interpretation of Jürgen Schneider's case differed markedly in western Germany and eastern Germany, in Frankfurt and Leipzig. These differences reflected the intra-national tensions and divisions that remained after German reunification.

Finally, the story of Jürgen Schneider must be seen in the context of the "triumph" of global capitalism following the collapse of socialism throughout central and eastern Europe in 1989. This earth-shattering event, together with the triumphalist discourses that accompanied it, endowed Schneider's performances with an air of legitimacy, for these performances were those of a quintessentially successful capitalist. Yet the theater surrounding Schneider—both the performance for attracting and accumulating capital as well as the media spectacle that ensued—suggests the degree of exuberance exhibited by triumphant capitalism: the suspension of rationality and orderly, transparent business practices, as in the cases of the Asian financial crisis of 1997 and the numerous business scandals in the United States after 2001. More generally, then, this story sheds light on discourses, practices, and cultures of neoliberal capitalism.

THE RISE AND FALL OF JÜRGEN SCHNEIDER

Born in Frankfurt in 1932, Jürgen Schneider got his start in his family's construction business, where the fact that he was paid far less than the other employees was a source of real pride for his domineering father. Indeed, the troubled father-son relationship pervades accounts of Schneider's life, including his own memoirs. His determination to surpass his father's success was a driving force of his own ambition; it pushed him to pursue a doctorate in political science at the University of Graz, earning him the coveted *Doktortitel* that would become part of his cultivated image and later the source of his media nickname, "Doc" Schneider. When he left his father's firm to form his own company in his late forties, his father not only cut him out of the family inheritance but also called upon his bank contacts, urging them not to loan his son any money. This appears to have only strengthened Schneider's resolve and ambition as he began to set his sights on large properties and substantial profits. Assisted by his wife's inheritance, he made his initial money through rental properties and condominiums; however, his particular passion was for the purchase and restoration of historically protected buildings. The extremely profitable renovation of the Frankfurt hotel "Fürstenhof," purchased by Schneider in 1986, was enough to persuade skeptical lenders that such historical restorations could be quite lucrative. Before long, Schneider had secured millions of Marks in bank loans for numerous projects in several German cities.

After German re-unification, Schneider's construction empire both benefited from and contributed to the building and investment boom in eastern German cities. "Hadn't the moment arrived," he recalled in his autobiography,

> when those of us who were spoiled by fate needed to return the blessings to our brothers and sisters in the East for which we had been envied for decades? . . . So I took the flag in my hand, called my people together and said, "we need to throw ourselves into the East and concentrate all our energy on one city, if possible. As builders we are the pioneers that others will follow." (Schneider 1999: 142)

As it happened, that city turned out to be Leipzig. When Schneider visited the old university town in October of 1990, it was love at first sight. "This old town rich in tradition was a sleeping princess of architectural beauty, and I was the prince who was willing and able to kiss her awake" (Schneider 1999: 143). Presenting himself as a selfless investor and the engine of "*Aufschwung Ost*" (eastern boom), Schneider purchased some of Leipzig's most historically significant structures, including the Mädlerpassage, with the famous Auerbach's Keller restaurant (scene of Goethe's Faust) and Barthels Hof. He was a welcome and frequent presence in the city, heralded as the "good man from Königstein" who "came, saw, and purchased" (Schulz 1993: 18). By 1994, Schneider owned nearly 40 percent of Leipzig's inner city old town and 10 percent of the city's buildings overall. A poster that was part of the city's urban renewal campaign ("Leipzig Kommt!") featured a quote from the property tycoon reflecting his position in Leipzig's future: "With its great architectural past, its infrastructure and its central location for East-West trade, Leipzig for us is the top address." Indeed, for many Schneider was the very embodiment of the "eastern boom" in its most negative and positive aspects, representing not only economic growth and the elegant renovation of Leipzig's dilapidated historical buildings, but also the influx and dominance of western capital and values; the metaphor of colonialism would be increasingly invoked to describe a growing resentment of the perceived arrogance and power of western investors.

In an effort to establish himself not only as an investor but also as an important benefactor, Schneider initiated several philanthropic ventures in Leipzig, including the sponsoring of art scholarships and archeological exhibits and a well-publicized subvention for a tenant whose doll repair business could no longer support the dramatic increase in rent. Such gestures were part of a conscious and carefully crafted image campaign, to which also belonged Schneider's self-presentation in pin-striped suits, gold Mercedes limousine, and easily recognizable toupee. "In my professional life I was a loyal toupee wearer," he wrote in his autobiography. "I liked myself tanned and with a full head of hair in the role of a successful businessman that I presented for those around me. The wig boosted my self confidence when dealing with business partners and thus fulfilled its purpose" (Schneider 1999: 56). In his quest for financial capital, Schneider's "economy of appearances" entailed dramatic performances and "the self conscious making of a spectacle" (to use Tsing's phrasing again). "I had the team and the image, and I got as much money from the banks as I wanted," he wrote (1999: 143). His particular strategy also tapped into national imaginations and narratives about authenticity, historical preservation (free of particular histories), and German economic power. The mass-mediated images of Schneider at ceremonies for completed projects (many of which were glittering shopping centers containing international retail outlets) confirmed and reiterated a dominant triumphalist narrative linking democracy and national legitimacy to economic prosperity and mass consumption—a discourse that was especially discernable in the immediate post-Wall German context (see Berdahl 2005a).

For example, the Mädlerpassage was exquisitely restored and housed some of the most exclusive shops from the West. It represented the triumph of western consumer society, giving the appearance of the economic recovery of the former East German city, apparently a seamless integration with the West. The appearances, however, were misleading, for with unemployment at nearly 20 percent, not many Leipzig residents could actually afford to shop there. A 1998 conversation with a woman in her mid-forties, employed as a librarian at the national library, called attention to this discrepancy. "Have you seen our downtown?" she asked. "Well, Leipzig does not consist of this glittering downtown alone. Beyond these colorful façades there is much depression. People can't participate in this prosperity. In fact, the different degrees to which people are excluded from this new prosperity is a source of depression, tension, and difficulty. We have a middle class and an unemployed class here, but neither group can truly afford to participate in the luxuries offered downtown" (Berdahl 2005a: 243).

Schneider's dramatic and economic performances in the pursuit of finance capital also entailed, however, corruption and deceit. By the early 1990s, Schneider had already accumulated significant debt from his undertakings in western Germany. Newly and easily available credit for construction projects in eastern Germany allowed him to continue borrowing to pay off existing debts and to pad his own cash accounts, which he in turn used as evidence of his assets when applying for more loans. Little did the banks realize that he was just showing them their own money.[2] His loan amounts almost always far exceeded the purchase price and renovation costs of his projects. Caught up in his own pyramid scheme, Schneider exaggerated the square footage of buildings he wanted to buy, inflated projected rental incomes, forged receipts from international companies, and inked out key information on blueprints (erasing the word "basement," e.g., to suggest another level of rental property). Yet throughout the early 1990s, the banks never questioned his numbers or credibility. One of the buildings that the Deutsche Bank financed with an understanding that it contained 20,000 square meters of retail space was a mere 5-minute walk from the bank's central offices in Frankfurt; a brief site visit would have revealed its size to be less than half of what the investor claimed. As Schneider wrote in his notes in 1993, "It is imperative now! Once again all the tricks—aggressively. Success is always paired with deception."[3]

His antics could not be sustained indefinitely, however, and in early 1994, banks started making more inquiries. At the beginning of April, Schneider notified the Deutsche Bank of his impending cash-flow crisis and requested financial assistance; his letter explained to the bank's board of directors that he would be withdrawing temporarily from business dealings for reasons of health. With nearly 6 billion Marks of debt owed to 50 German banks, Jürgen Schneider then vanished without a trace.

THE BARE TRUTH

Schneider's disappearance was followed by months of media speculation and public amusement concerning his whereabouts. Both the tabloid and mainstream press reported sightings in Iran, Canada, Paraguay, and the Philippines (among other places). An offhand remark of the chief spokesman for the Deutsche Bank, Hilmar Kopper, that the 50 million Marks owed to workers for unpaid contracts amounted to "peanuts" from the bank's perspective, became the German "Unwort des Jahres" (gaff-of-the-year) in 1994. Two and a half years later, it was the title of a "satirical comedy from German reality" based on the Schneider story: *Peanuts: The Bank Pays for Everything.* The film depicts an entrepreneur who is unsuccessful in obtaining loans for his projects until he comes upon the idea of donning a perky toupee, wearing custom-made business suits, and riding around in a limousine. Well received among audiences and critics alike, the movie highlighted a topic that would continue to dominate the Schneider legend, as the actor who starred in the film commented: "Façade over substance is the theme. Appearances matter more in the upper levels [of business]. Whoever wants to borrow over five million marks has to appear legitimate."[4]

Over a year after he fled Germany, Schneider and his wife were found and arrested in Miami, where they had been hiding the entire time. Charged with fraud and document forgery, they were jailed in Florida and extradited to Germany in early 1996. (Charges against his wife, Claudia, would later be dropped.) If the media spectacle surrounding Schneider's story and disappearance enhanced his mythic status, the property tycoon's trial in 1997 humanized him. While accepting responsibility for his actions, the defense strategy also sought to portray Schneider as a victim, accusing the banks of sharing the blame.[5] Bank officials' testimonies stressed the relationships of "trust" built up over the years, defending their failure to question his figures in terms of Schneider's image and reputation; as one official explained: "Schneider was regarded back then as the first address for real estate." Another bank representative maintained that "one simply had to trust the man who had built such glorious objects like the Fürstenhof in Frankfurt, the Mädlerpassage in Leipzig, the Kurfürsteneck in Berlin or the Frankfurter Zeilgalerie."[6] The failure of the banks to examine Schneider's assets itself reveals a fault-line in German economic reunion: he was trusted because he was an apparently successful West German businessman. The reconstruction of the East was seen to be a West German project, requiring western expertise and business experience. It is highly unlikely that any sound business plan submitted by an *Ossi* (East German) would have met with success with the banks and certainly would have been subjected to a rigorous analysis by bank officials.

Schneider himself appealed to the sympathy of the public and the presiding judge. Speaking in his own defense, he argued, "I put every Mark into my buildings. They are historical treasures in the heart of the cities . . . How do you quantify history, quality, and beauty in numbers?" (Schneider 1999: 332).

To a large extent, the strategy worked; Schneider was sentenced to a relatively light prison term of 6 years and 9 months, with credit for the 2 years already served before and during the trial. In his verdict, the presiding judge chastised the creditor banks for overlooking Schneider's shortcomings and for failing to check up on his false claims. While critical of the investor's fraudulent activities, the judge's ruling was largely sympathetic, mentioning Schneider's "father complex." "Who is this Dr. Schneider?" he asked.

> He was a workaholic who nevertheless shunned the high-life associated with his wealth. There was no golf club, no yacht, no Rolls Royce, no aircraft, not even a holiday in Acapulco. He is a vain man, always well groomed with many toupees, always well dressed . . . A man who places extreme value on the recognition and esteem of those around him . . . Everything that he surrounded himself with—doctorate, palace, historical landmarks, staff, foundation, and apparently the soaring bank account balances—these were all things he felt he needed to win this much-needed approval . . . Many have asked, not without some justification, if the banks didn't also belong at the defendant's table. (Quoted in Schneider 1999: 334)

The real loser in this process, then, turned out to be the German banks. Media accounts stressed the damaged reputation and image of German banks; a common saying was that time had become divided within the banking industry into "before Schneider" and "after Schneider." "The banks have lost the illusion of infallibility," one article proclaimed, "and it was a real-estate crook who exposed them."[7] An editorial in the Leipzig local paper focused on the arrogance of the bankers themselves: "[With the Schneider scandal] a dark spot on the white shirt of the finance industry became visible. The 'peanuts' comment of the Deutsche Bank spokesman trivialized the damages caused by the bankruptcy to which his company contributed. The arrogance of the banker was thus thrown into sharp relief and it will take some time for the industry to recover from the harm done to its image."[8] A special series in the weekly *Der Spiegel* on the Schneider case theorized it this way: "Jürgen Schneider is one of those enterprisers that a capitalist economic system needs so that its deadly serious drive for profits is infused with a breath of hilarity once in a while. He demonstrated that cockiness triumphs if the claims and stakes are high enough. It has to be that way so that the arrogance of power doesn't get the upper hand."[9]

Anna Tsing has suggested that the performative ability to blur the line between the "real and the fake" is a critical factor in attracting capital:

After the 1997 financial crises, we were told to distinguish between the real and the fake, but does not the whole design of these accumulation strategies work against our ability to draw this line? As in a beauty contest, artistry and drama are necessary to compete; spectacle and mystery, playing equally across the line of the real and the fake, establish the winning reality of performance. (Tsing 2000: 127)

In writing about the maintenance of empty business offices across the globe of Wall Street investment banks, Karen Ho has similarly pointed to this performative aspect of capitalism:

One of the main reasons why "flexible global presence" is an effective strategy is that it blurs the 'presences' that are substantial and those that are superficial or absent. It is precisely by exploiting the elusiveness between the real and the fake that investment banks are able to sustain and attract more business. This ambiguity is a necessary requirement for their often far-fetched performances of globe-reaching capabilities and potentials. (Ho 2005: 86)

The German banks' inability to make this distinction between appearances and reality was the key to Schneider's overwhelming success and ultimate downfall. His case not only exposed the connection between drama, spectacle, and capital accumulation, but the bare truth between the "real and the fake" itself, for which the toupee was an easy and ready-made symbol. After Schneider's arrest in Florida, the media speculated on whether he would return with or without his toupee, and a discourse of the bare-headed Schneider ran through much of the press coverage of the 1997 trial. A photo caption in the Leipzig newspaper, for example, read: "Lacking the customary toupee that he wore for his business appearances, real-estate investor Jürgen Schneider listens to the charges against him in the Frankfurt Regional Court." Just as the discarding of the hairpiece had uncovered Schneider's balding head, his accumulation strategies and performances had revealed the spectacle of finance capital and the workings of the banking industry, and he had been exposed as a fraud.

LOCAL HERO

In the postsocialist context of Leipzig, this distinction between real and fake took on somewhat different meanings. As in the rest of the country, Schneider's disappearance in April 1994 unleashed public resentment and outrage. The local edition of the tabloid newspaper, *Bild Leipzig,* for example, dramatically lamented: "Cranes are standing still and construction workers are crying. Construction firms are in a tailspin toward bankruptcy while bankers stare vacantly into space."[10] In a 2004 Leipzig newspaper article commemorating the 10-year anniversary of Schneider's disappearance, the city's mayor at that time recalled, "The shock was worse than the [actual] damage . . . [T]he reaction in the city, of the people, reflected shock and fear. There was a sense of a huge catastrophe."[11] For many local residents, Schneider represented the "ugly antics of capitalism" and the failed promises of *Aufschwung Ost.*[12] But their real anger was directed mostly at the banks. Indeed, Leipzig's mayor told *Der Spiegel* shortly after Schneider fled that the main responsibility for the crisis rested with the banks.

In fact, by the time of his arrest a year later, Schneider had been transformed into a local folk hero. Reflecting the shift in public opinion, a local magazine declared the bankrupt investor "a hero of our time." Alluding to national media coverage of his arrest in Florida, the article asserted in a slightly tongue-in-cheek style: "Jürgen Schneider—the incarnation of the 'eastern boom'—doesn't deserve this. Nobody likes him anymore; everyone is after him. But why? The monthly magazine *Kreuzer* reveals the real story. Perhaps Schneider is even a communist?" The piece went on to report on an alleged "renowned economist who prefers to remain nameless" who reportedly explained Schneider's strategy:

> His capitalist affectation was only a façade. Behind this lurked something like a primordial communist core. With the most modern methods of mass communication and PR, at the end of the 20th century Schneider resurrected Marxist theory and practice: the expropriation of the expropriators, or the exploitation of the exploiters.[13]

A month later, Schneider appeared on the magazine's cover again, this time under the headline "Jürgen Schneider: Superstar." A pop-art style cover image featured the folk hero's head surrounded by a halo of peanuts.

When he was released from prison in December 1999, the national weekly *Der Spiegel* described Schneider as "crafty, brutal, and greedy,"[14] while the local Leipzig monthly celebrated his release and love affair with the city. "My Leipzig, I praise thee," read the headline, a quotation from a scene in Goethe's *Faust*. This cover story featured words of praise and gratitude from local residents. "In his case he simply swindled for Leipzig. He's a great man who acted for the good of Leipzig," said the city tour guide who showed Schneider the city during his first visit to Leipzig, "and I would give him another tour if he came today—even without the toupee."[15]

Such testimonials were echoed in my conversations with Leipzig residents during fieldwork in 2001. As an employee of the local chamber of commerce told me when I asked him about Schneider:

> If I were mayor of Leipzig, I would make Schneider into an honorary citizen of this city. Now you can be amused or entertained by the criminal aspects of his investments, but he essentially acquired and renovated the objects that people obsessed with tax write-offs wouldn't touch . . . And these were the pearls of the city . . . If it hadn't been for Jürgen Schneider, we would never have the beautiful old town that we have now . . . From my perspective the banks were simply stupid and greedy. He didn't have that money in his pockets but raised it with elaborate psychological methods. In my view the whole thing showed that banks follow certain, almost criminal procedures. Of course he wanted to make money, too. But for the city of Leipzig something has remained in the end.

Although Schneider has not been granted honorary citizenship (at least not yet), since 1999 his story has been the subject of a monthly city walking tour sponsored by the Leipzig Tourist Service. Entitled "In the Tracks of Dr. Jürgen Schneider," the tour visits fifteen of the investor's most famous projects and reproduces a narrative that credits him with saving Leipzig's old town. "In 1989, Leipzig's baroque, classical and Jugendstil buildings were in complete disrepair," the tour description reads, and

> Dr. Jürgen Schneider—in the meantime a media legend—purchased the dilapidated treasures on credit . . . One of these was Barthels Hof. At the end of the 80's the building was totally run down, rotten. 147 million Marks later and with all historical preservation rules carefully observed, the stately courtyard shines a creamy yellow . . . The Teehaaus, Wünschmanns Hof, the Gasthof Joachimstal where Schiller lived, the Mädlerpassage with Auerbach's Keller, Steibs Hof of 1907 . . . all of these belonged to Schneider until he "disappeared."

Our tour guide proudly informed the group that while Schneider is a hero in Leipzig, he "can't show his face in Frankfurt." He went on to explain: "He had his hand in everything and was a little like Robin Hood. It doesn't matter how or where he found the money, the main thing is that he brought it here and did something with it."

Schneider's cult-like status was further confirmed when he returned to Leipzig in 2000 to promote his two books: one, an autobiography (*Bekenntnisse eines Baulöwen*, or "confessions of a real-estate tycoon"), whose title invokes Thomas Mann's *Felix Krull*, a novel about the career of a con-man extraordinaire (Schneider 1999); the second, a glossy coffee-table book entitled *All My Buildings: Modern Monuments in Germany* (Schneider 2000). At a reading attended by over a thousand residents who, according to the Leipzig newspaper, "surrounded the stage like the remaining hair around Schneider's bald head," he was greeted with applause, hugs, and requests for his return. "Leipzig was my Waterloo," he often said. "I met my end here, but I never stopped loving the city" (*Leipziger Volkszeitung* 2000).

Schneider's gift to Leipzig, for which he is revered and celebrated today, was not just his affection, money, and the revival of the city's most treasured landmarks, but also its recognition and visibility. "We should be proud of our Schneider," the magazine *Kreuzer* urged readers in 1995. "He made us all a little more important."[16] In the context of profound displacement and disillusionment following re-unification, involving, among other things, the devaluation of most things East German, the attention drawn to Leipzig through a common national currency of economic prosperity and mass consumption (reflected in national and international chain stores and elite boutiques that filled Schneider's renovated spaces) was an important boost for local identity and a sense of self, even for many local residents who were excluded from partaking in this largesse (see Berdahl 2005a). And the fact that this was achieved by a trickster who outsmarted the capitalists—even if he was a *Wessi* (West German), even if this economic prosperity was more appearance than reality—made it all the better.

CONCLUSION

It is often said that the popularity and cultural power of folk heroes stems from their ability to hold a mirror up to society, to serve as a reflection of our own hopes, dreams, disappointments, and nightmares. What are the implications, we may ask (as did many German media outlets), of Jürgen Schneider's story? What cultural logics are contained in the moral lessons spun around this tale? The polarizing figure of "Doc" Schneider—on the one hand an agent of West German capital who sacrifices his credibility and empire for something more important than money, on the other hand a conniving imposter and greedy crook—reflects some of the complex and contradictory workings of capitalism itself. Indeed, this ambivalence may underlie one of Leipzig's other commemorations of its real-estate tycoon: a mural in the famous restaurant Auerbach's Keller of a scene from Goethe's *Faust* in which Mephisto is depicted as a court jester with Schneider's face. Completed in 1999, the painting, which presents the man who once embodied western investment capital as the devil, suggests, perhaps, the Faustian bargain entailed in eastern Germany's perceived embrace of capitalism specifically, as well as the deceptions and performances required for success in a capitalist economy more generally. When seen through the eyes of people experiencing this for the first time (Verdery 1996), who, because of their experience of socialism, do not necessarily assume that capitalism is the natural order of things, the postsocialist context offers possibilities for understanding, critiquing, and de-naturalizing capitalism as a political and economic system. As John and Jean Comaroff have argued in writing about "millennial capitalism," we need to interrogate "the experiential contradictions at the core of neoliberal capitalism," suggesting that many of these contradictions are most visible in "so-called postrevolutionary societies." They continue by noting that "a good deal is to be learned about the historical implications of the current moment by eavesdropping on the popular anxieties to be heard in such places" (Comaroff and Comaroff 2000: 298–299).

There are those who have since argued that Schneider was a scapegoat; that he rode the wave of boom and bust along with countless other speculators, except that he got caught. The case thus also urges us to ask the question posed by Anna Tsing in the article I have found so useful for my analysis here: "Under what circumstances are boom and bust intimately related to each other? . . . [T]he whiggish acrobatics necessary to show how those very economies celebrated as miracles were simultaneously lurking crises hardly seem to tell the whole story" (Tsing 2000: 115).

Jürgen Schneider's story also illuminates capital's role in the production of locality and nation, and of locality in relation to nation. The unique reception of Schneider in Leipzig was both a reflection and product of East-West dynamics as well as the dreams and disappointments of the new society. The very "Germanness" of the affair—the German banks, German press, German courts, even German cultural references in news headlines, book titles, and wall murals—invoked and reinscribed the boundaries of the new nation. Thus, while there may be moments when processes and institutions we consider to be global, such as capitalism, mass consumption, finance capital, and investment banks, displace and replace national ones, we should also remain alert to those instances when the salience of the national in relation to these processes and institutions may be observed in particularly bold relief.

8
EXPRESSIONS OF EXPERIENCE AND EXPERIENCES OF EXPRESSION
Museum Re-Presentations of GDR History

IN THE HEART OF LEIPZIG'S DOWNTOWN, on the main street of the city's pedestrian zone, stands a statue called *The Step of the Century*. Completed in the mid-1980s by the renowned East German artist Wolfgang Mattheuer and erected at this location in 1999, the larger-than-life figure's right hand is extended in the Nazi salute while its left hand is clenched in a worker's fist; it steps forward, half dressed and half in military uniform, with its head hidden and barely visible, into an unknown future. Like many works of art, the statue has been subject to a range of interpretations. Mattheuer has described it as relating to his interest in "the significant tension between conformity and protest, between yes and no, which stimulates and sharpens our vision of the future"; others have read it as an "allegory of totalitarianism" or a "thought-image [*Denkbild*] for the eternal conflict between good and evil."[1] In the GDR, the sculpture was awarded a national prize for depicting the "clash during this century between fascism/nazism on the one side and Leninism/Stalinism on the other."[2] Yet the statue's placement in front of the Leipzig Forum of Contemporary History (Zeitgeschichtliches Forum Leipzig) in honor of the museum's opening in 1999 has invested it with yet another meaning—now the dominant interpretation—reflecting the museum's mission of portraying the "history of resistance and opposition in the GDR" and its underlying agenda of "comparative dictatorship studies." According to the museum director, the statue (one of his exhibit favorites) "demonstrates the German people's step away from two dictatorships."[3] Indeed, this or a similar explanation is frequently part of museum as well as Leipzig city tours. In its new context within the cultural landscape of re-united Germany, then, *The Step of the Century* is read as symbolizing the new Germany's step *out* of the last century, leaving behind its troubled pasts of Nazism and socialism.

I begin with this image for it illuminates and contextualizes several issues surrounding the politics of memory and museum representations that I address in this paper: the ongoing, often complex and contradictory struggles over the production of knowledge about the East German past, the contexts of this production, and the ways in which the struggles themselves shed light upon larger social and political processes within re-unified Germany more generally. The question of the relationship to and representation of the GDR past gained immediate relevance after the fall of the Berlin Wall in 1989 and has been the subject of significant popular as well as scholarly discussion and debate ever since.[4] I am interested here not just in the politics of memory making but also in the various domains in which memory is constructed and deployed, and in the cultural implications and effects of such memory-making practices. My aim here, then, is to interrogate the production of historical memory in the former GDR, and I do so by comparing two cases of the "museumification" of GDR history: the state-sponsored and officially sanctioned Forum of Contemporary History in Leipzig, and a local association's collection and exhibition of GDR material culture. My discussion is indebted to a large and burgeoning scholarship on museums, a field in which Ed Bruner has been an exemplary pioneer (Bruner 1993, 1994, 2005). Much of this work has viewed museums as critical sites for the convergence of social, cultural, and political forces: as arenas for the production of national identity, national citizens, and national "culture" (Dodd 1986; Duncan 1995); as objects of the tourist gaze (Urry 1990); as part of new disciplines of power (Bennett 1995); as spaces of cultural representation and contestation (Bruner 1993; Karp, Kraemer, and Lavine 1992; Kirschenblatt-Gimblett 1998; Lavin and Karp 1991; Stocking 1985). Yet as anthropologists Eric Gable and Richard Handler have pointed out, "most research on museums has proceeded by ignoring much of what happens in them" (1997). Stressing the advantages of an ethnographic approach to museum studies, Bruner has similarly argued, "This privileging of the specific leads to a consideration of the complexity of forces and multiplicity of voices and meanings at work. Audiences are not passive recipients of received wisdom and official views; the challenge is to understand the interpretations of the audience in particular instances" (Bruner 2005: 128).

Drawing on ongoing ethnographic fieldwork conducted since 2001 in the city of Leipzig, this essay explores discourses and practices surrounding two radically different representations of GDR history. Both contrasting cases, I argue, reflect ongoing contestations over the meanings of the GDR past as well as the significant power imbalances in which such struggles occur.

REPRESSION AND RESISTANCE:
THE ZEITGESCHICHTLICHES FORUM LEIPZIG (ZGF)

The sole satellite branch of the House of History (Haus der Geschichte) in Bonn (a project initiated by Helmut Kohl in 1982 with a conservative and hence controversial agenda that culminated in the opening of the museum in Bonn 8 years later),[5] the Leipzig Forum of Contemporary History is commonly described as the eastern counterpart to the Bonn original. It was opened with great fanfare in a ceremony attended by Chancellor Schroeder on October 9, 1999, the tenth anniversary of what is widely believed to be the "turning point" in the peaceful demonstrations of 1989 in Leipzig.[6] The city was selected as the site for the museum because of its role in this history.

As an institution, the ZGF describes itself as a "place of living remembrance." It thus strives to be more than a museum; it is also a memorial and a gathering place for lectures, discussions, and conferences. Indeed, the institution makes a very valuable contribution in this sense to intellectual life and historical work in Leipzig and beyond. Because the explicit focus of the museum is on "the history of resistance and opposition during the dictatorship of the Soviet occupation zone and the GDR," it commemorates a critical element of the East German experience as well as the earth-shattering events of 1989. Underlying this focus on repression and resistance is a scholarly interest in and commitment to what is sometimes called "comparative dictatorship studies"—a belief in the historical comparability of the Nazi and socialist regimes, with the latter described in the exhibit catalogue as the "second German dictatorship."[7]

These ideological underpinnings are evident throughout the chronologically organized exhibit, where stories and images of suffering, repression, and state violence are foregrounded alongside a narrative of resistance and opposition. Guided tours—frequently given by university students too young to have many memories of the GDR—often privilege the most gruesome or sensational installations, highlighting for visitors a sequential horror of socialist abuses. In addition to key events in political and economic history, exhibits contain several installations on political prisoners as well as the fortification of the inter-German border in the 1950s and the building of the Berlin Wall. An entire room, complete with a wall of video footage and a Soviet "division canon," is dedicated to the uprising on June 17, 1953, while another section focuses on the biographies of political dissidents and the work of oppositional peace and environmental groups. Displays representing GDR consumer culture and material scarcity are sandwiched between depictions of successful escapes and an exhibit devoted to the Stasi that includes cases of files, surveillance equipment and paraphernalia (containing, among other items, several odor specimens of regime opponents in canning jars[8] as well as actual State Security Police [Stasi] surveillance videos), and a van with a restructured interior to accommodate political prisoners without being recognizable as such on the outside. The narrative culminates in a triumphalist portrayal of 1989, the largest exhibit area in the museum, containing protest demonstration banners, a section of the Berlin Wall, the iconic Trabant car, and other artifacts of that eventful period. The last area of exhibit focuses on post-Wall eastern Germany, with displays on building booms, unemployment, and violence against foreigners that call specific attention to contemporary social issues and economic concerns but also risk naturalizing them in the larger context of the museum's teleological narrative.

Like many contemporary museums, the ZGF exhibits draw upon multiple media to invite active visitor participation and engagement. Audio stations, touch screens, video monitors, and interactive hands-on displays abound as part of the Haus der Geschichte's larger objective of enabling visitors to "experience history." This play with the senses surrounds visitors with images and sounds that can operate on many levels, sometimes eliciting emotional, even visceral reactions. Upon entering the exhibit area on the Berlin Wall, for example, one is confronted with videos of attempted escapes, with people screaming, hanging out of windows, or being mangled by barbed wire. The reverberations of tank rumblings and screeching provide the audio background for the June 17 uprising. With the exception of dissident songwriter Wolf Biermann's music, in fact, one's auditory experience of the museum is dominated by the sounds of bullets being fired, churches being blown up, and human cries. Taken together, these acoustic enhancements are carefully selected to conform to the museum's emphasis on repression and resistance, a narrative described by museum directors and employees as "the concept."[9]

This narrative concept is stressed repeatedly in the rigorous screening of museum guides. "You must agree with and stand by our concept," one university student was reportedly told firmly during her second round of interviews for a tour guide position. She was not offered the job after expressing reservations about her ability and willingness to comply with the strict guidelines. Indeed, the narrative of repression and resistance not only dominates the museum concept, but it can also be internalized and reproduced in personal accounts during guided tours. I was told, for example, of a visit to the museum by a group of local historians interested in initiating a conversation about representational practices at the exhibit. "Throughout the tour our guide grew increasingly excited and extreme," one of them recalled, "and when we came to the [Stasi van], she claimed that she had sat as a prisoner inside. I thought to myself: Wow! That is really awful. But then a member of our group exclaimed, 'No, Angelika, you sat in the Communist Party's (SED) district management office!' She turned bright red and just left." Pressure to adhere to the museum concept is reportedly felt very strongly by museum employees, allegedly creating an occasional atmosphere of fear and suspicion in the workplace. Most museum employees only wanted to speak off the record, for example, and I was especially alarmed to hear about rumors of wiretapping employee phone conversations.

Rumors and suspicion aside, it seems to me a more vexing issue is at stake here. While the museum's literature and staff are careful to point out that the focal point of the museum is "dictatorship and resistance" rather than "the history of the GDR," as the sole branch of the Haus der Geschichte national museum in the East (the "little brother" of the Haus der Geschichte in Bonn, I was sometimes told—a description that invoked the diminutive term used in referring to "brothers and sisters in the East"), and the only federally organized and funded museum dedicated exclusively to the GDR, the effect of this emphasis is to re-present GDR history in these terms. Media accounts of the museum's opening heralded it as an "exhibit and information center" that provides "a broad overview of the GDR and the division of Germany."[10] More specifically, the museum was applauded at its opening for its contribution to "the history of democracy in Germany"[11] and for demonstrating the "civil courage" of eastern Germans during the fall of 1989, an "unparalleled enrichment of German history."[12] In his speech at the opening ceremony, Chancellor Schroeder asked "not to be misunderstood" when he said that one could be "pleased to be a German today . . . to be proud of the realization of democracy."[13]

This adamant, indeed dogmatic, privileging of resistance at the museum may have as its subtext, it seems to me, the haunted past of the "first German dictatorship" and the question of German guilt. Conceptually and discursively linking the two regimes through the rhetoric of "a second German dictatorship" (a discourse in which comparability may be equated with commensurability, even if that is not its intended effect), the director of the Leipzig Forum writes in the exhibit catalogue:

> We have placed special emphasis on biographical approaches; it was however, clear that the isolated examples of bravery under the dictatorship stand for the courage of hundreds of thousands of other resisting East Germans. (Eckert 2000)

The privileged narrative here, then, is ultimately one of redemption: a new official history for the new Germany. The national director of the Haus der Geschichte, Hermann Schäfer, gestured toward this nationalizing project in describing the mission of the Leipzig ZGF:

> We want to break what the opinion research institutes have diagnosed as the wall of silence between East and West—break it by means of exhibitions, events and publications produced and sponsored by the new museum in Leipzig, in order to find a historical conception common to all Germans.[14]

Despite favorable ratings in museum visitor surveys (highly touted in the exhibit catalogue),[15] local reactions do not reveal that efforts to forge this "common historical conception" have been successful. In informal conversations as well as during interviews on other subjects, I often heard the ZGF described as a "victor's history." "It is purely propaganda from the western side," a man in his forties working for the chamber of commerce angrily explained. "It disgusts me just when I see the themes portrayed there: 'church in socialism,' 'resistance,' 'opposition.' All of this is a very western perspective." Outside of work, one of the most historically sophisticated of the ZGF tour guides agreed: "The museum conveys to visitors the impression that this is the history of the GDR, but it isn't. It is designed with a western view of GDR history. Many visitors from the East cannot find themselves here." An eastern German historian similarly suggested: "Actually I think it is kind of cute." He smiled and continued, "People in the GDR learned how to read things critically. I hope they apply those skills to this exhibit."

Another common local reaction—uttered in rage by some while exiting the exhibit area,[16] by others as a simple fact in subsequent conversations outside the museum: "that is not how I experienced the GDR!" "Sure there were people who were imprisoned or who were spied upon," one local merchant told me. "But that was not my experience. I'm sorry, but that was just not my experience." When I asked an artist in her late thirties about the emphasis on dictatorship and resistance exemplified by the Stasi van and border shootings, she answered:

> [In GDR times] you spent your days looking for the one detergent that was hard to get that didn't give your kids a rash. And then because you wanted your little ones to have some vitamins, you bought carrots, cleaned them, pressed them together with some apples, because that was how you could get juice. And when there was juice in the store, you took a box to the store and stood in line so that you could go for a while without having to press your own [juice]. THAT was daily life in the GDR.

The social and political context for these reactions is a much more general devaluation of East German histories since re-unification. As I have written about elsewhere (Berdahl 1999b), such practices have included the selling of East German factories to western companies, occasionally for next to nothing; the discrediting of the GDR educational system, particularly the *Abwicklung*[17] (restructuring) of the universities; the renaming of schools, streets, and other public buildings; the trial of Berlin border guards that for many eastern Germans represented a different sort of victors' justice; debates over what to do with and about East Germany's Stasi heritage that have often compared the GDR to the Third Reich; and discourses that ridiculed the backwardness of East German industry and consumer goods while ignoring the political and economic contexts that may have produced it. Although generated and experienced differently in form and content, such practices have generally been grouped together in eastern German discourses of oppositional solidarity against western hegemony—of which the ZGF has come to be viewed by many as an emblem.

BEARING WITNESS: THE *OSTALGIE* PROJECT

Since the mid-1990s a range of institutional and individual practices have emerged as part of a counternarrative to such hegemonic memory making and devaluations of the GDR. Commonly referred to as Ostalgie (nostalgia for the East), the production of counter-memories and identities has taken many forms: self-described "nostalgia cafés" that are decorated with artifacts from the socialist period and serve "traditional" GDR fare; dance parties ("*Ostivals*" or "Ostalgie Nights") featuring East German rock music; a double of Erich Honecker; numerous publications and trivia games recalling life in the GDR; supermarkets, mail order websites, and an annual "OstPro" trade show fair that specialize in East German products. The 1999 release and box-office success of two "Ostalgie films" (*Sonnenallee* and *Helden Wie Wir*) marked the emergence of Ostalgie as a truly mass cultural phenomenon. More recently, the critically acclaimed and top-grossing 2003 film *Good Bye, Lenin!* unleashed a new wave of Ostalgie, including a flurry of "Ostshows," featuring curiosities of life in the GDR, on at least five major German television networks.

What I want to focus on here, however, is a specific example of a counternarrative to the official histories and memories represented by the ZGF, a collection of East German "everyday objects" by a local non-profit organization. The collection reflects the privileging of material culture in eastern German historical memory (Betts 2000), the most extensive and sophisticated example of which is the Museum for East German Everyday Life Culture in Eisenhüttenstadt, a truly professional undertaking; its mission entails the "museumification of the world of GDR objects as an active and mutual communication that allows for reflective thought in a period of individual and often painful reorientation" (Ludwig 1996; Ludwig and Kuhn 1997a, 1997b). The "Zeitzeugen Ostalgie" project (Ostalgie Witnessess to History), however, is representative of more widespread practices of collecting, cataloging, and displaying "GDR everyday life." Voluntary associations dedicated to the documentation and preservation of "GDR everyday life," for example, allocate responsibilities among members for collecting everything from East German packaging materials to work brigade medals. Numerous makeshift museums, galleries, and displays in community centers or people's homes similarly contain various objects of the vanished state.[18]

The "Witnesses to History" collection is the product of government-subsidized make-work jobs (Arbeitsbeschaffungsmaßnahmen, or ABM); the purpose of the organization (whose name is "Neue Arbeit Wurzen") is in part is to generate jobs in the "second labor market," a term referring to the government-subsidized domain of employment. People employed as ABM do not consider themselves to be working in a "real job," as the man who picked me up from the train station explained immediately after introducing himself: "I am working in the second labor market," he said. "In capitalism there is a first labor market, but somehow there is still also a second one." As Angela Jancius has pointed out in her intriguing study of unemployment in the former GDR, workers employed in the second labor market perceive themselves as engaged in "useful but not productive labor" (Jancius 2002).

By any measure, the work of the three ABM staff employed at the "Zeitzeugen Ostalgie" project has been a labor of love. With no experience or training in exhibition design, they have painstakingly assembled a collection of GDR artifacts from the 1960s, 1970s, and 1980s ranging from food packaging to electronics to household furniture. In former classrooms of a vacated school building, the exhibit is comprised of reconstructed domestic living spaces as well as thematic clusters of particular items. A living room features a typical GDR upholstered sofa, side chairs on silver casters, coffee table, and wall unit displaying characteristic decorative objects; a kitchen is full of aluminum cooking pans and utensils, plastic kitchen gadgets and dinnerware, obsolescent appliances, and East German foodstuffs. The display items elicit what the exhibit organizers describe as an "Aha effect," a reaction that connects personal biographies to collective memory as visitors recognize and tell stories about familiar but forgotten cultural objects. These East German things are particularly effective *lieux de memoir* for what Paul Betts has insightfully termed their "aesthetics of sameness . . . That is, the very lack of product innovation and repackaging assured that these objects—however privately experienced and remembered—would function as transgenerational markers of East German culture and identity" (Betts 2000). A warehouse of discarded used furniture for low-income families, the vast majority of which are GDR products, occupies an adjacent room; a separate ABM project of the Neue Arbeit Wurzen, these items represent for many not only the throw-away mentality of today's consumer society, but also the dustbin of history to which the GDR and its products have been relegated, and from which the relics of Ostalgie have been culled.

The idea for the project came to one of the organization directors one day upon hearing what school children were learning about the GDR in class:

> I was interested in what the kids were learning about the GDR then, in the year 1997 or 1998. [My young relative] told me that there was nothing to eat, that people couldn't buy anything. Everything was dark and grey . . . And people weren't allowed to laugh and weren't able to laugh . . . And I thought to myself, this can't be true. So we brainstormed about how to turn this into an ABM project . . . what was daily life really like?

As we walked through the exhibit, my hosts repeatedly stressed that they did not want to "glorify the GDR," that this was intended as a completely "apolitical exhibit." As evidence of this, they cited their "strategic decision" not to include political memorabilia like pins, medals, uniforms, or FDJ scarves. In the kitchen area they described showing schoolchildren how juice was pressed, how fruits and vegetables were preserved "because you couldn't just go to the store and buy everything." The quaintness of socialist design was particularly highlighted in the electronics room, featuring, among other things, a square phonograph record. "We chose the name 'historical witnesses,'" one of the directors explained when I asked about the project title, "because we didn't want to write simply 'objects of utility' [*Gebrauchsgegenstände*] but also because these [things] really are witnesses."

But to what, we may ask, do these objects bear witness? Part of the answer to this question may lie in the comments and impressions of visitors left behind in the guestbook, which overwhelmingly revealed that the exhibit was far from "apolitical." Some examples:

> One can appreciate the meticulous effort and thoughtfulness that went into this [exhibit], but the strong ideological one-sidedness is very disturbing.

> Very nice . . . it recalls memories, above all how the prices remained stable for years.

Remember this? We used to cook with it. And this we used to wash with. The shampoo wasn't bad either . . . but it was only available under the table.

Because this is also a part of my life, I was very happy to see this exhibit.

Many thanks for taking on the important task of collecting and preserving things from a distant epoch. One shouldn't think of this in terms of Ostalgie, but as a piece of identity preserved.

What emerges in these comments—as in many other practices of Ostalgie—is a sense of a highly complicated relationship between personal histories, disadvantage, dispossession, the betrayal of promises, and the social worlds of production and consumption. As I have argued elsewhere about Ostalgie more generally (Berdahl 1999b), such practices must be seen in the context of feelings of profound displacement and disillusionment following re-unification, reflected in the popular saying that we have "emigrated without leaving home." As one university student said to me in a conversation about the subject in the spring of 2001:

Everything simply disappeared. When you leave your past behind, you can normally go home again, look at it—at your Heimat and so forth. But in this case everything just disappeared.

The focus on East German things may also recall an identity as producers that has been lost in this transition. In a society where productive labor was a key aspect of state ideology and where the workplace was a central site for social life, the high incidence of unemployment throughout eastern Germany has undermined profoundly many peoples' sense of self and identity. It is no accident, then, that a collection emphasizing the products of East German labor emerged in the context of the "second labor market," where feelings of disillusionment, devalued selves, and betrayal often prevail. There is something strikingly poignant in this self-validating effort to recall and preserve a distinctive and honorable past, it seems to me—in this work created for and performed by those considered "unemployable" in the "first labor market": "I was born in 1961," one of the project participants told me,

Those whole years I was a child, youth, adult—school, studies, work. It is a part of my life. The predominant part of my life. This Ostalgie is for me also a piece of my own life, my own identity . . . Those were formative years, that's how I would see it.

The frequent reference to GDR consumer culture in the guestbook comments as well as in the exhibit tour and demonstration is also significant. The fact that East German things have become mnemonics must be viewed in relation to larger historical and political processes and contexts. The dominant narrative in the Ostalgie collection is not one of a repressive dictatorship, as at the ZGF, but of a regime that, quite literally, failed to deliver the goods. In this sense, the emphasis on quaint East German things and their scarcity under socialist rule in implicit or explicit contrast to the plentiful supply of ever new and improved products in the West affirms and perpetuates a narrative of "democratization" and national legitimacy in which access to consumer goods and consumer choice are defined as fundamental rights and democratic expressions of individualism. Indeed, many observers have since suggested that the transitions of 1989 were not about demands for political or human rights, but for consumer rights.[19] As the historian Ina Merkel has observed: "The struggle between the systems did not take the form of armed conflict, but was rather shifted to the marketplace. And it was here, in the sphere of consumerism, that the battle was won" (Merkel 1998). In the context of this postwar relationship between political legitimacy and mass consumption, such re-presentations of the GDR not only contribute to the production of new (counter) memories and histories; they contribute to the production of citizen-consumers as well (see Berdahl 2005a).

CONCLUSION: FASHIONING THE PAST

To conclude, I turn to an event in which these various domains and practices of memory converged: a fashion show of East German clothing styles held at the Leipzig Forum of Contemporary History during the Leipzig "museum night," an evening for promoting city museums with special presentations, exhibits, and long opening hours. The master of ceremonies was an extremely animated local celebrity (and former SED Party member), Paul Fröhlich, whose energetic performance enlivened the packed house of onlookers. "Good evening ladies and gentlemen," he began. "Welcome to the Zeitgeschliches Forum! . . . We would like to transport you this evening to the fashion and Zeitgeist of the GDR." While GDR tunes blasted over loudspeakers and period photos were projected onto a nearby screen, models strode down the runway outfitted in exemplary GDR fashion design. The running commentary of the host had the audience laughing and applauding at nearly every example, as Fröhlich drew upon a culturally shared knowledge of socialist products, cultural images, and party rhetoric. Full of irony, he brilliantly played with the history of socialist industrial design ("Here we have a multifunctional downhill and cross country ski"), often explicitly fetishizing the objects on display: "Please look, with an eye for detail, at these buttons. Look at these, as one says today, 'cool'[20] buttons. These are simply erotic details from GDR designer times!" In another instance, he had the audience in stitches with a demonstration of the sexual eroticism of a GDR vacuum cleaner. (Hint: the vacuum cleaner bag inflates upright.)

The repeated references to GDR consumer culture required a shared and privileged knowledge that excluded any audience member—real or imagined—who had not experienced socialism, creating a strong sense of solidarity among those in the know. It would be easy, therefore, to categorize this performance as another instance or commodification of Ostalgie. More than this, however, the show was also a playful appropriation and ironic parody of Ostalgie. In this context, East German things became "camp" rather than objects of nostalgic longing or counter-memory. Thus, although one of the ZGF historians described the show as not fitting into the concept—he suggested to me that its presentation was a subversive act because it was an attempt by several staff members to address critiques of the ZGF by bringing in the "everyday" and because the museum director did not approve of the idea—the mocking tone and the focus on the quaint, hopelessly backward, and outdated GDR styles were, in fact, quite in line with the institutional agenda of creating a "historical conception common to all Germans." Although it did not stress the museum's focal point of dictatorship and resistance, the show not only underscored the relationship between national legitimacy and mass consumption, it also belittled and dismissed eastern German critiques of hegemonic memory making contained in many Ostalgic practices. Indeed, poking fun at Ostalgie is fast becoming almost as profitable a cottage industry as Ostalgie itself. Lyrics to a 2001 Leipzig cabaret song, for example, reflect this satirizing sentiment:

> Good federal republic citizens the Ossis want to be
> Yet they buy only eastern products on their department-store
>   shopping sprees
> Spee and Florena, Rotkäppchen and Fit[21]
> How long will the Office for Constitutional Protections
> put up with it?[22]

The parodies of Ostalgie contained in the fashion show and cabaret song signal one of the latest waves in the ongoing negotiation of memory in the former GDR. Indeed, together with the two cases of "museumification" I have discussed here, they reflect the multiple, fluid, shifting, complex, and often contradictory forms and domains of memory production—and consumption—in postsocialist eastern Germany. When viewed in this way, the work and the politics of memory and museums can be a window onto larger political processes and landscapes of nation building, identity formation, and belonging in a period of social change and discord.

9

GOODBYE LENIN, AUFWIEDERSEHEN GDR

On the Social Life of Socialism

IN THE YEARS SINCE ITS COLLAPSE, socialism has become the object of significant historical curiosity, memory making, and contestation. In addition to more public sites like the Museum of Communism in Prague (next to a McDonald's) or the Budapest Statue Park and House of Terror (to name just a few examples), the cultural landscape of postsocialist memory also includes private exhibitions of socialist material culture or Communist kitsch (depending on the context and the eye of the beholder) (Ten Dyke 2001; Berdahl 2005b), published personal memoirs (Hensel 2002), mass-mediated images in film or television, commemorations, silences, and an ongoing dynamic between individual biographies and collective histories—between personal narratives and public re-presentations. Of course socialism was being remade into memory from the very beginnings of its end, as new histories were created out of unsanctioned memories of the past (Watson 1994), in emergent nationalizing projects (Wanner 1998), and in symbolic acts of legitimizing new states (Verdery 1999). In the realm of memory, then, socialism has had a complex and often unpredictable social life.

My aim in this essay is to reflect upon the social life of socialism by focusing on memory and the present in a context with which I am most familiar: post-Wall Germany. In his work on commodities in cultural perspective, Appadurai has shown that the social life of things is subject to longer-term shifts in value and demand (Appadurai 1986). I am arguing that the same processual approach is relevant for understanding the production and circulation of historical memory: the social life of socialism has been, and continues to be, a process informed by large-scale political shifts, economic developments, and cultural dynamics.

My use of the concept of memory refers to practices, performances, representations, and other modes of shaping images of the past. Memory, although it may be a "reservoir" of history (Watson 1994), is not the same as history. Instead, history may be viewed as a particular configuration of historical representation—usually in written or narrative form, including "official histories" of the socialist states—that itself is open to questions of interpretation and interpretive authority (D. Cohen 1994: 130). Memory, on the other hand, is a more infinitely malleable, contestable, interactive, and social phenomenon. Produced and constructed on a variety of fronts, memory can be personal as well as public, individual as well as collective. Museums, commemorations, and monuments give an important physicality to memory, but they are not necessarily separate from history; indeed such representations may also entail in a dynamic relationship between both memory and history, between public and private. (See also D. Cohen 1994; Connerton 1989; Davis and Starn 1989; Huyssen 1995; Watson 1994.) Whether deployed strategically in everyday practices or constructed through mass-mediated narratives and images, memory puts the past into dialogue with the present. To what ends, we should then ask, and with what effects?

I attempt to address these and other questions through a reading of the wildly successful German film *Good Bye, Lenin!* released in 2003. I am an anthropologist with admittedly no training in film theory, so I ask for readers' patience as I make my way through this analysis. But, I should add, as an anthropologist, this film is a kind of "in-your-face" ethnographic object that cannot be ignored. Its production and reception in a post-Wall Germany still fraught with East-West tensions both reflect and constitute historically specific negotiations, discourses, and debates about the meanings of memory, nostalgia, and the politics of the present. The film also represents the apex of the postsocialist cultural phenomenon known in Germany as *Ostalgie,* to which I shall return later.

VIRTUALLY EXISTING SOCIALISM

Good Bye, Lenin! is the story of an East German family during the tumultuous year of the *Wende* (turning point, the term used in referring to the events surrounding the fall of the Berlin Wall). The mother, Christiane, is a devout and active party loyalist who has been deeply committed to the socialist state since the departure of her husband for West Germany in 1978. Eleven years later, in October 1989, she is on her way to celebrate the fortieth anniversary of the GDR with party dignitaries and observes her young adult son, Alex, clash with police during a pro-democracy protest march. The trauma of seeing her son among the demonstrators, combined with the shock of witnessing the brutality of the regime, causes her to have a heart attack and sends her into a coma for the next 8 months. While she is sleeping, the Berlin Wall falls, eastern Germans embrace western capitalism and consumerism, and Germany is catapulted toward re-unification. Alex loses his job in the state-owned television repair service and begins selling satellite dishes, while his sister starts sleeping with a *Wessi* (West German) and abandons her studies in order to work at Burger King. When Christiane emerges from her coma, doctors warn her children that any unexpected shock could complicate her recovery and potentially prove fatal. Her son Alex thus resolves to recreate the GDR in her bedroom, concealing from his mother all the changes of the past 8 months. Western-style IKEA furniture is hastily replaced with East German particleboard, venetian blinds are pulled down and polyester curtains are put up, and the socialist iconographic hero Che Guevara goes back up on the mustard-colored floral wallpaper. Within this 79-square-meter apartment, then, the GDR lives on.

Alex's efforts to make time stand still grow increasingly complicated as his bed-ridden mother's health improves. With East German products gone from the store shelves following the currency union in July of 1990 when West German companies took over distribution networks, he frantically searches for familiar goods, repackaging foodstuffs and refilling pickle jars from the recycling bin with Dutch imports to satisfy his mother's craving for Spreewald gherkins. He enlists friends and family members to participate in the lie: demanding that visitors wear eastern German clothing, paying former pupils to perform pioneer songs for her birthday, and encouraging a neighbor to take dictations of *Eingaben* (legally sanctioned complaints) to state authorities, for which his mother had been well known before her illness. With the help of an aspiring West German filmmaker friend from his new job, Alex fabricates GDR newscasts for his mother to view on a TV that is linked to a VCR machine in an adjacent room.

The dizzying pace of change and a few puzzling encounters make it progressively challenging to continue his fantasy, but whenever his mother comes close to figuring out the truth, Alex invents a plausible explanation. The unfurling of a Coca-Cola banner on a nearby building that had been draped in a Communist Party red banner just months before—a powerful visual metaphor embodying the cultural and political upheaval—is explained in the next day's fake news bulletin as being a result of a recent discovery that the formula for Coke was actually an East German invention. The presence of westerners in East Berlin is attributed to a decision by President Erich Honecker to grant asylum to those disillusioned with capitalism. With his filmmaker friend posing as the news anchor, the fictitious Aktuelle Kamera report explains:

> Unemployment, dire prospects for the future, and the increasing electoral success of the neonazi *Republikaner* have moved the clearly unsettled West German citizens to turn their backs on capitalism and attempt a new beginning in the worker and peasant state.

Several months into his charade Alex realizes that the fantasy is as much for himself as for his mother, admitting that "the GDR I created for my mother was increasingly becoming the GDR that I might have wished for myself."

Indeed, Alex ultimately rewrites the end of the Cold War, casting communism as the victor. In his final fake newscast, intended to put an end to his deception by informing his ailing mother that the border between East and West Germany is gone, Alex creates a narrative in which Erich Honecker resigns and his childhood hero, the cosmonaut Sigmund Jähn, assumes leadership of the party and the GDR. Alex solicits Jähn's help after a chance encounter with him (or a convincing Doppelgänger) as a taxi driver one evening. While the GDR national anthem plays in the background, Jähn delivers his scripted speech in Vogtland dialect (which had become identified with eastern Germans and mocked in the West) to the nation:

> Dear citizens of the GDR. Once you have experienced the miracle of seeing our planet from the cosmos, you see things differently. . . . When viewed from outer space, this is a very small country, and yet thousands of people have come to us in the past year. People whom we used to see as the enemy and who want to live with us today. . . . socialism means not to be fenced in. Socialism means approaching others, living with other people. Not only to dream of a better world, but to make it come true. I have thus decided to open the borders of the GDR.

The anchor's commentary is juxtaposed with well-known footage of November 9, with Germans dancing on the Berlin Wall and climbing up the western side:

> In the first hours since the borders opened, thousands of citizens from the Federal Republic of Germany have already taken the opportunity to visit the German Democratic Republic. Many want to stay. They are searching for an alternative to the brutal struggle for survival in the capitalist system. Not everyone wants to participate in the addiction to career and the terror of consumerism. Not everyone is made for the elbow society. These people want a different life. They realize that cars, videorecorders, and televisions are not everything. They are prepared to build a different life with nothing but goodwill, determination, and hope.

Christiane dies 3 days after Germany is re-unified, blissfully unaware, Alex believes, of the truth. In a small ceremony of family and friends, her ashes are scattered over Berlin by the kind of rocketship that Alex used to play with as a child, a fitting and proper sendoff for his mother, his childhood, and his country.

THE LONG GOODBYE

After its premiere in February 2003, *Good Bye, Lenin!* quickly became one of the most successful films in German movie history, breaking box-office records and garnering multiple national and international awards. Crowds flocked to see it in East and West (unlike the 1999 GDR retro film *Sonnenallee,* which was popular in eastern Germany but criticized in the West for glorifying the socialist regime); theaters were packed and shows regularly sold out. Critics talked about its "cathartic release" and attempted to find meaning in its unprecedented success: for some, the passage of time had allowed for enough critical distance to produce a "requiem for the failed Honecker state" or a "dirge for the century of communism" (Von Vestenberg 2003). For others, the film's success could be explained by an enduring nostalgia for the socialist past, or Ostalgie, a term that plays with the German words for East, *Ost,* and nostalgia, *Nostalgie.* While these are important observations (and I shall return to them momentarily), they fail to capture the multiplicity of meanings underlying this film as a cultural document and cultural event.

To begin with, there are several recurring themes in the film that make it particularly effective and resonant across generational and East-West divides.

A major motif involves the tensions and gaps between appearance and reality, between fact and fiction. This theme invokes a dominant discourse about socialism and its demise: socialism collapsed, goes this argument, because of this ever-widening gap. The film's central premise of the fabricated GDR that Alex creates for his mother is echoed in parallel stories of family secrets and lies: toward the end of her life, Christiane confesses to her children that their father had not fled to the West for another woman, as they had been led to believe, but that his departure had been planned with the intention of having the family follow him as soon as possible. After he was gone, she tells them, she lacked the courage to go through with the plan; his unopened letters to the children are hidden behind a cupboard in the kitchen. Another layer of the confusion between appearance and reality comes at the end of the film when it is revealed that, unbeknownst to Alex, his mother is aware and deeply appreciative of his charade.

It is the film's central premise, however, that begins to explain its resonance by allowing for different readings and receptions. On the one hand, the GDR is nothing but a façade or a childhood fantasy—an interpretation that would arguably confirm many perceptions and stereotypes among eastern but mostly western Germans. On the other hand, the sense of promise and possibility contained in Alex's phantasmagorical recreation of a GDR that never existed accesses for many eastern Germans shared sentiments of loss and longing in the context of the broken promises and disillusionments of re-unification. With very few exceptions, this nostalgia did not reflect a longing to return to the GDR, but a sense of lost possibilities and critiques of the present.

Dominant discourses of East-West relations are most effectively addressed in the film, however, by not addressing them explicitly. Indeed, re-unification is celebrated as a joyful moment, with a newly reconfigured family from East and West (including the father from West Berlin with whom Alex has made contact, and the West German boyfriend who is the father of Alex's sister's baby). In Alex's new workplace, sales teams consist of one eastern and one western German, and his filmmaker friend and Aktuelle Kamera accomplice is a co-worker from the West.

More effectively, however, it is the narrative device of a subplot focusing on Alex's childhood idol, the cosmonaut Sigmund Jähn, and the metaphor of space travel that is subtly suggestive of East-West dynamics. Jähn had been the first German to travel in space, a battleground of the Cold War, aboard Soyuz 31. It is a moment that Alex characterizes as the "GDR attaining a world standard"; it is also a moment that Alex connects to his father's flight to the West, for he learns of his father's departure while watching television coverage of Jähn's historic flight in space. The analogy between the West and outer space would be recognizable to many eastern Germans, for whom West Germany before 1989 seemed to be, in a common phrase, "as far away as the moon." It is no coincidence, then, that Jähn is the apparent taxi driver who takes Alex to his father's home in West Berlin. Similarly, Jähn answers Alex's question about what it was like "up there" by simply replying "really nice, only a long way from home," a description that would echo a widespread and frequently articulated sentiment among eastern Germans about having "emigrated without leaving home."

A leitmotif connected to this subplot concerns the children's television bedtime character the Sandmann. Jähn brings the Sandmann with him on his voyage and Alex sends him off into space in a homemade rocketship. The figure also makes an appearance when Alex shows up at his father's house unannounced and finds himself watching the show with his father's young children. For many eastern Germans, the Sandmann is a potent symbol and cultural icon. Under socialism, East German school children were frequently subjected to the "Sandmann Test" until it became legal to watch western television in 1971. An artefact of the Cold War waged on the front of mass media, both East and West German television aired their own brief children's show, *Der Sandmann,* before the evening news. Following the show, a clock would appear on the screen until the beginning of the news broadcast. The West German clock had small lines in place of numbers, the East German clock small dots. In school, teachers would ask children if the clock after their "sandman" had dots or lines, thus forcing children to reveal unwittingly whether parents were watching western television. After 1989 the East German sandman was one of the few cultural and political institutions that didn't lose out to western forms, and there are few eastern Germans who will not mention with pride that "our" sandman prevailed if the subject arises.

This kind of shared, insider knowledge works effectively to produce feelings of solidarity and belonging among eastern German audiences. The film's attention to detail, ranging from East German products and repeated references to GDR consumer culture to party rhetoric and socialist icons, excludes any viewer—real or imagined—who has not experienced socialism. In a context where, almost overnight, the value of eastern Germans' cultural capital plummeted—or, as a GDR trivia game explained, around 50 percent of the knowledge East Germans acquired during the course of a lifetime was rendered useless through sudden and unforeseen events—the portrayal of everyday socialist objects and practices produced a privileged knowledge for those in the know. Although critics may have hailed the film for uniting easterners and westerners in laughter, *Ossis* and *Wessis* were frequently laughing at very different things. When describing their reactions to the film, for example, eastern Germans I talked to often spoke with pride about moments when Wessis were unable to appreciate the humor in particular cultural references. Laughter—who laughed and at what—emerged as an important gauge of a newly recognized cultural competence, and quickly became a key topic of post-film discussions and discourses.

In order to understand the film's resonance with eastern German audiences, however, it is most critical to point out how *Good Bye, Lenin!* gives expression to the largely unacknowledged and forgotten experiences and memories of eastern Germans during a period of dizzying change. The complicated and often contradictory feelings of euphoria, bewilderment, possibility, and loss are captured in the film's careful attention to detail, ranging from the disappearance of *Spreewaldgurken* to billboards in which Trabants morph into western cars. As one audience member remarked, "Hopefully our fellow citizens from the old federal states [western Germany] will also see this film in order to understand how it really was." Similarly, another commented: "A film for every Ossi and those who want to learn more about us." When asked about the fact that the director was a Wessi, eastern Germans often replied that he had clearly done his "homework" and deserved to be an "honorary Ossi."

The re-presentation of GDR culture at the moment of its vanishing relates to another dominant theme and cultural meaning of the movie as a ritual of farewell (cf. Ivy 1995). There are many goodbyes in this film: to childhood, family secrets, fantasies, a mother, a state. All of these converge in the mother as symbol, whose ashes are rocketed into space during a rooftop ceremony at the end of the film. An earlier symbolic gesture of letting go occurs in a scene where Alex tosses 30,000 Marks of his mother's eastern German currency, now valueless and unexchangable because of a missed deadline, from the roof, like confetti in the wind.

The film's most memorable farewell is, to borrow a phrasing of Katherine Verdery's, a "corpse on the move" (Verdery 1999). In this key scene, Christiane ventures out of her reconstructed GDR (while Alex is sleeping) into an entirely new world, full of western neighbors, consumer goods, automobiles, and advertisements. The influx of western capitalism and consumer culture is set against a backdrop of socialist waste, signified by heaps of discarded GDR furniture. A bewildered Christiane wanders through this unfamiliar landscape and observes the torso of a Lenin statue, an icon familiar to most inhabitants of the former eastern bloc, being transported by helicopter across the East Berlin skyline. Lenin floats by, hand extended in a gesture of both ephemeral greeting and long goodbye. As her frantic children rush to rescue their mother from possible injury as well as from the shattering of an illusion, Lenin vanishes into the sunset.

Verdery has written eloquently about the political symbolism of dead bodies in the postsocialist period, arguing that reburials of particular human remains and the dismantling of iconic statues have been widespread and important "foundational acts of new states" (Verdery 1999: 21). The image of Lenin in the film partakes of and comments on this larger iconoclasm, invoking not only earlier foundational acts of the new state, but providing a powerful visual metaphor for saying goodbye to an old, and, in some cases virtually lingering one.

Indeed, as I mentioned earlier, one explanation for the film's unprecedented success is its cultural meaning as a sendoff—for an imagined GDR, I would add, in whatever form. The film's director, Wolfgang Becker, acknowledged in an interview that there had been no time for a proper funeral for the East German state. Other critics have expressed the hope that the film will put an end to East-West divisions, finally bringing together what belongs together. The actress Katrin Saß, a former GDR film star who plays Christiane, similarly said:

"One should see in *Good Bye, Lenin* how actors from East and West tell a story about our history. Perhaps we will finally succeed in putting this era [of division] behind us" (Saß 2008). Indeed, this might have been part of the intention behind a collective viewing of the film by 180 members of the German parliament, a "work outing" (*Betriebsausflug*) characterized by a headline in *Der Spiegel* as "The Bundestag bids farewell to Lenin" (*Der Spiegel* 2008).

ACTUALLY EXISTING POSTSOCIALISM

The cultural practices surrounding the film have not just been about saying goodbye, but are also about an *Aufwiedersehen* in the literal sense of the word (see you again). The premiere and success of *Good Bye, Lenin!* unleashed a new wave of Ostalgie throughout post-Wall Germany. Keeping with its tagline, "The GDR lives on," theaters across eastern Germany were decorated with GDR paraphernalia. National and multinational movie theater chains featured displays of GDR memorabilia—old East German newspapers, party medallions and certificates, consumer goods—and often included a small living area (10 square meters) of "GDR." Theater employees and audience members donned young pioneer scarves, Free German Youth shirts, or NVA uniforms and were encouraged to bring in East German souvenirs; during the first week of the film's showing a theater in Berlin accepted admission in now defunct eastern Marks. A theater entrance in Leipzig was adorned with a Lenin bust from a building at the old trade fair (*Messe*), on loan from the collection of a Wessi who normally has it sitting in his garden alongside other objects of the vanished state.

In the aftermath of *Good Bye, Lenin*'s success, Ostalgie has become an even more widespread merchandising industry. *Ostalikers,* as practitioners of Ostalgie are called, can now rent out the film set and throw an Ostalgie party. Local, national, and international retail businesses as well as internet websites feature a seemingly endless supply of books, games, music, and other mementos, including a "GDR in a box" kit to "help you discover the Ossi in yourself," complete with Mocca-fix, plastic chicken eggcups, and a *Neues Deutschland* newspaper. In the summer of 2004, *Ostshows* premiered on six major television networks featuring ice-skating princess Katarina Witt wearing a Free German Youth shirt, a parade of Trabant cars, Communist Party songs and slogans, and other cultural references. For a brief period, there was serious discussion of building a GDR theme park in eastern Berlin, complete with grumpy guards, socialist songs piped throughout the park, and of course spluttering Trabant cars. Ostalgie, then, in its many manifestations, meanings, and practices, has become a highly visible cultural phenomenon in the actually existing postsocialist landscape.

To dismiss this as history returned as farce, however, would ignore the historically specific cultural contexts and asymmetrical relations of power in which many such practices have emerged. As I have argued elsewhere, earlier forms of Ostalgie that emerged in the mid-1990s—including a re-invention, re-production, and mass merchandising of East German products, and the collecting, cataloging, and "museumification" of GDR everyday life—captured feelings of profound loss, longing, and displacement in a period of intense social discord. Ostalgie in this sense echoed Kathleen Stewart's definition of nostalgia: "a cultural practice, not a given content . . . In positing a 'once was' in relation to a 'now,' it creates a frame for meaning, a means of dramatizing aspects of an increasingly fluid and unnamed social life" (Stewart 1988: 227).

While earlier sentiments and practices that transformed socialist rhetoric and symbols into nostalgic icons endure, Ostalgie in its current incarnation is frequently dominated by a certain cynicism, irony, and parody. There is widespread awareness reflected in discourses about Ostalgie, for example, of the ironic fact that the bust of Lenin is now an "advertising gag" for the film, that many of these East German products are now often produced by western German firms, sold by western German internet businesses, or stocked by Walmart. In its hypercommercial and self-parodying form, then, current practices of Ostalgie celebrate and naturalize capitalism as the inevitable outcome of socialism's demise.

Quite predictably, the film *Good Bye, Lenin!* and the subsequent Ostalgie boom have re-ignited familiar debates about the meanings, memories, and representations of the socialist past. One of the principal criticisms of Ostalgie is that it provides a means of eliding questions of complicity, responsibility, and accountability in relation to a burdened GDR past; in other words, that it glorifies what had been a brutal regime. While these observations raise legitimate concerns about representations of the past and thereby contribute to ongoing debates about historical memory, dismissals and attempts to belittle Ostalgie may also be viewed as part of a larger hegemonic project to devalue eastern German critiques of the politics of re-unification. More generally, the allegations of "mereness" and accusations of neglect, as well as the culturally specific practices of Ostalgie, both reflect and constitute struggles over the control and appropriation of historical knowledge, shared memories, and personal recollections—all of which interact in highly complicated ways (cf. Lass 1994).

The anthropologist Caroline Humphrey has recently asked whether the category "postsocialism" still makes sense given the diverse range of postsocialist contexts and trajectories (Humphrey 2001). It's a reasonable question, and something people like us should probably think about. Like Humphrey, though, I would argue that the category retains its usefulness for a number of reasons, particularly as long as the socialist past remains a prime reference point for many people in their own personal histories and memories as they struggle to make sense of the present. The category will remain compelling, it seems to me, as long as socialism continues to have an active social life that people engage and make meaningful in cultural practices and productions.

But it remains important for another, perhaps more pressing, reason; postsocialism, with its implicit temporal positioning of relating to the present in terms of the past, offers the possibility of positing socialism in relation to its world historical other: capitalism. Verdery has argued that "the context in which we should assess postsocialism's emerging forms is—far more than before—the international one of global capital flows" (Verdery 1999: 25). I would expand on this insight to suggest that it also works the other way around: postsocialism's "emerging forms" provide a means of assessing and critiquing global capitalism.

This brings us, in a rather roundabout way, back to the topic of memory, nostalgia, and the present. For it is in the realm of memory—whether through routine cultural practices like the consumption or display of East German things or mass-mediated representations—that capitalism's world historical other (socialism) is given meaning and significance, even if a parodied one. The various domains in which memory is produced, negotiated, and deployed can be where capitalist forms and practices are both contested *and* affirmed.

In a rich article on millennial capitalism, John and Jean Comaroff aim to interrogate "the experiential contradictions at the core of neoliberal capitalism," suggesting that many of these contradictions are most visible in "so-called post-revolutionary societies" (Comaroff and Comaroff 2000: 298). They continue by noting that "a good deal is to be learned about the historical implications of the current moment by eavesdropping on the popular anxieties to be heard in such places" (299). Following their lead, in addition to the fieldwork I have conducted in different regions of the former GDR, I also attempted a form of "eavesdropping" in its "postmodern" version: by "lurking" on internet bulletin boards and discussion groups focusing on themes of Ostalgie and German-German relations. In a lengthy internet forum devoted to the film, located on the *Good Bye, Lenin!* website (www.good-bye-lenin.de), I "overheard" mostly enthusiastic reviews of the film as well as predictable debates about the phenomenon of Ostalgie. There were also voices like "Eike," articulating a minority but not uncommon sentiment:

> The fall of the Wall that was staged for the mother's benefit at the end of the film is exactly what I might have wished for myself.... Whoever criticizes the GDR for being oppressive and undemocratic has NOT TRULY lived and worked in capitalism.

Other postings expressed similar reactions: "I could have cried during Sigmund Jähn's speech," one contributor wrote, "it really spoke to me"; or, "the perspective of a society with no terror of consumerism" or "elbow society broadens one's horizons, especially now when capitalism isn't functioning very well anymore."

Such are the contexts, large and small, for the production and circulation of historical memory. My suggestion for thinking about the role of memory in the postsocialist present calls for us to think out of what Bruce Grant has called the "socialist-postsocialist box" and engage with larger theoretical debates about the meanings of the market, the contradictions of millennial capitalism, and the cultures of neoliberalism, among other topics (Grant 2006). Following the social life of socialism through its various forms, uses, and trajectories has the potential of illuminating these and other phenomena. As one instantiation of socialism's social life, *Good Bye, Lenin!* as a mass-mediated history of the present has contributed to the construction of cultural realities that themselves are a function of the political landscape they inhabit and reproduce.

NOTES

—⁂—

INTRODUCTION

1. "Historical Memory/Historisches Gedächtnis." Conference held at the Internationales Forschungszentrum Kulturwissenschaften (IFK), Vienna, March 19–21, 1998.

1. VOICES AT THE WALL

1. An alphabetical directory of names assists visitors in locating an individual name on the Wall by indicating the panel and line number where the name is inscribed.

2. A tomb honoring an unknown Vietnam soldier was dedicated at Arlington National Cemetery in 1984.

3. I use the term "dominant narrative" in a manner similar to the way it is employed by Edward M. Bruner in his discussion of narrative structures, their influence on ethnography, and how these change over time (Bruner 1986b).

4. "Of Heart and Mind: The Serene Grace of the Vietnam Men," *Washington Post,* May 16, 1981, B4.

5. I have based my account of the memorial's dedication and National Salute to Vietnam Veterans on the extensive coverage of the events in the *Washington Post;* reports in popular periodicals such as *Time, Newsweek, U.S. News and World Report;* Scruggs and Swerdlow's book; and discussions with people who participated in the ceremonies, including veterans, National Park Service volunteers, Jan Scruggs, and Robert Doubek.

6. A firebase was a safe place, an artillery base camp, where soldiers were relieved of their responsibilities of combat, escaped the war, and could be together.

7. Defined by Barbara Myerhoff: "Definitional ceremonies deal with problems of invisibility and marginality; they are strategies that provide opportunities for being seen and in one's own terms, garnering witnesses to one's worth, vitality, and being" (Myerhoff 1986: 267).

8. *Washington Post,* November 15, 1982, 1A.

9. VVMC is an abbreviation for Vietnam Veterans Memorial Collection; the number following the x (e.g., x1901) indicates the accession number assigned to a particular item by the collection curator. I have indicated items I saw at the memorial during fieldwork simply with a VVMC because I do not know their accession numbers.

10. This was pointed out to me by Steve Bavisotto and Duery Felton, curators of the Vietnam Veterans Memorial Collection.

11. "Remembrance on a Train: From Seattle and the Plains, Vietnam Veterans Make Pilgrimage to a Reunion at the Wall," *Washington Post,* November 10, 1984.

12. MIA/POW (missing in action/prisoner of war) groups are permitted to set up tables at a prescribed distance from the memorial to educate the public on the issue of American servicemen still missing in Southeast Asia. Many of the tables are manned by Vietnam veterans. The first such group set up a 24-hour vigil at the memorial soon after its dedication, vowing to remain there until all missing servicemen were identified or returned.

At times there may be six separate groups distributing literature, talking with visitors, and selling bracelets with the name of a missing serviceman or T-shirts. Differing in political perspectives and fund-raising techniques as well as strategies for change, there is much infighting among these groups.

13. However, suicides that occurred in Vietnam are included among the names of the casualties.

14. Haines argues the memorial has produced a consensual memory of Vietnam and that the theme of healing is an "administrative version" of Vietnam that serves dominant political interests. This argument is based solely upon literature about the memorial rather than any time spent there. My fieldwork experience disproves Haines's thesis; any attempts to impose meaning on the memorial by "administrative power" to fit conservative political agenda have not been successful. Indeed, Reagan's visits and speeches at the memorial have been criticized and even ridiculed.

15. The late Pegi Donovan also compiled information on local, state, and international Vietnam veterans memorials for future publication, which she generously shared with me.

16. The articles' titles are also indicative of the discourse's emphasis on individual memories of the war: "From Voices Free or Fettered Comes a Call to Remember" and "Catching Up with Life: The Return of Everett Alvarez," in the *Washington Post*, Sunday, November 12, 1989.

2. CONSUMER RITES

1. I have chosen the hyphenated terms "re-unification" and "re-unified" to refer to the union of the FRG and GDR on October 3, 1990. Although I am aware of the arguments pointing to the teleological and ideological implications of the term "reunification" as well as the fact that the territories united in 1990 do not represent Germany in an earlier state, I am also concerned that the omission of any term reflecting a previous union of this region as one country silences critical elements of Germany's past as well: the fact, for example, that Germany was divided in 1945 for a reason. Further, the area that I discuss in this book has experienced a resumption of earlier economic and social ties across regional, religious, and former national borders. My use of the hyphen is thus a sort of compromise, an effort to avoid the naturalizing connotations of "re-unification" while reflecting an awareness of certain histories of divisions and recent restorations. At times I do use the word "unity," however, as a literal translation of the official German term *Einheit*.

2. Advertisers targeting Ossis were particularly focused on this theme, best exemplified by the cigarette brand West billboards throughout the GDR in the years after the Wende: "Test the West."

3. The emergence of consumption as an important topic for study in the context of postsocialist transitions is highlighted, among others, by Berdahl, Bunzl, and Lampland 2000; Berdahl 1999b and 2005b; Creed 2002; Humphrey 2002; Konstantinov 1996; Mandel and Humphrey 2002; Patico and Caldwell 2002; and Verdery 1996.

4. See Bauman 1992; Borneman 1991; Drakulić 1991.

5. See Berdahl 1999a; Friedman 1994; Liechty 2003; McKracken 1988; D. Miller 1994, 1995a, 1995b; Orlove and Rutz 1989.

6. On consumption and resistance, see, for example, Fiske 1989; Hebdidge 1988; McRobbie 1989; Willis 1990.

7. See Berdahl 1999a; Caldwell 2004; Dunn 2004; Hann 1993; Lampland 1995; Nagengast 1991; Verdery 1996.

8. My understanding of the borderland concept owes much to Gupta and Ferguson (1992) and Rosaldo (1989), among others.

9. See Borneman (1991: 130–149) for a discussion of East Germans' need for "the fantasyland" of the West.

10. In German: Überholen ohne einzuholen.

11. "Camp" has been a topic for American cultural critics as well as anthropologists (cf. Ivy 1995; Ross 1980; S. Stewart 1993). Most relevant to my understanding here is Ross's observation that camp parodies "the thing on its way out" (in Ivy 1995: 56).

12. See Wilk 1994 for a discussion of temporal meanings of goods in a colonial context.

13. Stein (1993) and Brednich (1990) discuss in detail Trabi jokes and their identification of East Germans with "the inferior product of their state" (Stein 1993: 40).

14. Stein (1993) points out the DM-nationalism was not a new phenomenon in the West, and argues that Trabi jokes were an expression of a perceived threat to this West German identity.

15. As one popular saying described the election results: *Nur Kohl bringt die Kohle* (Only Kohl will bring us the money/cabbage) (in Borneman 1991: 231).

16. See also Korff 1990.

17. This practice stems from a socialist economy of scarcity, when the issue was not where a product might be but whether a store even had it.

18. William Kelleher (2003) similarly points out how boundary maintenance in Northern Ireland is sustained through the reading of bodies.

19. Numerous writings on the politics of everyday life in socialist societies have highlighted as well as nuanced an "us versus them" opposition between citizens and the state. A very limited sampling includes Drakulić 1991; Kideckel 1993; Lampland 1995; Milosz 1991; Nagengast 1991; Verdery 1996; Watson 1994.

20. In *Der Spiegel* 27 (1995), p. 95.

21. This field of play is largely new here: under socialism, when commodities and clothing were either uniform or scarce, people took what they could get. Most villagers' taste in clothing, for example, was determined by the hand-me-downs sent by western relatives. "I used to wear that dress every day," one woman recalled, pointing to an old photograph of herself, "just because it was from the West. Now of course I know they just sent us the things they didn't want any more." While people creatively used their limited resources to shape different styles and expressions of distinction under socialism, the range of possibilities—and the meanings of those possibilities—have changed.

22. See, for example, DeSoto 1994; Einhorn 1993; Funk and Mueller 1993; Gal 1994; Rosenberg 1991; Verdery 1996.

23. *Frühschoppen* is the name of the Sunday morning festivities during Kirmes (the annual celebration in honor of the church's dedication) when, traditionally, lots of alcohol gets consumed by the male participants.

24. For a brief history of *Gleichstellungsstellen*, with its origins in 1980s West Germany, and an analysis of differences and conceptualizations of these offices after re-unification as reflective of differences among feminist concerns in the old and new federal states, see Ferree 1991.

25. *Abwicklung,* meaning "to unwind" as well as "to liquidate," entailed the restructuring of East German universities through the dissolution of departments and institutes, dismissal of East German faculty members (20% of professors and 60% of Mittelbau or intermediate ranks [Maier 1997: 305]), and the recruitment of West German academics and concomitant influx of West German research agendas.

26. The Berlin examples stem from an article in *Der Spiegel* 27 (1995). In the last 10 years, this cultural phenomenon of Ostalgie has expanded enormously, resulting in trivia games, books, mail order catalogs, exhibits, and television programs, among many other products. The commodification of Ostalgie arguably reached its peak in 2004 with the release of the widely popular and critically acclaimed film *Good Bye, Lenin!* For more on the shifting meanings and practices of Ostalgie, see Berdahl 1999b, 2005b.

27. For a notable exception, see, for example, Mintz 1985.

28. Defined by Herzfeld as a "collective representation of an Edenic order—a time before time—in which the balanced perfection of social relations has not yet suffered the decay that affects everything human" (1997a: 109).

29. For a sensitive and incisive account of the history and complexities of production ideologies in relation to actual labor practices in the GDR, see Lüdtke 1994.

30. For discussions of the causes and consequences of East Germany's deindustrialization, see De Soto (2000b) and Geyer (1994).

31. In "Wehre dich täglich," *Der Spiegel* 52 (1993), pp. 46–48.

32. To transform a concept suggested by Fredric Jameson (1989).

33. The cult of the Trabi continues to this day, although most commonly in the form of parody and camp. Several eastern German cities offer "Trabi Tours" or "Trabi Safaris," and the "two stroke" is exhibited in many museum displays. There are websites and clubs for Trabi fans, who meet to exchange memories and auto parts. For more on the Trabi, see Berdahl 2001.

34. Indeed, there was much grumbling in eastern Germany about the fact that the western German music video station refused to play Nieman's song.

3. *"(N)OSTALGIE"* FOR THE PRESENT

This chapter is based on ethnographic fieldwork in the city of Leipzig during the summer of 1998 as well as research conducted since 1990 in the former East German border village of Kella, including an extended stay in 1990–1992 and follow-up research visits in 1994, 1996, and 1998 (see Berdahl 1999a). Earlier versions were presented at the 1997 meetings of the American Anthropological Association, a conference on historical memory sponsored by the Internationales Forschungszentrum Kulturwissenschaften in Vienna, Austria, and the European Cultural Studies Workshop at the University of Michigan, Ann Arbor; I wish to thank members of those audiences for their comments and questions. My thanks also go to John Baldwin, Matti Bunzl, Richard Handler, Bruce Owens, and the four anonymous reviewers for *Ethnos* for their incisive comments on various versions of this essay.

1. *Ossi* is a colloquial term for eastern Germans.

2. Post-communist nostalgia is not unique to the GDR, although very little has been written about this phenomenon here or elsewhere in eastern Europe. For a very different angle, see Boym 1995.

3. The paper is thus also situated within contemporary discussions of history and

memory, a literature too vast to cite here. A relevant limited sample includes: discussions of "official" and "unofficial" memories (Watson 1994); collective memory (Connerton 1989; Halbwachs 1992; Nora 1989); the dialogical relationship between objects and memories (Berdahl 1994; Sturken 1997); commemorations and national memory (Bodnar 1991; Zerubavel 1995); history and memory in relation to Germany's burdened past (Maier 1988); oppositional and counter-memories (Bunzl 1998; Foucault 1977; Popular Memory Group 1982; Watson 1994).

4. "Camp" has been a topic for American cultural critics as well as anthropologists (cf. Ivy 1995; Ross 1980; Stewart 1984). Most relevant to my understanding here is Ross's observation that camp parodies "the thing on its way out" (in Ivy 1995: 56).

5. For an illuminating discussion of immediate post-Wall consumerism, see Borneman 1991 and 1992.

6. One of the tragic stories about the disposal of East German products during this period concerned the discarding of books published in the GDR. There were reports of authors going to waste dumps to retrieve their published works.

7. Although Trabi jokes predate re-unification and were told throughout the GDR immediately following the fall of the Wall, they took on new meaning when re-appropriated in the tellings of West Germans. For more on jokes (including Trabi jokes) in the first years after the Wende, see Brednich 1990 and Stein 1993.

8. *Abwicklung*, meaning "to unwind" as well as "to liquidate," entailed the restructuring of East German universities through the dissolution of departments and institutes, dismissal of East German faculty members (20% of professors and 60% of Mittelbau or intermediate ranks [Maier 1997: 305]), and the recruitment of West German academics and concomitant influx of West German research agendas.

9. "Turning point," the term used to refer to the fall of the Berlin Wall and collapse of socialist rule.

10. For a sensitive and incisive account of the history and complexities of production ideologies in relation to actual labor practices in the GDR, see Lüdtke 1994.

11. For discussions of the causes and consequences of East Germany's deindustrialization, see De Soto (2000b) and Geyer (1994).

12. For example, the exhibits Wunderwirtschaft: DDR Konsumkultur und Produktdesign in den 60er Jahren in Berlin; and Tempolinsen und P2: Altagskultur der DDR, first in Eisenhüttenstadt and then Berlin.

13. Defined by Herzfeld as a "collective representation of an Edenic order—a time before time—in which the balanced perfection of social relations has not yet suffered the decay that affects everything human" (1997a: 109).

14. In this sense, my analysis of nostalgia in the context of radical deindustrialization in the GDR resonates with Steinmetz's provocative analysis of right-wing violence ("nostalgia expressed as violence") in the context of contemporary Germany's transition from Fordism to Postfordism (Steinmetz 1994).

15. *Junge Pioneere* (Young Pioneers) and *FDJ* (*Freier Deutscher Jugend*) were two of three socialist youth organizations in the GDR.

16. In *Der Spiegel* 55 (1996).

17. The East German Film Society.

18. *Eigen-Sinn* (one's own sense or one's own meaning) is a multi-faceted term denoting self-will, self-affirmation, re-appropriation, and playful autonomy. It is a central concept in Lüdtke's analysis of workers' everyday life and shopfloor dynamics (Lüdtke 1993a;

see also Lüdtke 1993b), but has far broader and very useful implications for theorizing the dynamics of power, alienated social relations, and the politics of everyday life more generally.

19. *Freitag,* December 20, 1996, p. 19.

20. To transform a phrase of the Comaroffs (1991).

21. In *Tagesspiegel,* March 11, 1997, p. 26.

4. "GO, TRABI, GO!"

1. I have chosen the hyphenated terms "re-unification" and "re-unified" to refer to the union of the FRG and GDR on October 3, 1990. Although I am aware of the arguments pointing to the teleological and ideological implications of the term "re-unification" as well as the fact that the territories united in 1990 do not represent Germany in an earlier state, I am also concerned that the omission of any term reflecting a previous union of this region as one country silences critical elements of Germany's past as well: the fact, for example, that Germany was divided in 1945 for a reason. My use of the hyphen is thus a sort of compromise, an effort to avoid the naturalizing connotations of "re-unification" while reflecting a sensitivity to certain histories of divisions and recent restorations.

2. I should also add at the outset that the idea for this paper is not my own. It stems from a lively conversation that took place 9 years ago near the bike racks by Haskell Hall at the University of Chicago. Jim Fernandez and I had each just returned from relatively brief visits to a Germany still in the throes of immediate post-Wall euphoria, disorientation, and unease. During the course of our conversation he suggested writing, and perhaps co-authoring, a paper on the Trabi. It has taken me a while to get around to doing this, but, like much of Jim's other commentary and advice over the years, the idea stuck with me.

3. *Auto Zeitung* magazine gave the Trabi honorary top billing in its 1989 test results, for example, and a Trabi was included in the centerfold of *Autobild's* "Best Autos of 1989" (*Time,* January 1, 1990, p. 39).

4. *Time,* January 1, 1990, p. 39.

5. On Trabi jokes, see Brednich 1990 and Stein 1993.

6. *Abwicklung,* meaning "to unwind" as well as "to liquidate," entailed the restructuring of East German universities through the dissolution of departments and institutes, dismissal of East German faculty members (20% of professors and 60% of Mittelbau or intermediate ranks [Maier 1997: 305]), and the recruitment of West German academics and concomitant influx of West German research agendas.

7. Although generated and experienced differently in form and content (Abwicklung was viewed as an affront and degradation by eastern German academics, e.g., whereas the toppling of socialist monuments and memorials was divisive and often done by GDR anticommunists), such practices have generally been grouped together in an eastern German discourse of oppositional solidarity against western hegemony.

8. Trabi fan clubs do exist in West Germany and elsewhere, although they are mostly concentrated in the former GDR.

9. I am drawing here on media representations and individual accounts.

10. In *Neue Revue* 27 (July 1, 1999).

11. In *Die Welt,* November 26, 1999.

12. "Das Rote Gespenst," *Der Spiegel* 10 (March 1, 1999), pp. 22–33.

13. Christiane Peitz, "Alles so schön grau hier," *Die Zeit* 45 (October 28, 1999).

14. See Rofel (1998) on nostalgic narratives in post-Mao China.

5. MIXED DEVOTIONS

This chapter is part of research that has been funded by the Fulbright Commission, the University of Chicago Division of Social Sciences, and a James Bryant Conant Fellowship in German and European Studies at the Center for European Studies, Harvard University. I am deeply grateful to these institutions for their support. Thanks as well to John N. Baldwin, Edward M. Bruner, Hermine De Soto, Nora Dudwick, Renate Lellep Fernandez, Kari Robinson, and Siegfried Weichlein for their helpful comments and insights. I dedicate this piece, with love and admiration, to the two strong women who inspired it.

1. Critiques of ethnography that have called these dichotomies (observer/observed, insider/outsider, self/other) into question have argued that they are products of a notion of ethnographic authority that has been used to perpetuate an ideal (and arguably fiction) of objectivity. See Clifford 1983, 1986; Dubisch 1996; Handler 1993; as well as more general examinations of the fieldwork encounter (Crapanzano 1980; Myerhoff 1978; Rabinow 1977). Because feminist ethnography has often been particularly concerned with the implications and transgressions of "self" versus "other" or "West" versus "the Rest" dichotomies (Abu-Lughod 1990b, 1991; Behar 1993; Behar and Gordon 1995; Tsing 1993), feminist ethnographers have more frequently described their relationships in the field as friendships (e.g., Abu-Lughod 1995; Behar 1993; McBeth 1993).

2. Anthropologists who have worked intensively with a particular individual, as in a life-history project, are also more likely to address issues of attachment, distance, and friendship in relation to a specific relationship and/or the fieldwork encounter in general. See, for example, Behar 1993; Crapanzano 1980; Dwyer 1982; McBeth 1993. See also Silverman 2000.

3. The village in which I conducted my fieldwork is located within the Eichsfeld region, for centuries a Catholic enclave in Protestant central Germany with its origins as an ecclesiastical territory. A large majority of village residents are practicing Catholics. See Berdahl 1999a.

4. The *Focolare* movement, started in southern Italy in 1943 and officially sanctioned by Pope Jean Paul II, now exists in over 180 countries with several million "adherents" and 80,000 core members (Urquhart 1995: 6).

5. Complaints of the movement's divisiveness are not unique to this congregation (cf. Urquhart 1995).

6. The Catholic church, it should be noted, was a minority religion in the GDR. Whereas in 1986 the Protestant church claimed 6.5 million members (Ramet 1991), there were only 1 million Catholics, or approximately 6% of the population, in the GDR (Fischer 1991).

7. One of the principal reasons for this, I was told, is that Father Münster had an unfortunate tendency to ignore the confessional oath of secrecy; occasionally items discussed in confession were included in his sermons. Although the identities of the persons involved were never revealed, in a small community like this one, they didn't have to be.

8. My husband, John, was especially affected by this. Because the priest was often engaged in power struggles with several village husbands over the time commitments of their wives to the Focolare movement, for example, Father Münster often used John's support of me and my research as an example of the independence all men should give their wives. On the day John left Germany, the priest falsely told a community gathering about a glowing assessment John had given of the Focolare movement. It may be

that Father Münster focused on John more frequently because their relationship was less problematic than the one between me and the priest (John was not the one asking probing questions of the priest and his parishioners), although I was not immune to similar misrepresentations.

9. I have since learned that the Focolare movement actively enjoins its members to rid themselves of all "attachments," including to things, persons, ideas, work, or relatives, that interfere with fulfilling the movement's ideals (Urquhart 1995: 18). Father Münster was thus largely echoing instructions of the movement's leaders.

10. Although the kitchen was frequented primarily by villagers most actively involved in the church as members of the parish council, board of directors, or Focolare discussion group, Father Münster's efforts to create a relaxed atmosphere in which many people felt at home at his house made the kitchen more accessible than in many parish rectories.

11. From the beginning, Father Münster had addressed us with the informal pronoun *Du* rather than the formal *Sie* he used with all parishioners. It was a gesture of multiple, if not fully conscious, intentions that initiated our relationship as one of equals distinct and separate from others in the community, thereby extending to us a welcome approval from a visible authority figure as well as constructing an association with us that I believe the priest found useful.

12. While it was true that Johanna's husband rarely acknowledged or discussed her illness with her, I believe this was a product of his own fear, denial, and emotional capacities rather than indifference.

13. I recognize that a similar situation could easily occur in the context of research in the United States and am not attributing this dilemma to cultural differences among Europe, Germany, and the United States (a notion that implies a certain boundedness and homogeneity of "culture" that I reject), but to cultural differences in class, education, and religion stemming in part from divergent life experiences under two different political economic systems as well as subsequent negotiations of change following the collapse of socialism described here.

14. For discussions of the particular challenges of doing fieldwork in Europe, see, for example, Herzfeld 1987; Jaffe 1993; de-Pina-Cabral and Campbell 1992; Sheehan 1993.

15. For a compelling account of mutual expectations in fieldwork, see Kondo 1990.

16. I am indebted to Behar's (1991) discussion of displaced emotions in relation to her grandfather's death and her study of death and memory in a Spanish village for inspiring much of my perspective here.

17. For a more detailed analysis of these transformations, particularly in relation to a dynamic between popular faith and institutionalized religion, see Berdahl 1999a.

18. As a village in the high-security border zone, this community was especially the object of state efforts to root out religion in the GDR. The local pilgrimage chapel was enclosed by the border fence, for example, thus making it inaccessible for nearly 40 years, and church services were occasionally prohibited here during the 1950s.

19. "Popular religion," Caroline Brettell writes, "applies to any social situation where a conflict or dialectic emerges between official religious models proposed by the ecclesiastical hierarchy and 'unofficial' forms" (Brettell 1990: 55). Constraints of space prevent me from going into detail here about the changing dynamics of, and interplay between, popular faith and institutionalized religion before and after the collapse of socialism (see Berdahl 1999a).

20. See Berdahl 1999a.

21. Telephone ethnography, a relatively new phenomenon that is particularly pertinent for anthropologists working in Europe, has interesting implications for the changing dynamic between "ourselves" and "the field" by extending relationships beyond the ethnographer's departure from the field through the immediacy of telephone communication. In this sense, telephone ethnography arguably has contributed to the blurring of boundaries between these two traditionally opposed categories.

22. Renato Rosaldo (1984), in his poignant and well-known essay "Grief and a Headhunter's Rage," was one of the first anthropologists to reflect on how experiences of people and ideas in the field may shape an anthropologist's sense of self and life events. See also Abu-Lughod 1995; Kondo 1990; Riesman 1977; Dubisch 1996.

23. From personal letter to Edward M. Bruner, excerpted in Bruner 1993.

6. THE SPIRIT OF CAPITALISM AND THE BOUNDARIES OF CITIZENSHIP IN POST-WALL GERMANY

Different versions of this paper were presented at meetings of the Council of European Studies, at a conference on German national identity at Emory University, and at the Center for 21st Century Studies at the University of Wisconsin–Milwaukee. I am grateful to these audiences as well as to two anonymous *CSSH* reviewers for their probing questions and incisive comments. I also thank Robert Berdahl, Kriszti Fehervery, Andreas Glaeser, and Alf Lüdtke for conversations that have enriched this work. Thanks also to Ursula Dahlinghaus for her assistance in the final preparation of this manuscript. Funding for the research was provided by a University of Minnesota McKnight Land-Grant Professorship and a Fulbright Fellowship. Finally, as always, I owe a debt of gratitude to John Baldwin, who made this research, and so much more, possible.

1. See also Robert Foster's recent and ethnographically rich study of the place of commodities and consumption in Papua New Guinean nation building (2002).

2. T. H. Marshall's 1949 lectures on "Citizenship and Social Class" have provided the starting point most contemporary citizenship debates. Marshall traces the progression of citizenship as an expansion of rights: civil rights, originating in eighteenth-century Enlightenment thought; political rights, stemming from the French Revolution and involving the participation in politics through voting or representation; and social rights, or the guarantee of economic welfare and social security by the twentieth-century welfare state.

3. See Zunz (1999) and L. Cohen (2003); see also debates about links between the consumer and industrial revolution (McKendrick, Brewer, and Plumb 1982).

4. Robert Foster has similarly argued: "Commodity consumption, or the decline thereof for many people, has thus become a politically charged arena in which frustrations about the nation-state are often expressed" (Foster 2002: 9).

5. See Borneman (1991: 130–149) for a discussion of East Germans' "need" for the "fantasyland" of the West.

6. I have chosen the hyphenated term "re-unified" in the paper to refer to the union of the FRG and GDR on October 3, 1990. Although I am aware of the arguments pointing to the teleological and ideological implications of the term "reunification" as well as the fact that the territories united in 1990 do not represent Germany in an earlier state, I am also concerned that the omission of any term reflecting a previous union of this region as one country silences critical elements of Germany's past as well: for example, the fact that Germany was divided in 1945 for a reason. My use of the hyphen is thus a compromise, an

effort to avoid the naturalizing connotations of "re-unification" while reflecting an awareness of certain histories of divisions and recent restorations.

7. See Berdahl (1999b) for a discussion of the connections between eastern products, memory, and identity in the former GDR.

8. The term stems from Joseph (1999), who borrows from Appadurai's taxonomy of "scapes" (1996) to describe "vignettes of nomadic citizenship in ambivalent relations to official and available discourses about private and public citizenship" (1999: 13). My usage of the term is slightly different here and is intended to suggest multiple articulations of global flows and nationalizing processes through which contemporary citizenship discourses and practices are produced.

9. Betts also makes the similar point that "East Germany's political destiny, too, was built with the very mortar of western social politics for the last half-century, namely, consumerism as political legitimacy."

10. Much recent literature has richly addressed socialist consumer culture. See Merkel (1998), Kaminksy (2001), Pence (2001), and for the GDR, Stitziel (2003).

11. German: "*Ich leiste was, ich leiste mir was,*" 10th SED Parteitag Poster, 1981.

12. This 17% unemployment figure is actually quite modest in eastern Germany, where some regions suffer double that level.

13. Much of downtown property in Leipzig was owned by Jewish families who perished in the Holocaust. Tracing heirs has been difficult and time-consuming.

14. Initial expectations for economic growth have not materialized, however, and investment and construction in Leipzig has exceeded demand. Many new and renovated office and retail spaces, hotel rooms, and living quarters remain empty.

15. It should be noted that the experience of these transitions has been very generation-specific. Although a younger generation of eastern Germans in their twenties and early thirties have little memory of life in the GDR and lead lives that look very much like their peers in western Germany, their cultural identities and political outlooks are very much shaped by the experience of unemployment, disillusionment, and resentment of western German hegemony throughout the former GDR.

16. See the special 2002 theme issue of *Ethnos,* "Consumers Exiting Socialism: Ethnographic Perspectives on Daily Life in Post-Communist Europe," edited by Jennnifer Patico and Melissa L. Caldwell (67[3]: 285–294).

17. Thanks to Gerald Creed for this anecdote.

7. LOCAL HERO, NATIONAL CROOK

1. *Der Spiegel* 28 (July 8, 1996), p. 98

2. *Der Spiegel* 17 (July 1, 1996), p. 95.

3. *Der Spiegel* 28 (July 8, 1996), p. 91.

4. In http:/rhein-zeitung.de/freizeit/kino/galerie/peanuts/rezpeanu.html.

5. And indeed it appears that banks knew about his tricks and decided to play along (Daniel Sturm, personal communication).

6. In *Leipziger Volkszeitung,* July 1, 1997, p. 11.

7. *Der Spiegel* 21 (1995), p. 99.

8. *Leipziger Volkszeitung,* December 24, 1997, p. 1.

9. *Der Spiegel* 27 (July 1, 1996), p. 93.

10. In *Kreuzer* 1 (20/00), p. 19. It should be noted that immediately after Schneider's

disappearance, local institutions in Leipzig—including the chamber of commerce, the municipal government, and workers' unions—banded together to address the crisis. A telephone hotline for abandoned workers was created, taxes were deferred, and the city as well as several local firms assumed responsibility for many of the unfinished building projects. As a result, no local businesses were forced to close because of Schneider's failures.

11. *Leipziger Volkseitung,* April 9, 2004.

12. In *Kreuzer* 6 (1995), p. 20.

13. *Kreuzer* 6 (1995), p. 21.

14. *Der Spiegel* 49 (December 6, 1999), p. 112.

15. In *Kreuzer* 1 (2000), p. 19.

16. *Kreuzer* 7 (1995), p. 11.

8. EXPRESSIONS OF EXPERIENCE AND EXPERIENCES OF EXPRESSION

Funding for this research was provided by a Fulbright grant and a University of Minnesota McKnight Land-Grant Professorship. This article is a revised version of a paper that was presented at the University of Michigan–Dearborn in March 2002 and at the University of Michigan–Ann Arbor in April 2004. I thank the audiences at these lectures for their valuable questions and comments. Above all, I thank Ed Bruner for introducing me to anthropology and encouraging me to make it my profession.

1. BerlineOnline: Romantiker im Jahrhundertschritt: Der Maler und Grafiker Wolfgang Mattheuer wird heute 70. http://www.berlinonline.de/ . . . ner_zeitung/archiv/1997/kultur/0002/.

2. Http://www.dhm.de/lemo/html/biograpfien/MattheuerWolfgang.

3. In Express Online, wysiwyg://235/http:www.express.de/bonn/museen/1392214 .html.

4. See, for example, Berdahl 1997; Betts 2000; Ten Dyke 2001; Silberman and Hermand 2000.

5. For a sophisticated discussion of the Bonn museum origins in the context of wider debates about the politics of German history and memory, see Maier 1988.

6. Leipzig, known as the "city of heroes," was where the Monday demonstrations of 1989 began. On October 9, over 70,000 citizens of the city took to the streets despite warnings of orders to police to shoot; the absence of violence on this date signaled that the demonstrations against the state could proceed peacefully, and participant demands and numbers grew after that.

7. Hanna Schissler (2001) has pointed to the dangers of perpetuating Cold War narratives through such comparisons.

8. One of the many elaborate surveillance practices of the Stasi entailed the collection of scent specimens of regime opponents in preserving jars for use with scent detection dogs.

9. This notion of the concept is consistent with the Bonn museum's agenda and discourse as well. (See Maier 1988.)

10. *Neue Zürcher Zeitung,* November 19, 1999, p. 5.

11. Rainer Eckert quoted in *Der Spiegel* 41 (October 1999), p. 19.

12. Associated Press World Stream—German. October 10, 1999.

13. In Christian Schmidt, "Leipzig: Die Siege rim Freudentaumel," *Junge Welt,* October 11, 1999. http://www.jungewelt.de.

14. Schäfer quoted on Haus der Geschichte website, http://www.hdg.de/Final/eng/oage 141.htm.

15. Deutschland, Stiftung Haus der Geschichte der Bundesrepublik 2001. Einsichten: Diktatur und Widerstand in der DDR. Leipzig: Reclam Verlag.

16. This was reported to me by an employee of the museum shop, located at the exit to the exhibits.

17. *Abwicklung,* meaning "to unwind" as well as "to liquidate," entailed the restructuring of East German universities through the dissolution of departments and institutes, dismissal of East German faculty members (20% of professors and 60% of mid-level lecturers), and the appointment of West German academics and concomitant influx of West German research agendas. See Maier 1997.

18. See also Ten Dyke 2001.

19. For example, Bauman 1992; Betts 2000; Borneman 1992; Drakulić 1991.

20. The play with words cannot be captured in translation here as the German term, "geil," draws on the different colloquial meanings of "cool" and "horny."

21. These are well-known brand names of East German products.

22. German:

> Sie möchten gute Bundesbürger sein
> Und kaufen in der Kaufhalle Ostprodukte ein
> Spee und Florena, Rotkäppchen und Fit
> Wie Lange macht das der Verfassungsschutz noch mit?

REFERENCES

—᠁—

Abu-Lughod, Lila. 1990a. "The Romance of Resistance: Tracing Transformations of Power through Bedouin Women." *American Ethnologist* 17: 41–55.

———. 1990b. "Can There Be a Feminist Ethnography?" *Women and Performance* 5(1): 7–27.

———. 1991. "Writing against Culture." In Richard Fox, ed., *Recapturing Anthropology*. Santa Fe, N.M.: School of American Research Press, 17–43.

———. 1995. "A Tale of Two Pregnancies." In Ruth Behar and Deborah Gordon, eds., *Women Writing Culture*. Berkeley: University of California Press.

Anzaldúa, Gloria. 1987. *Borderlands/La Frontera: The New Mestiza*. San Franciso: Spinsters/ Aunt Lute Books.

Appadurai, Arjun. 1986. "Introduction: Commodities and the Politics of Value." In Arjun Appadurai, ed., *The Social Life of Things: Commodities in Cultural Perspective*. Cambridge: Cambridge University Press, 3–63.

———. 1996. *Modernity at Large*. Minneapolis: University of Minnesota Press.

Asad, Talal, ed. 1973. *Anthropology and the Colonial Encounter*. London: Ithaca Press.

Badone, Ellen, ed. 1990. *Religious Orthodoxy and Popular Faith in European Society*. Princeton, N.J.: Princeton University Press.

Bakhtin, Mikhail. 1968. *Rabelais and His World*. Cambridge, Mass.: MIT Press.

———. 1981. *The Dialogic Imagination*. Austin: University of Texas Press.

Basso, Keith. 1984. "'Stalking with Stories': Names, Places and Moral Narratives among the Western Apache." In Edward Bruner, ed., *Text Play and Story: The Construction and Reconstruction of Self and Society*. Washington, D.C.: American Ethnological Society.

Baudrillard, Jean. 1988. *Selected Writings*. Mark Poster, ed. Stanford, Calif.: Stanford University Press.

Bauman, Zygmunt. 1992. *Intimations of Postmodernity*. New York: Routledge.

———. 1998. *Work, Consumerism and the New Poor*. Buckinghamshire, England: Open University Press.

Behar, Ruth. 1991. "Death and Memory: From Santa Maria Del Monte to Miami Beach." *Cultural Anthropology* 6(3): 346–384.

———. 1993. *Translated Woman: Crossing the Border with Esperanza's Story*. Boston: Beacon Press.

———. 1995. "Introduction: Out of Exile." In Ruth Behar and Deborah Gordon, eds., *Women Writing Culture*. Berkeley: University of California Press, 1–32.

Behar, Ruth, and Deborah Gordon, eds. 1995. *Women Writing Culture*. Berkeley: University of California Press.

Bellah, Robert. 1970. *Beyond Belief*. New York: Harper & Row.

Bennett, Tony. 1995. *The Birth of the Museum: History, Theory, Politics*. London: Routledge.

Berdahl, Daphne. 1994. "Voices at the Wall: Discourses of Self, History, and National Identity at the Vietnam Veterans Memorial." *History & Memory* 6(2): 88–124.

———. 1995. "Where the World Ended: Identity, Differentiation, and Unification in the German Borderland." Dissertation, Department of Anthropology, University of Chicago.

———. 1997. "Dis-Membering the Past: The Politics of Memory in the German Borderland." In Scott Denham, Irene Kacandes, and Jonathan Petropoulos, eds., *A User's Guide to German Cultural Studies*. Ann Arbor: University of Michigan Press, 309–332.

———. 1999a. *Where the World Ended: Re-Unification and Identity in the German Borderland*. Berkeley: University of California Press.

———. 1999b. "*(N)Ostalgie*' for the Present: Memory, Longing, and East German Things." *Ethnos* 64(2): 192–211.

———. 1999c. "Citizenship and Mass Consumption in Post-Wall Germany." Paper presented at the Department of Anthropology, University of Illinois, September 9, 1999.

———. 2000. "Introduction." In Daphne Berdahl, Matti Bunzl, and Martha Lampland, eds., *Altering States: Ethnographies of Transition in Eastern Europe and the Former Soviet Union*. Ann Arbor: University of Michigan Press.

———. 2001. "'Go, Trabi, Go!': Reflections on a Car and Its Symbolization over Time." *Anthropology and Humanism* 25(2): 131–141.

———. 2005a. "The Spirit of Capitalism and the Boundaries of Citizenship in Post-Wall Germany." *Comparative Studies in Society and History* 47(2): 235–251.

———. 2005b. "Expressions of Experience and Experiences of Expression: Museum Re-Presentations of GDR History." *Anthropology and Humanism* 30(2): 156–170.

Berdahl, Daphne, Matti Bunzl, and Martha Lampland, eds. 2000. *Altering States: Ethnographies of Transition in Eastern Europe and the Former Soviet Union*. Ann Arbor: University of Michigan Press.

Berlant, Lauren. 1997. *The Queen of America Goes to Washington City: Essays on Sex and Citizenship*. Durham, N.C.: Duke University Press.

Bertsch, Georg. 1990. "The Galapagos Islands of the Design World?" In Georg Bertsch, Ernst Hedler, and Matthias Dietz, eds., *SED: Stunning Eastern Design*. Cologne: Taschen Verlag.

Betts, Paul. 2000. "The Twilight of the Idols: East German Memory and Material Culture." *Journal of Modern History* 72(3): 731–765.

Blum, Shirley Neilson. 1987. "The National Vietnam War Memorial." *Arts Magazine* 59.

Bodnar, John. 1991. *Remaking America: Public Memory, Commemoration, and Patriotism in the Twentieth Century*. Princeton, N.J.: Princeton University Press.

Borneman, John. 1991. *After the Wall: East Meets West in the New Berlin*. New York: Basic Books.

———. 1992. *Belonging in the Two Berlins*. Cambridge: Cambridge University Press.

Bourdieu, Pierre. 1977. *Outline of a Theory of Practice*. Cambridge: Cambridge University Press.

———. 1984. *Distinction: A Social Critique of the Judgment of Taste*. Cambridge, Mass.: Harvard University Press.

Boyer, Dominic. 2008. "Nostomania for the Present." Paper presented at the Annual Meeting of the American Anthropological Association, San Francisco, November 19–23.

Boym, Svetlana. 1995. "From the Russian Soul to Postcommunist Nostalgia." *Representations* 49 (Winter): 133–166.

Brednich, Rolf. 1990. "Trabi-Witze: Ein populäres Erzählgenre in der Gegenwart." *Volkskunde in Niedersachsen* 7(1): 18–35.

Brettell, Caroline. 1990. "The Priest and His People: The Contractual Basis for Religious Practice in Rural Portugal." In Ellen Badone, ed., *Religious Orthodoxy and Popular Faith in European Society*. Princeton, N.J.: Princeton University Press, 55–75.

Brown, Keith. 2000. "Would the Real Nationalists Please Step Forward: Destructive Narration in Macedonia." In Hermine DeSoto and Nora Dudwick, eds., *Fieldwork Dilemmas: Anthropologists in Postsocialist States*. Madison: University of Wisconsin Press.

Broyles, William. 1986. "A Ritual for Saying Good-Bye." *U.S. News and World Report*, November 19.

Bruner, Edward M. 1984. "The Opening Up of Anthropology." In Edward Bruner, ed., *Text, Play and Story: The Construction and Reconstruction of Self and Society*. Washington, D.C.: American Ethnological Society.

———. 1986a. "Introduction." In Victor Turner and Edward M. Bruner, eds., *The Anthropology of Experience*. Urbana: University of Illinois Press.

———. 1986b. "Ethnography as Narrative." In Victor Turner and Edward M. Bruner, eds., *The Anthropology of Experience*. Urbana: University of Illinois Press, 139–155.

———. 1990. "Introduction: The Ethnographic Self and the Personal Self." In P. Benson, ed., *Anthropology and Literature*. Urbana: University of Illinois Press, 1–26.

———. 1993. "Lincoln's New Salem as a Contested Site." *Museum Anthropology* 17(3): 14–25.

———. 1994. "Abraham Lincoln as Authentic Reproduction: A Critique of Postmodernism." *American Anthropologist* 96(2): 397–415.

———. 2005. *Culture on Tour: Ethnographies of Travel*. Chicago: University of Chicago Press.

Bruner, Edward, and Phyllis Gorfain. 1984. "Dialogic Narration and the Paradoxes of Masada." In Edward Bruner, ed., *Text, Play and Story: The Construction and Reconstruction of Self and Society*. Washington, D.C.: American Ethnological Society.

Bunzl, Matti. 1998. "Counter-Memory and Modes of Resistance: The Uses of Fin-de-Siècle Vienna for Present-Day Austrian Jews." In Dagmar Lorenz and Renate Posthofen, eds., *Transforming the Centre, Eroding the Margins: Essays on Ethnic and Cultural Boundaries in German-Speaking Countries*. Columbia, S.C.: Camden House.

Burawoy, Michael, and János Lukács. 1992. *The Radiant Past: Ideology and Reality in Hungary's Road to Capitalism*. Chicago: University of Chicago Press.

Caldwell, Melissa. 2004. *Not by Bread Alone: Social Support in the New Russia*. Berkeley: University of California Press.

Canclini, Néstor García. 2001. *Consumers and Citizens: Globalization and Multicultural Conflicts*. George Yúdice, trans. Minneapolis: University of Minnesota Press.

Carter, Erica. 1997. *How German Is She? Postwar West German Reconstruction and the Consuming Woman*. Ann Arbor: University of Michigan Press.

Cheree, Carlson, and John Hocking. 1988. "Strategies of Redemption at the Vietnam Veterans Memorial." *Western Journal of Speech Communication* 52 (September): 203–215.

Clifford, James. 1983. "On Ethnographic Authority." *Representations* 1(2): 118–146.

———. 1986. "Introduction: Partial Truths." In James Clifford and George Marcus, eds., *Writing Culture: The Poetics and Politics of Ethnography*. Berkeley: University of California Press, 1–26.

Clifford, James, and George Marcus, eds. 1986. *Writing Culture: The Poetics and Politics of Ethnography*. Berkeley: University of California Press.

Cohen, David William. 1994. *The Combing of History*. Chicago: University of Chicago Press.

Cohen, Lizabeth. 1998. "The New Deal State and the Making of Citizen Consumers." In Susan Strasser, Charles McGovern, and Matthias Judt, eds., *Getting and Spending: European and American Consumer Societies in the Twentieth Century*. Cambridge: Cambridge University Press, 111–126.

———. 2003. *A Consumers' Republic: The Politics of Mass Consumption in Postwar America.* New York: Knopf.

Comaroff, Jean, and John L. Comaroff. 1991. *Of Revelation and Revolution: Christianity, Colonialism, and Consciousness in South Africa,* vol. 1. Chicago: University of Chicago Press.

———. 2000. "Millennial Capitalism: First Thoughts on a Second Coming." *Public Culture* 12(2): 291–343.

Connerton, Paul. 1989. *How Societies Remember.* Cambridge: Cambridge University Press.

Crain, Mary. 1991. "Poetics and Politics in the Ecuadorean Andes: Women's Narratives of Death and Devil Possession." *American Ethnologist* 18: 67–89.

Crapanzano, Vincent. 1980. *Tuhami: Portrait of a Moroccan.* Chicago: University of Chicago Press.

Creed, Gerald. 2002. "(Consumer) Paradise Lost: Capitalist Dynamics and Disenchantment in Rural Bulgaria." *Anthropology of East Europe Review* 20, 2: at http://condor.depaul .edu/%7Errotenbe/aeer/v20n2/Creed.pdf.

Darnton, Robert. 1991. *Berlin Journal.* New York: Norton.

Davis, Belinda. 1996. "Food Scarcity and the Empowerment of the Female in World War I Berlin." In Victoria De Grazia, ed., *The Sex of Things: Gender and Consumption in Historical Perspective.* Berkeley: University of California Press, 287–310.

Davis, Natalie Zemon, and Randolph Starn, eds. 1989. "Memory and Counter-Memory." *Representations* 26(1), theme issue.

De Grazia, Victoria, ed. 1996. *The Sex of Things: Gender and Consumption in Historical Perspective.* Berkeley: University of California Press.

De Pina-Cabral, Joao, and Campbell, John, eds. 1992. *Europe Observed.* London: Macmillan.

DeSoto, Hermine. 1994. "'In the Name of the Folk': Women and Nation in the New Germany." *UCLA Women's Law Journal* 5(1): 83–102.

———. 2000a. "Crossing Western Boundaries: How East Berlin Women Observed Women Researchers from the West After Socialism, 1991–1992." In Hermine DeSoto and Nora Dudwick, eds., *Fieldwork Dilemmas: Anthropologists in Postsocialist States.* Madison: University of Wisconsin Press.

———. 2000b. "Contested Landscapes: Reconstructing Environment and Memory in Post-Socialist Saxony-Anhalt." In Daphne Berdahl, Matti Bunzl, and Martha Lampland, eds., *Altering States: Ethnographies of Transition in Eastern Europe and the Former Soviet Union.* Ann Arbor: University of Michigan Press.

Deutschland, Stiftung Haus der Geschichte der Bundesrepublik. 2001. *Einsichten: Diktatur und Widerstand in der DDR.* Leipzig: Reclam.

Dodd, Philip. 1986. "Englishness and the National Culture." In R. C. a. P. Dodd, ed., *Englishness: Politics and Culture 1880–1920.* London: Routledge, 1–28.

Drakulić, Slavenka. 1991. *How We Survived Communism and Even Laughed.* New York: Norton.

Dubisch, Jill. 1995. "Lovers in the Field: Sex, Dominance, and the Female Anthropologist." In Don Kulick and Margaret Wilson, eds., *Taboo: Sex, Identity, and Erotic Subjectivity in Anthropological Fieldwork.* London: Routledge, 29–50.

———. 1996. *In a Different Place: Pilgrimage, Gender, and Politics at a Greek Island Shrine.* Princeton, N.J.: Princeton University Press.

Duncan, Carol. 1995. *Civilizing Rituals: Inside Public Art Museums.* London: Routledge.

Dunn, Elizabeth. 2004. *Privatizing Poland: Baby Food, Big Business, and the Remaking of Labor.* Ithaca, N.Y.: Cornell University Press.

Dwyer, Kevin. 1982. *Moroccan Dialogues.* Baltimore, Md.: Johns Hopkins University Press.

Eckert, Rainer. 2001. "Repression und Widerstand in der zweiten deutschen Diktatur." In S. H. d. G. d. B. Deutschland, ed., *Einsichten: Diktatur und Widerstand in der DDR.* Leipzig: Reclam, 16–22.

Edelman, Bernard. 1985. *Dear America: Letters Home from Vietnam.* New York: Norton.

Einhorn, Barbara. 1993. *Cinderella Goes to Market: Citizenship, Gender and Women's Movements in East Central Europe.* London: Verso.

Ezell, Edward Clinton. 1987. *Reflections on the Wall: The Vietnam Veterans Memorial.* Harrisburg, Pa.: Stackpole Books.

Falk, Richard. 1994. "The Making of Global Citizenship." In Bart van Steenburgen, ed., *The Condition of Citizenship.* London: Sage, 127–140.

Ferguson, James. 1988. "Cultural Exchange: New Developments in the Anthropology of Commodities." *Cultural Anthropology* 3(4): 488–513.

Fernandez, James. 1986. *Persuasions and Performances: The Play of Tropes in Culture.* Bloomington: Indiana University Press.

———. 1990. "Enclosures: Boundary Maintenance and Its Representations over Time in Asturian Mountain Villages (Spain)." In Emiko Ohnuki-Tierney, ed., *Culture Through Time: Anthropological Approaches.* Palo Alto, Calif.: Stanford University Press, 94–127.

Ferree, Myra Marx. 1991. "Institutionalizing Gender Equality: Feminist Politics and Equality Offices." *German Politics and Society* 24 and 25: 55–65.

Fischer, H. F. 1991. "The Catholic Church in the GDR: A Look Back in Anger." *Religion in Communist Lands* 19(3–4): 211–219.

Fish, Lydia. 1987. *The Last Firebase: A Guide to the Vietnam Veterans Memorial.* Shippensburg, Pa.: Self-published.

Fiske, John. 1989. *Reading the Popular.* Boston: Unwin Human.

Foss, Sonja. 1986. "Ambiguity as Persuasion: The Vietnam Veterans Memorial." *Communication Quarterly* (Summer): 326–340.

Foster, Robert. 2002. *Materializing the Nation: Commodities, Consumption, and Media in Papua New Guinea.* Bloomington: Indiana University Press.

Foucault, Michel. 1977. "Counter-Memory: The Philosophy of Difference." In Donald Bouchard, ed., *Language, Counter-Memory, Practice: Selected Essays and Interviews.* Donald Bouchard and Sherry Simon, trans. Ithaca, N.Y.: Cornell University Press.

Friedman, Jonathan, ed. 1994. *Consumption and Identity.* London: Harwood Press.

Friends of the Vietnam Veterans Memorial. n.d. "Among Friends: News of the Friends of the Vietnam Veterans Memorial."

Funk, Nanette, and Magda Mueller, eds. 1993. *Gender Politics and Post-Communism.* New York: Routledge.

Gable, Eric, and Richard Handler. 1997. *The New History in an Old Museum: Creating the Past at Colonial Williamsburg.* Durham, N.C.: Duke University Press.

Gal, Susan. 1994. "Gender in the Post-Socialist Transition: The Abortion Debate in Hungary." *East European Politics and Societies* 8(2): 256–286.

Gal, Susan, and Gail Kligman. 2000. *The Politics of Gender After Socialism.* Princeton, N.J.: Princeton University Press.

Geertz, Clifford. 1983. "From the Native's Point of View: On the Nature of Anthropological Understanding." In Clifford Geertz, *Local Knowledge: Further Essays in Interpretive Anthropology*. New York: Basic Books.

Geyer, Michael. 1994. "Industriepolitik in der DDR. Von der großindustriellen Nostalgie zum Zusammenbruch." In Jürgen Kocka and Martin Sabrow, eds., *Die DDR als Geschichte: Fragen-Hypothesen-Perspektiven*. Berlin: Akadamie Verlag.

Gillis, John, ed. 1994. *Commemorations: The Politics of National Identity*. Princeton, N.J.: Princeton University Press.

Graf, William, William Hansen, and Brigitte Schulz. 1993. "From the People to One People: The Social Bases of the East German 'Revolution' and Its Preemption by the West German State." In Hermine DeSoto and David Anderson, eds., *The Curtain Rises: Rethinking Culture, Ideology, and the State in Eastern Europe*. Atlantic Highlands, N.J.: Humanities Press.

Grant, Bruce. 2006. "Cosmopolitan Baku." Paper presented at the conference "Post-Communist Nostalgia." University of Illinois at Urbana-Champaign, April 7–8.

Griswold, Charles. 1986. "The Vietnam Veterans Memorial and the Washington Mall: Philosophical Thoughts on a Political Landscape." *Critical Inquiry* 12.

Gupta, Akhil, and James Ferguson. 1992. "Beyond 'Culture': Space, Identity and the Politics of Difference." *Cultural Anthropology* 7(1): 6–23.

Haines, Harry. 1986. "What Kind of War? An Analysis of the Vietnam Veterans Memorial." *Critical Studies in Mass Communication* 3.

Halbwachs, Maurice. 1992. *On Collective Memory*. Chicago: University of Chicago Press.

Handler, Richard. 1993. "Fieldwork in Quebec, Scholarly Reviews, and Anthropological Dialogues." In Caroline Brettell, ed., *When They Read What We Write: The Politics of Ethnography*. Westport, Conn.: Bergin & Garvey, 67–74.

Hann, Chris, ed. 1993. *Socialism: Ideals, Ideologies and Local Practice*. London: Routledge.

Hebdidge, Dick. 1988. "Object as Image: The Italian Scooter Cycle." In *Hiding in the Light*. London: Routledge.

Hensel, Jana. 2002. *Zonenkinder*. Reinbek, Germany: Rowohlt.

Herzfeld, Michael. 1987. *Anthropology Through the Looking-Glass: Critical Ethnography in the Margins of Europe*. Cambridge: Cambridge University Press.

———. 1997a. *Cultural Intimacy: Social Poetics in the Nation-State*. New York: Routledge.

———. 1997b. "Anthropology and the Politics of Significance." *Social Analysis* 41(3): 107–138.

Hess, Elizabeth. 1987. "Vietnam: Memorials of Misfortune." In Reese Williams, ed., *Unwinding the Vietnam War*. Seattle: Real Cornet Press.

Ho, Karen. 2005. "Situating Global Capitalism: A View from Wall Street Investment Banks." *Cultural Anthropology* 20(1): 68–96.

Holston, James, and Arjun Appadurai. 1996. "Cities and Citizenship." *Public Culture* 8: 187–204.

Humphrey, Caroline. 1995. "Creating a Culture of Disillusionment: Consumption in Moscow, a Chronicle of Changing Times." In Daniel Miller, ed., *Modernity Through the Prism of the Local*. London: Routledge.

———. 2001. "Does the Category 'Postsocialist' Still Make Sense?" In C. N. Hann, ed., *Postsocialism: Ideals, Ideologies, and Practices in Eurasia*. London: Routledge, 12–15.

———. 2002. *The Unmaking of Soviet Life*. Ithaca, N.Y.: Cornell University Press.

Huyssen, Andreas. 1995. *Twilight Memories: Marking Time in a Culture of Amnesia.* New York: Routledge.

Ingersoll, Daniel, and James N. Nickel. 1987. "The Most Important Monument: The Tomb of the Unknown Soldier." In Daniel Ingersoll and Gordon Bronitsky, eds., *Mirror and Metaphor: Material and Social Constructions of Reality.* Lanham, Md.: University Press of America.

Ivy, Marilyn. 1995. *Discourses of the Vanishing: Modernity, Phantasm, Japan.* Chicago: University of Chicago Press.

Jaffe, Alexandra. 1993. "Involvement, Detachment, and Representation on Corsica." In Caroline Brettell, ed., *When They Read What We Write.* Westport, Conn.: Bergin & Garvey, 51–66.

Jameson, Fredric. 1989. "Nostalgia for the Present." *South Atlantic Quarterly* 88(2): 517–537.

Jancius, Angela. 2002. "Social Markets and the Meaning of Work in Eastern Germany." In U. Kockel, ed., *Culture and Economy: Contemporary Perspectives.* Hampshire, England: Ashgate.

Joseph, May. 1999. *Nomadic Identities: The Performance of Citizenship.* Minneapolis: University of Minnesota Press.

Kaminsky, Annette. 2001. *Wohlstand, Schönheit, Glück. Kleine Konsumgeschichte der DDR.* Munich: C. H. Beck.

Kämper, Andreas, and Reinhold Ulbrich. 1995. *Wir und unser Trabant.* Berlin: Rowohlt.

Karnow, Stanley. 1983. *Vietnam: A History.* New York: Viking Press.

Karp, Ivan, Christine Mullen Kraemer, and Steven D. Lavine. 1992. *Museums and Communities: The Politics of Public Culture.* Washington, D.C.: Smithsonian Institution Press.

Katakis, Michael. 1988. *The Vietnam Veterans Memorial.* New York: Crown.

Kelleher, William. 2003. *The Troubles in Ballybogoin: Memory and Identity in Northern Ireland.* Ann Arbor: University of Michigan Press.

Kideckel, David. 1993. *The Solitude of Collectivism.* Ithaca, N.Y.: Cornell University Press.

Kirshenblatt-Gimblett, Barbara. 1998. *Destination Culture: Tourism, Museums, and Heritage.* Berkeley: University of California Press.

Kondo, Dorinne. 1990. *Crafting Selves: Power, Gender, and Discourses of Identity in a Japanese Workplace.* Chicago: University of Chicago Press.

Konrád, George, and Ivan Szelényi. 1979. *Intellectuals on the Road to Class Power: A Sociological Study of the Role of the Intelligentsia in Socialism.* New York: Harcourt, Brace, Jovanovich.

Konstantinov, Yulian. 1996. "Pattern of Interpretation: Trader-Tourism in the Balkans (Bulgaria) as Picaresque Metaphorical Enactment of Post-Totalitarianism." *American Ethnologist* 23(4): 762–782.

Koppel, Ted. 1987. *Nightline.* Television program. June.

Korff, Gottfried. 1990. "S-Bahn Ethnologie." *Österreichische Zeitschrift für Volkskunde* 44: 5–26.

Kornai, Janos. 1992. *The Socialist System: The Political Economy of Communism.* Princeton, N.J.: Princeton University Press.

Kubik, Jan. 1994. *The Power of Symbols against the Symbols of Power.* College Park: Pennsylvania State University Press.

Lampland, Martha. 1995. *The Object of Labor: Commodification in Socialist Hungary.* Chicago: University of Chicago Press.

Lass, Andrew. 1994. "From Memory to History: The Events of November 17 Dis/membered." In Rubie Watson, ed., *Memory, History, and Opposition under State Socialism*. Santa Fe, N.M.: School of American Research, 87–104.

Lavin, Steven, and Ivan Karp. 1991. *Exhibiting Cultures: The Poetics and Politics of Museum Display*. Washington, D.C.: Smithsonian Institution Press.

Leach, Edmund. 1984. "Realm of Folly." In Edward Bruner, ed., *Text Play and Story: The Construction and Reconstruction of Self and Society*. Washington, D.C.: American Ethnological Society.

Liechty, Mark. 2003. *Suitably Modern: Making Middle-Class Culture in a New Consumer Society*. Princeton, N.J.: Princeton University Press.

Löfgren, Orvar. n.d. "Creativity and Consumption: Some Reflections on the Pairing of Two Concepts." Paper.

Lopes, Sal. 1987. *The Wall: Images and Offerings from the Vietnam Veterans Memorial*. New York.

Lüdtke, Alf. 1993a. *Eigen-Sinn: Fabrikalltag, Arbeitererfahrungen und Politik vom Kaiserreich bis in den Faschismus*. Hamburg: Ergebnisse Verlag.

———. 1993b. "Polymorphous Synchrony: German Industrial Workers and the Politics of Everyday Life." *International Review of Social History* 38: 39–84.

———. 1994. "'Helden der Arbeit'—Mühen beim Arbeiten. Zur mißmutigen Loyalität von Industrialarbeitern in der DDR." In Hartmut Kaelble, Jürgen Kocka, Hartmut Zwahr, eds., *Sozialgeschichte der DDR*. Stuttgart: Klett-Cotta.

Ludwig, Andreas. 1996. *Alltagskultur der DDR: Begleitbuch zur Ausstellung "Tempolinsen und P2."* Berlin-Brandenburg: be.bra-Verl.

Ludwig, Andreas, and Gerd Kuhn. 1997a. *Alltag und Soziales Gedächtnis*. Hamburg: Ergebnisse Verlag.

———. 1997b. "Sachkultur und DDR-Alltag: Versuch einer Annäherung." In Andreas Ludwig and Gerd Kuhn, *Die DDR Objektkultur und ihre Musealisierung*. Hamburg: Ergenisse Verlag.

Lutz, Catherine. 1988. *Unnatural Emotions: Everyday Sentiments on a Micronesian Atoll and Their Challenge to Western Theory*. Chicago: University of Chicago Press.

Maier, Charles. 1988. *The Unmasterable Past: History, Holocaust, and German National Identity*. Cambridge, Mass.: Harvard University Press.

———. 1997. *Dissolution: The Crisis of Communism and the Collapse of the East German State*. Princeton, N.J.: Princeton University Press.

Mandel, Ruth, and Caroline Humphrey, eds. 2002. *Markets and Moralities: Ethnographies of Postsocialism*. Oxford: Berg.

Marshall, T. H. 1992. "Citizenship and Social Class." In T. H. Marshall and Tom Bottomore, *Citizenship and Social Class*. London: Pluto Press, 1–51.

Marx, Karl. 1972. "On the Jewish Question." In Robert C. Tucker, ed., *The Marx-Engels Reader*. New York: Norton, 24–51.

McBeth, Sally. 1993. "Myths of Objectivity and the Collaborative Process in Life History Research." In Caroline Brettell, ed., *When They Read What We Write: The Politics of Ethnography*. Westport, Conn.: Bergin & Garvey, 145–162.

McCracken, Grant. 1988. *Culture and Consumption*. Bloomington: Indiana University Press.

McElvoy, Annie. 1992. *The Saddled Cow*. London: Faber & Faber.

McGovern, Charles. 1998. "Consumption and Citizenship in the United States, 1900–1940." In Susan Strasser, Charles McGovern, and Matthias Judt, eds., *Getting and Spending: European and American Consumer Societies in the Twentieth Century*. Cambridge: Cambridge University Press, 37–58.

McKendrick, Neil, John Brewer, and J. H. Plumb. 1982. *The Birth of a Consumer Society: The Commercialization of Eighteenth-Century England*. Bloomington: Indiana University Press.

McRobbie, Angela. 1989. "Second-Hand Dresses and the Role of the Ragmarket." In Angela McRobbie, ed., *Zoot-Suits and Second-Hand Dresses*. London: MacMillan.

Merkel, Ina. 1998. "Consumer Culture in the GDR, or How the Struggle for Antimodernity Was Lost on the Battleground of Consumer Culture." In Susan Strasser, Charles McGovern, and Matthias Judt, eds., *Getting and Spending: European and American Consumer Societies in the Twentieth Century*. Cambridge: Cambridge University Press, 281–300.

———. 1999. *Utopie und Bedürfnis: Die Geschichte der Konsumkultur der DDR*. Cologne: Böhlau.

Miller, Daniel. 1994. *Modernity, an Ethnographic Approach: Dualism and Mass Consumption in Trinidad*. Oxford: Berg.

———. 1995a. "Consumption Studies as the Transformation of Anthropology." In Daniel Miller, ed., *Acknowledging Consumption*. London: Routledge.

———. 1995b. "Consumption and Commodities." *Annual Review of Anthropology* 24: 141–161.

Miller, Daniel, ed. 1995c. *Worlds Apart: Modernity Through the Prism of the Local*. New York: Routledge.

Miller, Toby. 1993. *The Well-Tempered Self: Citizenship, Culture, and the Postmodern Subject*. Baltimore, Md.: Johns Hopkins University Press.

Mills, Mary Beth. 1997. "Contesting the Margins of Modernity: Women, Migration, and Consumption in Thailand." *American Ethnologist* 24(1): 37–61.

Milosz, Czeslaw. 1991. "Ketman." In Gale Sokes, ed., *From Stalinism to Pluralism*. New York: Oxford University Press.

Mintz, Sidney. 1985. *Sweetness and Power: The Place of Sugar in Modern History*. New York: Penguin.

Molyneux, Maxine. 2000. "Comparative Perspectives on Gender and Citizenship: Latin America and the Former Socialist States." In J. Cook, J. Roberts, and G. Waylen, eds., *Toward a Gendered Political Economy*. New York: St Martin's Press, 121–144.

Mosse, George. 1990. *Fallen Soldiers: Reshaping the Memory of the World Wars*. New York: Oxford University Press.

Myerhoff, Barbara. 1978. *Number Our Days*. New York: Dutton.

———. 1986. "'Life Not Death in Venice': Its Second Life." In Victor Turner and Edward M. Bruner, eds., *The Anthropology of Experience*. Urbana: University of Illinois Press.

Nagengast, Carol. 1991. *Reluctant Socialists, Rural Entrepreneurs: Class, Culture, and the Polish State*. Boulder, Colo.: Westview Press.

Narayan, Kirin. 1993. "How Native Is a 'Native' Anthropologist?" *American Anthropologist* 95: 671–686.

National Geographic. 1985. *Vietnam Veterans Memorial: America Remembers*. May (special issue).

National Review. 1981. "Stop That Monument." September 16.

NGBK [Neue Gesellschaft für Bildende Kunst], ed. 1996. *Wunderwirtschaft: Konsumkultur in den 60er Jahren.* Cologne: Böhlau Verlag.

Nickel, Hildegard Maria. 1993. "Women in the German Democratic Republic and in the New Federal States: Looking Backward and Forward (Five Theses)." In Nannette Funk and Magda Mueller, eds., *Gender Politics in Post-Communism.* New York: Routledge.

Nora, Pierre. 1989. "Between Memory and History: Les Lieux de Memoire." *Representations* 26 (Spring): 7–25.

Ong, Aihwa. 1996. "Cultural Citizenship as Subject-Making: Immigrants Negotiate Racial and Cultural Boundaries in the United States." *Current Anthropology* 37(5): 737–762.

———. 1999. *Flexible Citizenship: The Cultural Logics of Transnationality.* Durham, N.C.: Duke University Press.

Orlove, Benjamin, ed. 1997. *The Allure of the Foreign: Imported Goods in Postcolonial Latin America.* Ann Arbor: University of Michigan Press.

Orlove, Benjamin, and Henry Rutz, eds. 1989. *The Social Economy of Consumption.* Lanham, Md.: University Press of America.

Ortner, Sherry B. 1995. "Resistance and the Problem of Ethnographic Refusal." *Comparative Studies in Society and History* 37(1): 173–193.

Palmer, Laura. 1988. *Shrapnel in the Heart.* New York.

Patico, Jennifer, and Melissa Caldwell. 2002. "Consumers Exiting Socialism: Ethnographic Perspectives on Daily Life in Post-Communist Europe." *Ethnos* 67(3): 285–294.

Patton, Cindy, and Robert L. Caserio. 2000. "Introduction: Citizenship 2000." *Cultural Studies* 14(1): 1–14.

Pence, Katherine. 2001. "'You as a Woman Will Understand': Consumption, Gender and the Relationship between State and Citizenry in the GDR's Crisis of 17 June 1953." *German History* 19(2): 218–252.

Popular Memory Group. 1982. "Popular Memory: Theory, Politics, Method." In Richard Johnson, Gregor McLennan, Bill Schwarz, and David Sutton, eds., *Making Histories: Studies in History-Writing and Politics.* London: Hutchinson.

POW/MIA Common Cause. n.d. *Vietnam in Poems.*

Rabinow, Paul. 1977. *Reflections on Fieldwork in Morocco.* Berkeley: University of California Press.

Ramet, S. P. 1991. "Protestants in East Germany, 1949–89: A Summing Up." *Religion in Communist Lands* 19(3–4): 160–194.

Riegelhaupt, Joyce. 1984. "Popular Anti-Clericalism and Religiosity in Pre-1974 Portugal." In Eric Wolf, ed., *Religion, Power, and Protest in Local Communities: The Northern Shore of the Mediterranean.* Berlin: Mouton, 83–114.

Riesman, Paul. 1977. *Freedom in Fulani Life: An Introspective Ethnography.* Chicago: University of Chicago Press.

Rofel, Lisa. 1999. *Other Modernities: Gendered Yearnings in China After Socialism.* Berkeley: University of California Press.

Rosaldo, Michelle. 1984. "Toward an Anthropology of Self and Feeling." In Richard Shweder and Robert LeVine, eds., *Culture Theory: Essays on Mind, Self & Emotion.* Cambridge: Cambridge University Press.

Rosaldo, Renato. 1984. "Grief and a Headhunter's Rage: On the Cultural Force of Emotions." In Edward Bruner, ed., *Text, Play and Story.* Washington, D.C.: American Ethnological Society, 178–198.

——. 1989. *Culture and Truth.* Boston: Beacon Press.

——. 1994. "Cultural Citizenship and Educational Democracy." *Cultural Anthropology* 9(3): 402–441.

Rosenberg, Dorothy. 1991. "Shock Therapy: GDR Women in Transition from a Socialist Welfare State to a Social Market Economy." *Signs* 17(1): 129–151.

Ross, Andrew. 1980. *No Respect: Intellectuals and Popular Culture.* New York: Routledge.

Sahlins, Marshall. 1981. *Historical Metaphors and Mythical Realities.* Ann Arbor: University of Michigan Press.

——. 1988. "Cosmologies of Capitalism: The Trans-Pacific Sector of the World System." *Proceedings of the British Academy* 74: 1–51.

Sampson, Steven. 1991. "Is There an Anthropology of Socialism?" *Anthropology Today* 7(5): 16–19.

Saß, Katrin. 2008. "Interview mit Katrin Saß." Electronic document, http://www.good-bye-lenin.de/int-sass.php, accessed February 21.

Schissler, Hanna. 2001. *The Miracle Years: A Cultural History of West Germany, 1949–1968.* Princeton, N.J.: Princeton University Press.

Schneider, Jürgen. 1999. *Bekenntnisse eines Baulöwen.* Munich: Ullstein.

——. 2000. *Alle meine Häuser: Moderne Denkmale in Deutschland.* Zurich: Vaw.

Schulz, Christian. 1993. "Der gute Mensch aus Königstein." *Kreuzer* 6: 18–20.

Scruggs, Jan, and Joel Swerdlow. 1985. *To Heal a Nation.* New York: Harper & Row.

Shafir, Gershon. 1998. "Introduction: The Evolving Tradition of Citizenship." In Gershon Shafir, ed., *The Citizenship Debates.* Minneapolis: University of Minnesota Press, 1–28.

Sheehan, Elizabeth. 1993. "The Student of Culture and the Ethnography of Irish Intellectuals." In Caroline Brettell, ed., *When They Read What We Write.* Westport, Conn.: Bergin & Garvey, 75–90.

Silberman, Marc, and Jost Hermand. 2000. *Contentious Memories: Looking Back at the GDR.* New York: Peter Lang.

Silverman, Carol. 2000. "Researcher, Advocate, Friend: An American Fieldworker among Balkan Roma, 1980–1996." In Hermine DeSoto and Nora Dudwick, eds., *Fieldwork Dilemmas: Anthropologists in Postsocialist States.* Madison: University of Wisconsin Press.

Sommers, Margaret. 1993. "Citizenship and the Place of the Public Sphere: Law, Community, and Political Culture in the Transition to Democracy." *American Sociological Review* 58(5): 587–620.

Soysal, Yasemin. 1994. *Limits of Citizenship: Migrants and Postnational Membership in Europe.* Chicago: University of Chicago Press.

Spiegel, Der. 2003. "Der Bundestag nimmt Abschied von Lenin." Spiegel Online, April 3, 2003. Electronic document, http://www.spiegel.de/kultur/gesellschaft/0,1518,243206,00.html, accessed February 21, 2008.

Stein, Mary Beth. 1993. "The Present Is a Foreign Country: Germany After Unification." *Journal of Folklore Research* 30(1): 29–43.

Steinmetz, George. 1994. "Fordism and the (Im)Moral Economy of Right-Wing Violence in Contemporary Germany." *Research on Democracy and Society* 2: 277–315.

Stewart, Kathleen. 1988. "Nostalgia: A Polemic." *Cultural Anthropology* 3(3): 227–241.

Stewart, Susan. 1993. *On Longing: Narratives of the Miniature, the Gigantic, the Souvenir, the Collection.* Durham, N.C.: Duke University Press.

Stitziel, Judd. 2003. "On the Seam between Socialism and Capitalism: East German Fashion Shows." In David Crew, ed., *Consuming Germany in the Cold War.* Oxford: Berg.

Stocking, George, ed. 1985. *Objects and Others: Essays on Museums and Material Culture.* Madison: University of Wisconsin Press.

Strait, Jerry, and Sandra Strait. 1988. *Vietnam War Memorials: An Illustrated Reference to Veterans Tributes throughout the United States.* Jefferson, N.C.: McFarland & Co.

Sturken, Marita. 1997. *Tangled Memories: The Vietnam War, the AIDS Epidemic, and the Politics of Remembering.* Berkeley: University of California Press.

Ten Dyke, Elizabeth. 2000. "Memory, History and Remembrance Work in Dresden." In Daphne Berdahl, Matti Bunzl, and Martha Lampland, eds., *Altering States: Ethnographies of Transition in Eastern Europe and the Former Soviet Union.* Ann Arbor: University of Michigan Press.

———. 2001. *Dresden: Paradoxes of Memory in History.* London: Routledge.

Tsing, Anna. 1993. *In the Realm of the Diamond Queen: Marginality in an Out-of-the-Way Place.* Princeton, N.J.: Princeton University Press.

———. 2000. "Inside the Economy of Appearances." *Public Culture* 12(1): 115–144.

Turner, Bryan. 1994. "Post Modern Culture/Modern Citizens." In Bart van Steenbergen, ed., *The Condition of Citizenship.* London: Sage, 153–168.

Turner, Terence. 1997. "The Dithering Away of the State? Social Theory, Cultural Consciousness and Class Perspectives in the Contemporary World System." Lecture presented at Massachusetts Institute of Technology, March.

Urquhart, Gordon. 1995. *The Pope's Armada.* London: Bantam Press.

Urry, John. 1990. *The Tourist Gaze: Leisure and Travel in Contemporary Society.* London: Sage.

Verdery, Katherine. 1996. *What Was Socialism, and What Comes Next?* Princeton, N.J.: Princeton University Press.

———. 1998. "Transnationalism, Nationalism, Citizenship, and Property: Eastern Europe Since 1989." *American Ethnologist* 25(2): 291–306.

———. 1999. *The Political Lives of Dead Bodies.* New York: Columbia University Press.

———. 2000. Review of *Where the World Ended. American Ethnologist* 27(2): 545–546.

Von Vestenberg, Nikolaus. 2003. "Kinder haften für ihre Eltern." *Der Spiegel,* March 24, 114–116.

Wagner-Pacifici, Robin, and Barry Schwartz. 1991. "The Vietnam Veterans Memorial: Commemorating a Difficult Past." *American Journal of Sociology* 97: 376–420.

Wanner, Catherine. 1998. *Burden of Dreams: History and Identity in Post-Soviet Ukraine.* University Park: Pennsylvania State University Press.

Warner, W. L. 1962. *American Life: Dream and Reality.* Chicago: University of Chicago Press.

Watson, Rubie, ed. 1994. *Memory, History, and Opposition under State Socialism.* Santa Fe, N.M.: School of American Research.

Wilk, Richard. 1994. "Consumer Goods as Dialogue about Development." In J. Friedman, ed., *Consumption and Identity.* London: Harwood Press.

Williams, Reese, ed. 1987. *Unwinding the Vietnam War: From War into Peace.* Seattle: Real Cornet Press.

Willis, Paul. 1990. *Common Culture.* London: Open University Press.

Yudice, George. 1995. "Civil Society, Consumption, and Governmentality in an Age of Global Reconstruction." *Social Text* 45: 1–25.

Zerubavel, Yael. 1995. *Recovered Roots: Collective Memory and the Making of Israeli National Tradition.* Chicago: University of Chicago Press.

Zivkovic, Marko. 2008. "Tales of Mega Jury-Rigging: Trabi, Fića and Diana in Comparative Perspective." Paper presented at the Annual Meeting of the American Anthropological Association, San Francisco, November 19–23.

Zunz, Oliver. 1999. *Why the American Century?* Chicago: University of Chicago Press.

INDEX

NEW ANTHROPOLOGIES OF EUROPE

DAPHNE BERDAHL, MATTI BUNZL, AND MICHAEL HERZFELD,
FOUNDING EDITORS

DAPHNE BERDAHL (1964–2007) was Associate Professor of Anthropology and Global Studies at the University of Minnesota. She was author of *Where the World Ended: Re-Unification and Identity in the German Borderland* and editor (with Matti Bunzl and Martha Lampland) of *Altering States: Ethnographies of Transition in Eastern Europe and the Former Soviet Union.*

—∭—

MATTI BUNZL is Professor of Anthropology at the University of Illinois. He is author of *Symptoms of Modernity: Jews and Queers in Late-Twentieth-Century Vienna* and *Anti-Semitism and Islamophobia: Hatreds Old and New in Europe.*

—∭—